Praise for *Digital Marketing Analytics*

"The first edition of this book set the bar for brands and agencies looking to understand how to analyze the impact of digital marketing. What is remarkable is that it hasn't needed a new edition since it was published in 2013, given the pace of change in this marketplace.

"While DMA 2.0 does represent a root and branch update and moves the authors' thinking on in significant ways—covering new platforms, new metrics, new ways of measuring—its essential common sense and no-nonsense approach remains constant. Chuck and Ken lead marketers clearly and efficiently through the minefield of digital marketing measurement. And they do so with a lightness of touch and absence of jargon so rare in this overhyped, much-misunderstood ecosystem. To be recommended."

—**Sam Knowles**, Founder & MD of Insight Agents; author of *Narrative by Numbers: How to Tell Powerful & Purposeful Stories with Data*

"This book is more vital and important than ever. Hemann and Burbary go beyond the basics to show you precisely how to measure every element of your digital marketing. A must-read!"

—**Jay Baer**, Founder of Convince & Convert

"While a lot of the tactics of digital marketing have changed since the first edition of this book, two things haven't: the need to measure the *right* things, and my trust that Chuck and Ken have you covered, right here in the pages of this new edition. Indispensable for the modern, data-driven marketer."

—**Tom Webster**, Senior Vice President, Strategy and Marketing, Edison Research

Digital Marketing Analytics

Making Sense of Consumer Data in a Digital World

Second Edition

CHUCK HEMANN
KEN BURBARY

Digital Marketing Analytics

ISBN-13: 978-0-7897-5960-3
ISBN-10: 0-7897-5960-8

Library of Congress Control Number: 2018932445

01 18

Trademarks

Warning and Disclaimer

Special Sales

For information about buying this title in bulk quantities, or for special sales opportunities (which may include electronic versions; custom cover designs; and content particular to your business, training goals, marketing focus, or branding interests), please contact our corporate sales department at corpsales@pearsoned.com or (800) 382-3419.

For government sales inquiries, please contact governmentsales@pearsoned.com.

For questions about sales outside the U.S., please contact intlcs@pearson.com.

Editor-in-Chief
Greg Wiegand

Executive Editor
Laura Norman

Development Editor
Malobika Chakraborty

Managing Editor
Sandra Schroder

Senior Project Editor
Lori Lyons

Copy Editor
Paula Lowell

Indexer
Lisa Stumpf

Proofreader
Jeanine Furino

Technical Editor
Kevin Johnson

Cover Designer
Chuti Prasertsith

Compositor
codemantra

Que Biz-Tech Editorial Board
Michael Brito
Jason Falls
Rebecca Lieb
Simon Salt
Peter Shankman

CONTENTS AT A GLANCE

CONTENTS

3   Choosing Your Analytics Tools   43

4   Digital Analysis: Brand   59

5   Digital Analysis: Audience   75

6 Digital Analysis: Ecosystem   93

7 Return on Investment   99

8 Understanding Digital Influence   115

9   How to Use Digital Analytics to Inform Marketing Programs   131

10   Improving Customer Service   145

11   Using Digital Analytics to Anticipate a Crisis   157

12   Launching a New Product   173

13   Building Your Research Plan   189

Foreword

Now is your time. The time to be challenged, and your time to rise.

Yes, your time. Never before has a marketer been given so many digital tools to reach customers all around the world. Never before has a marketer been saddled with an overwhelming amount of technologies, choices, and data.

If you're like me, it's hard to keep up with the explosion of new technologies. They're coming from every direction, and at an increasing pace. First, we started with the Internet, then we saw the rise of social media (where I was an industry analyst focused on the Interactive Marketer as a Forrester Analyst), and then we saw the rise of the Collaborative Sharing Economy where customers required on-demand models, subscription models, marketplaces, and new crowd-based models.

While many companies and marketers have adopted these new technologies, there are even more technologies coming, many of which could disrupt the very fabric of our business models, supply chain, and products—technologies like block-chain, cryptocurrencies, mixed reality, drones, self-driving cars, chatbots, machine learning, and other artificial intelligence systems. There are undoubtedly more technologies coming as they embed under our skin, in our brains, and in our environment—everything that can be digitized will be.

Yet, these technologies come and go—some are impactful to our business and some aren't. Now more than ever, the digital marketer has the eye of certainly the CMO and more often the CEO. Executives are looking at the digital marketing group as the first troops to test, analyze, and determine if these are worthwhile for your businesses. The eyes are on you, and you must be ready.

It's both a blessing and a curse that the role of marketing has expanded. Marketing is not just limited to pre-sales and demand generation, but it's also what we do that impacts customer care, supply chain, and even the actual products and services. The whole of the company is seeking our guidance, and you may find leaders from all departments of the company knocking on your door.

That's why we need accountability and the ability to measure. That's why you need this book, but qualified practitioners, and thought leaders, who have experience and insight on how those who are leading the way, are best deploying. As a technology leader, you must measure so you can manage, and this requires returning to the basics to apply sensible business practices to measure—regardless of what new technology emerges from emerging startups.

In our research on how companies are innovating, we've found that the number one issue isn't technology or budget, but actually a culture of resistance to change. Making change to digital systems requires a mindset change, and established processes will resist this.

The best way to overcome cultural resistance is to lead with real data, showing what's working and what's not. This is your opportunity to bring internal stakeholders along, by using data. It's important to do this now, as with the rise of connected IoT technologies, we'll see even more data as machines create massive amounts.

This leads us to the future, which this book covers in the latter chapters. The future of digital will certainly bring forward strong Artificial Intelligence systems with vast amounts of data that are able to Machine Learn and start to make recommendations to you, the leader.

The sentient machine is still a few decades off, but the early predecessors are here today. And this is why measurement is key—now. We must be ready to make decisions based off real-world digital data and using our human insights to derive the right recommendations.

It's a time of never-ending change, a time of incredible technology, and a time for you to stand and rise to the occasion. Now is your time.

—**Jeremiah Owyang**
Founder, Catalyst Companies and Kaleido Insights
Former Founding Partner and Industry Analyst, Altimeter Group
Senior Analyst, Forrester Research

About the Authors

Chuck Hemann, Managing Director of Analytics/Head of Digital Analytics for W2O, has spent the past 14 years providing strategic counsel on digital analytics, measurement, online reputation, and social media. He was previously Global Director of Digital and Paid Media Analytics at Intel Corporation. He has worked with global brands from Intel to P&G to Verizon.

Ken Burbary, Consultant and Digital Marketing Professor at Cornell Johnson Graduate School of Management, has 20+ years of online marketing and advertising experience, including a deep background in digital and social media. He served as VP–Group Director, Strategy and Analysis at Digitas, working with global brands from American Express and Bank of America to P&G and GM.

Dedication

This book is dedicated to my mom, grandmother, and grandfather. Without their consistent encouragement and guidance, I would not be where I am today. There is not a day when I am not thankful for everything you have done for me.

—Chuck

This book is dedicated to my family. They gave me the inspiration to embark on this journey and provided much support, encouragement, and understanding throughout the process. I would not have been able to do this without their love.

—Ken

Acknowledgments

From Chuck

Raise your hand if you have ever thought about writing a book. The number of you now raising your hands is probably pretty small. Raise your hand if you have ever thought about writing two? I'm guessing the number is now almost none. At the time of the publishing of our first book, it was the most professionally gratifying thing I had ever done. That is, until we set forth on the journey to publish the second edition of *Digital Marketing Analytics*. The second edition afforded me the opportunity to help further advance my profession based on first-hand knowledge of how large marketing organizations think about analytics.

A book like this does not happen without a lot of support. First and foremost, I would like to thank my mom and sister Marie for being amazing cheerleaders. They are always there, checking on progress and offering encouragement throughout my career. There were many who suggested we write this book, but the loudest voice was Alejandra Hernandez—I would like to extend a special thank you to your constant encouragement.

Thank you to Jim Weiss, Jenn Gottleib, Bob Pearson, and Seth Duncan at W2O Group for not only supporting me in this endeavor, but also bringing me to such an incredible firm now multiple times. I have learned a lot while working for you and appreciate everything you have done for me. Also, a huge thank you to my team at W2O and Intel (current and former)—Dan Linton, Sara Vlasach, Bethany Bengston, Michael Hall, Skylar Fogel, Vani Petkar, Christina Flint, Jessica Hastings, Allison Barnes, Robert Rose, Jonathan Isernhagen, and Meredith Owen—who have supported me throughout this project.

I would also like to thank Scott Chaikin, Chas Withers, Keith Mabee, and Rob Berick for giving me my first agency job at Dix & Eaton. If you had not taken a chance on me back then, I would not be where I am today.

Thank you to Becky Brown, who brought me to Intel in 2014 and taught me how marketing organizations should be run within large companies. Thank you also to Geoff Ivey, Scott Jaworski, Julie Keshmiry, Scott Rosenberg, Laura-Ann Mitchell, and Justin Huntsman, who were great peers and friends during my time at the company.

I also want to thank several friends and mentors who provided support for me throughout my career. Thank you to Marcel Lebrun, David Alston, Tom Webster, Tamsen Snyder Webster, Justin Levy, Michael Brito, Kyle Flaherty, Greg Matthews, Colin Foster, Jason Falls, Lauren Warthan, Amanda Vasil, Adam Cohen, Jaime Punishill, Jim Storer, Adrian Parker, and Lisa Grimm. I very much appreciate all you have done to support me.

Thank you to Laura Norman, our acquisitions editor, who patiently worked with us every step of the way. This book would not have happened without the faith you have put in us. I cannot thank you enough. Thank you also to Malobika Chakraborty, our development editor, and Kevin Johnson, our technical editor, for their tireless work in making sure this book sings for the reader.

Thank you also to Ken Burbary, my co-author, for agreeing to embark on this journey with me a second time. It could not have been completed without your expertise and knowledge. You have been a great friend for many years.

Finally, I would like to say thank you to all the clients I have worked with over the years. All of you have taught me a lot about business and marketing, and I hope I have added value to your business during our relationship.

From Ken

When Chuck and I were in the middle of the writing process of this second edition, bogged down in work and seeing little to no light at the end of the tunnel, it's easy to question yourself, "Why am I doing this?". Chuck reminded me of a quote from one of his colleagues and author as well, Bob Pearson. "We don't write books like these for economic gain or celebrity, we write them to give back and further the industry, help move it forward." That resonated deeply within me and helped serve as a reminder during the rough patches of the writing process. This book may not contain or touch on every single part of the digital analytics current universe, but we believe that it does cover a wide swath of digital marketing topics and will surely help marketers advance and improve their company's ability to utilize digital analytics tools, frameworks, and resources to become data-driven marketers. If it does, we've achieved our aim to help advance the industry in our own small way.

Writing a book can be fun, really! That said, no book gets to the finish line without support and hard work from a big cast of characters, not just the authors. I owe a great many thanks to some very special people in my life for providing the unwavering support and encouragement that I needed to stay focused; eyes on the prize. For that, I want to thank my wife, Shauna Burbary—this book would not have happened without you. You deserve so much more credit than you'll ever receive; working in the same industry has brought us both a wealth of shared knowledge, giving greater context to both our disciplines. I also want to thank my mother, Debbie Burbary, for doing what moms do best—checking-in, staying positive, and sharing proud moments of encouragement that helped keep me moving forward.

Big thanks to our main point of contact with Pearson and acquisitions editor, Laura Norman. Your engagement and responsiveness to all of our questions and issues served as the rock for keeping everything organized and running smoothly. Thank you as well to Malobika Chakraborty, our development editor, and Kevin Johnson, our technical editor: this book would not have happened without all of your contributions.

Thank you also to Chuck Hemann, my co-author, for being an excellent partner in co-authorship and beyond. It could not have been completed without your expertise and knowledge and more importantly, your patience (not my strong suit)! I couldn't have known I was gaining a lifelong friend so many years ago when we were just two geeks working on a social listening framework. You're a terrific friend, and I'm lucky to be able to call you one.

I'd like to thank many other people, from friends to professional mentors and peers, but there simply isn't enough room to mention them all. Through meetings, phone calls, one-on-one conversations, or simply me learning from what these people publish and share on a regular basis, their advice, opinions, and expertise have influenced my perspective and content in this book. For that I want to give a special thank you to the following people: Thank you James Sanders, Branden Bauer, Jane Ansara, Adam Cohen, Lucy Shon, Jim Storer, Rachel Happe, Jordan Bitterman, Amber Naslund, Avinash Kaushik, Rishad Toboccowala, Tom Webster, Aaron Strout, Noah Mallin, Paul Mabray, Jeremiah Owyang, Lee Odden, Tamsen Webster, Larry Kim, and Bill Silarski.

Reader Services

Register your copy of *Digital Marketing Analytics* at informit.com for convenient access to downloads, updates, and corrections as they become available. To start the registration process, go to informit.com/register and log in or create an account*. Enter the product ISBN, 9780789759603, and click Submit. Once the process is complete, you will find any available bonus content under Registered Products.

*Be sure to check the box that you would like to hear from us in order to receive exclusive discounts on future editions of this product.

Understanding the Synergetic Digital Ecosystem

The growth and sophistication of digital platforms have grown substantially since the first edition of this book. Although these changes have brought with them new opportunities for marketers and brands—while growing several major platforms such as Facebook, Instagram, and LinkedIn—they have largely exacerbated many issues and challenges that companies face when planning and executing digital initiatives. The original promise of digital channels we described four years ago—"to deliver the right message to the right audience at the right time"—is truer than ever, but the complexity associated with doing so is greater than ever.

The Evolution of the Digital Ecosystem

The digital ecosystem has grown dramatically, both in the number of major platforms that marketers must focus on, but also in defining what digital even means. The evolution of digital as a simple, owned media property like your brand website, to the inclusion of email marketing, paid media (paid search and all variants of paid display), and video advertising, was seemingly manageable before the introduction of social media and the crop of major social platforms that now dominate consumers' digital daily lives. Extending digital technologies and tools beyond marketing into other parts of the enterprise, such as customer service and support, product development, and consumer insights, has led to expanding the definition of digital in 2018 and beyond.

Look no further than how the term *digital transformation* dominates industry headlines to understand how broad and pervasive the digital ecosystem currently is. Delivering on the promise of digital isn't impossible but can certainly be far more difficult now than it used to be. However, by using many of the approaches and techniques that we cover in detail throughout this book, you can arm yourself with the knowledge and perspective to confidently navigate putting together your own plans for achieving digital success.

The relentless and rapid introduction of new platforms, tools, data sources, and media distribution vehicles (such as messaging apps or chatbots) has created a digital ecosystem that can make any marketer's head spin. The nature of the challenge that you face hasn't changed, only the number of options you have to choose from. For any marketer or brand, the challenge still lies in identifying the unique combination of the digital channels, platforms, and partners that is required to produce the outcomes needed to realize your digital marketing, customer experience, or business transformation goals and objectives. The answer to that question will be unique for every organization. Think of it as your brand's digital fingerprint; that is, unique to that brand.

Something else that is new and worth noting since the first edition of this book—we've deliberately included partners in the scope of how you define your digital initiatives. Partnering with other firms for technology or data you don't have is the new normal in digital marketing. Marrying your organization's assets (technology, data, IP) with a complementary partner's assets can yield enormous benefits, particularly in the areas of audience insights (enhancing your understanding of a target audience by combining your audience data with audience data from a DMP [data management platform] or CDP [customer data platform]) and is one of the more common ways companies are currently seeking to differentiate themselves and achieve a single, unified view of the customer. Why? To get closer to realizing that digital promise: "deliver the right message, to the right audience, at the right time." The modern manifestation of that concept is highly personalized experiences and content that are contextually relevant in the moment for a single consumer. Most companies need help to achieve this manifestation. When looking across the digital ecosystem, be sure you're also looking at the right partners that can catapult you to success versus going it alone as was traditionally the accepted approach.

Data Growth Trends

As the digital ecosystem has evolved, the types and the volume of data that is generated have grown. For example, at the 2018 Consumer Electronics Show in Las Vegas, Intel shared its projections on data growth trends. Intel projected that by 2020, in two years, the average consumer will generate 1.5 Gigabytes of data per day from their associated Internet activities.

Marketers collect, analyze, and report on digital data that describes who you are, what you like and dislike, your brand affinities, your expectations and needs for brand experiences, and where you've been. This includes behavior both online and offline because ad trackers are implemented on more than 75% of websites, according to a January 2018 study published by eMarketer, and geolocation data that's appended to other behaviors or activities (think of the location and time-stamp included with every photo you take on your smartphone)[1]. The tasks of determining what data assets exist, figuring out which of those you need, and learning how to manage and use them are now part of every marketer's job.

Stepping back a moment outside of a marketing-focused perspective, it's important to note that data is increasingly critical to how companies compete in nearly every meaningful way. Here are some different examples of how data is fueling strategic initiatives across enterprises:

- **Business strategy:** This includes pulling consumer and industry data and insights to the forefront of business planning, influencing everything from product development to product ownership experiences with customers to marketing investment allocations. Some guiding questions include:

  - What are consumers most stressed about right now?

  - How are consumers using or talking about using our products right now?

  - What is most important to our consumers when it comes to (our industry/current strategic focus)?

  - What areas of our owned channels perform best? Get the most relevant traffic? Why? Is this an asset or opportunity to reduce friction?

- **Data strategy:** Companies like Amazon and Google are built on data strategy; it's core to their DNA. Data is increasingly an asset for all organizations and therefore should be considered not only as fuel for insights, but also for productization. This idea is core to digital business transformation. Some guiding questions include:

  - If there are going to be cuts to the campaign-style reporting, what specifically might get cut?

- Social sentiment?

- Major traffic spikes on our owned, earned, and paid channels? (Why?)

- Low engagement on our owned, earned, and paid channels? (Why?)

- Based on what consumers complain most about (data source examples: social sentiment, reviews, chatbots), how might we improve products or ownership experiences?

- **Communications strategy:** This includes communications across all channels, focused on all relevant company stakeholders, from shareholders to recruitment efforts to consumer messaging. Converged ecosystems mean brands must speak with one voice, giving consideration to all stakeholders for all outward-facing communications. Example guiding questions include:

  - What impact might these insights have for the full industry?

  - How could we focus to activate these insights and impact needs within our talent pool?

  - What is the language our customers are using? It is critical we speak their same language.

- **Media strategy:** Objectives should be set before a campaign ever reaches the ideation stage. (This sounds obvious, but we still see this common mistake among many organizations.) This organizing objective should be supported with a specific approach, and key performance indicators (KPIs) should ladder up to this. An example structure might be:

  - Organizing objective, approach/behavior, KPI

These examples cover four main areas that most enterprises will likely have a need for. This book can help you work smarter by providing you with the approach and information you need to successfully harness the data assets that exist across the entire digital ecosystem. Hopefully, the digital promise will become a reality for you, and your organization will develop a data-driven approach to marketing planning and execution.

Digital Media Types

As we've already noted, media types are evolving, and fast. The digital medium has permeated nearly every traditional media experience (be it from a consumer experience perspective, analytically, or both). The growth and pervasiveness of the digital experience in all of its forms—media, content, Internet of Things, artificial intelligence–driven virtual assistants—contribute to the data revolution we're in the midst of.

In only five years since the first edition of this book, marketers find themselves collecting and analyzing multi-channel consumer interaction data from more sources than ever before (tens if not hundreds of data sources are normal for some organizations). If you want a comprehensive view of the *entire* landscape, then look no further than Figure 1.1, which is Scott Brinker's "chiefmartec.com Marketing Technology Landscape," currently known as the Martech 5000 because it contains nearly 5,000 different marketing technologies, vendors, and marketing automation tools across 50 unique categories in various digital channels and platforms. Each of these has its own data generation and collection mechanism and analytics capabilities. It's mind numbing to consider the effort alone needed to catalog and produce this; tip of the cap to Scott for updating and publishing it every year.

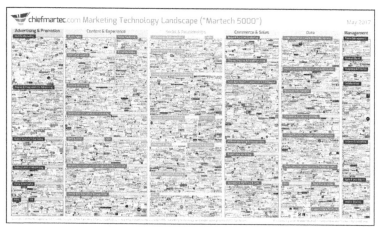

Source: Chiefmartec.com/2017/05/marketing-technology-landscape-supergraphic-2017/

Figure 1.1 *ChiefMartec.com 2017 Marketing Technology Landscape.*

As we outlined in the first edition of this book, going back a decade or more in digital, there were only two dominant media types, although they've been renamed through the years. The first is *paid media*, either in the form of paid search (think Google AdWords) or display advertising (think Display banner ads, or more recently Video ads). Paid media is literally just that—digital media channels that a brand pays to get their message, offer, or branded content in front of an audience they believe it will resonate with.

The second is *owned media*. This is a generic term for any media asset or property that a company owns, controls, and utilizes to reach a prospective audience. Some of the most common forms of owned media are dot-com brand websites; email marketing to subscribers; company blogs; or even branded apps for smartphones, tablets, or IoT devices such as Amazon's Alexa or Google Home. For both paid and owned media, clickstream data has ruled as the dominant data to collect and analyze. Tracking what happens after a user clicks on a link can be useful, but it can't answer all the questions. New and other ways exist to fill in the gaps for a more complete picture by using a variety of digital data sources.

Due primarily to the emergence and growth of social platforms, *earned media* has risen in importance and in the effect it has on other media types. By definition, earned media is something generated by word of mouth, buzz, or a communication "going viral."

With Facebook encompassing 2 billion users, Instagram more than 800 million, and Twitter more than 325 million, owned and earned media are now richer sources of data that include new data types that weren't available to marketers in the past—specifically those types that involve user behaviors, intentions, and affinities, which when properly captured and analyzed, can yield a better understanding of consumer intent. The new era of engagement has resulted in a data explosion that takes us well beyond focusing on clicks, advertising impressions, or website page views.

The data and tools available today can give you the insight you need to improve marketing and advertising performance; improve customer experiences across all touchpoints; and identify the specific details needed to personalize content, experiences, and messaging on an individual consumer basis. Simply put, marketers have never been better suited to generate their desired outcomes and predict future consumer behavior thanks to the robust ecosystem of data and analytics tools available to them. Over the course of the next several chapters we will dive into the tools, which include search analytics, media analytics, social listening, and social media engagement.

Each media type contains several channels that serve a purpose and play a role in your unique digital media mix. The data and analytics associated with each helps you determine how much or how little of a role each should play, enabling you to develop an omni-channel strategy that fits your audience. No digital strategy can succeed based on purely one media type. The world has changed and consumer behavior has radically altered as new platforms and technologies have emerged to enable consumer mobility and accessibility.

Paid Media

Paid media is a more mature media type than some of the other digital media types, with some notable exceptions, as the paid media universe has also exploded over the past several years with many of the major platforms such as Facebook, You-Tube, Twitter, and even Snapchat all experimenting with new types of advertising units. Not all of those come with the transparency around performance and data you might want or are used to getting. Paid media has well-established and robust methods of targeting, audience segmentation, and measurement. Additionally, paid media programs contain real-time measurement capabilities, which allow companies the opportunity to assess and change course on the fly if necessary.

Paid search is far from its shiny object heyday; nevertheless, it is still one of the best places to get insights and understanding about an audience and their intentions. Several search engine and third-party analytics tools work with search data to identify user, behavioral, and intention insights.

Paid display, otherwise known as banner advertising, is suffering these days due to a few factors, but the primary reason is they have been replaced with more compelling rich media ad units or video ad units. Combine that with consumer banner blindness and you have a decline in the efficacy of paid display advertising. Banner blindness happens for one very clear reason: utter saturation of the digital landscape with all types of banner advertising units, including standard ads, interactive game ads, and social ads. Consumers have become so attuned to seeing display ad units on web pages that they block them out. Banners are essentially background noise most of the time. The net effect is declining views and click-through rates (CTRs). This was all true even before the ad blocker wars began. Ad blockers are third-party extensions or plug-ins that consumers can install on their web browsers to automatically scrub any ad content from every web page they visit. There has been an ad blocker war between blockers and publisher websites ever since, with many brand websites asking consumers to whitelist them or denying access to their content unless the ad blocker is disabled. Ad blockers have gained in popularity throughout the past few years, and reached 25% market penetration as of 2017, according to eMarketer.[2]

Performance of banner ads varies due to many factors as well as the banner type. The average CTR for a standard banner ad unit is estimated to be around 0.1% or 0.2%, depending on banner type. This means that if 1,000 people see a banner, only 1 or 2 people click it. This is subpar performance by any standard, and it compares unfavorably to seemingly less attractive digital options, such as email (or even traditional marketing options such as direct mail). The upside of the paid display market is its well-established methods for targeting and measurement. It's easy to get your ad in front of the right audience with this targeting.

Publishers and ad tech platforms have become quite advanced in their usage of cookies for collecting data and tracking audiences. In fact, it's bigger business than ever. According to a joint 2017 study by the IAB (Interactive Advertising Bureau), Winterberry Group, and DMA (Data & Marketing Association), U.S. companies spent more than $10 billion in 2017 on third-party data intended to provide audience insights. They also spent an additional $10 billion on data activation efforts to put those audience insights into practice. This is just further validation that audience data continues, and will continue, to be a main focus for marketers into 2018 and beyond (eMarketer, 2017).[3]

Targeting occurs through a combination of both first- and third-party data. What does this mean? It means the company (first party) that owns the website you land on is directly capturing data about you and your visit. Third-party collection is responsible for the lion's share of the data collection growth. Targeting is done through a variety of creative cookie wrangling and device ID matching, and has been aided by the integration of social data and tools into owned media assets.

An example of targeting that is quite common is via popular social sharing widgets such as ShareThis. It's a simple proposition for website owners: A company makes it easy for you to install a preconfigured social sharing widget to allow sharing of your brand content across major social networking platforms and/or email. ShareThis is free, and it takes little time to get it installed and running. There is no free lunch, and in this case you're paying for lunch with data. There is a catch, and it is data leakage. The sharing widgets are voluntarily leaking data about users to third parties and generating revenue by doing so.

In exchange for freely distributing a sharing widget, companies like ShareThis target users by tracking users' sharing activity through the network of websites that have the widget installed. They collect data about what users like, read, share, save, and more. This data is then augmented with additional targeting or audience data and sold at a premium.

The end result is a robust data set that can be sliced and diced using data management platforms (DMPs), of which there are many: Adobe, Oracle, MediaMath, and Salesforce to name just a handful. DMPs are cookie data warehouses married to analytics engines that have massive horsepower. They are designed to clean, manage, and integrate data with all different types of first-party and third-party data that a company might have or purchase. The DMP vendor landscape has unsurprisingly changed considerably since the first edition of this book. Significant merger and acquisition activity occurred as well as innovation of DMP features and capabilities. Specifics for choosing a DMP is outside the scope of this chapter but we can point you to relevant and helpful resources to aid you in that journey. Forrester Research does a regular assessment of the DMP vendor landscape and highlights the strengths and weaknesses of each DMP vendor in a buying guide they call "Forrester Wave—Data Management Platforms." You can easily find it on the Forrester Research website for free with a subscription or purchase it individually.

DMPs also offer advanced capabilities to find trends and to understand and segment audiences based on consumer data attributes, media consumption habits, and much more. Many large corporations with complex segmentation needs, such as those within the Fortune 100, have standardized on utilizing DMPs to increase performance and improve efficiency through optimization and targeting.

Owned Media

The emergence of earned media is not all that is new to the digital data and analytics landscape. Due to continued enhancements such as audience analytics, cross-user tracking, and advanced segmentation in web analytics platforms like Google Analytics and Adobe Analytics, owned media assets offer more options than ever to gather competitive intelligence, user experience feedback, content analytics, and real-time site analytics; test for site optimization; and provide richer-than-ever-before clickstream activity analysis.

Your goal should be to tie the insights and data from each media channel to one another to tell a deeper story. These are not redundant analytics options, meant to be an either/or decision. Remember, they complement one another. Think additive; each data source reveals a piece of the picture.

Trying to decide which of the data and analytics options to implement can be overwhelming. What should determine those choices for you is your previously defined goals and learning agenda. You can read more about the details of defining clear and specific objectives in Chapter 2, "Understanding Digital Analytics Concepts."

Developing a learning agenda is a useful technique in defining the boundaries of where to focus your analytics efforts. It acts as your guide and helps keep you from going down an irrelevant but interesting rabbit hole with analysis or insights exploration. A learning agenda essentially defines the specific questions you are trying to answer about your audience and as a result keeps you relentlessly focused on answering those during your analysis.

> ✉ *Note*
>
> It's now the big data era. Massive amounts of data and processing are available, but that doesn't mean you need all of it. In fact, you likely need a lot less than you think. Many companies are struggling with digital analytics because they are trying to collect, analyze, and manage all the data they can get their hands on. Resist the urge to collect and analyze all the data these platforms make available. Remember that although they're interesting, many digital data sources are diagnostic measures at best, and do not deliver data that is actionable. Applying the "So what?" test is a simple and helpful way to avoid chasing shiny objects that have no real business value. Ask yourself, "So what? What action can I take based on this data that will further me down the path of achieving my goals?" If the answer isn't clear, you're probably just playing with a tool that outputs data rather than valuable insights. Don't be data rich and insights poor; apply discipline with your data collection efforts.

In the following few sections, we dive into each of the considerations for analytics on your owned media properties.

Competitive Intelligence

Keeping an eye on competitors is nothing new. There is more than a bit to pay attention to these days, and many tools are aimed at helping you understand what your competitors are doing on both their owned media assets and social media platforms. You can use a combination of free and paid tools to access the data you need for competitive intelligence.

✉ *Note*

You'll see that using a combination of free and paid tools to perform adequate analyses is a theme of this book. We deliberately chose this approach so that it works for both bigger organizations and smaller ones with perhaps a smaller budget or fewer resources to spend on tools.

Free tools from Google, Alexa, and SimilarWeb can provide competitor website and audience profile data. Paid versions of these tools offer more robust data on consumer behavior data that you can use to answer specific questions such as these:

- Which audience segments are competitors reaching that you are not?
- What are the top referring sources to your website?
- What keywords are successful for your competitors?
- What sources are driving traffic to your competitors' websites?

Gathering competitive intelligence data is not difficult in regard to social media. Most of this data is freely available to anyone who is interested in it. Quick-and-dirty approaches using free versions of tools such as SimplyMeasured can provide a wide range of competitive intelligence across several social platforms, including the following:

- Facebook page analysis
- Facebook insights analysis
- Facebook competitive analysis
- Facebook content analysis
- Instagram follower analysis
- YouTube competitive analysis

- YouTube channel analysis

- Twitter profile analysis

These higher-level reports do not always provide the depth you need. To get more information, you can use specialty tools that focus on particular social platforms and can provide more detailed data and metrics. For example, SocialBakers "Measure & Benchmark" solution focuses on social analytics that benchmark performance across all major social platforms for a specific industry and compares them to your brand page. Reports like these provide analysis and insight into post-grading, page recommendations, trending of post performance over time, and keyword engagement analysis.

Clickstream (Web Analytics)

Web analytics are the old man of the digital analytics community. However, being the wise and experienced older member of the community, web analytics still have a lot to offer in regard to analytics and insights, despite a shifting focus to content engagement and content analytics by many marketers as time spent time on social platforms has outpaced time spent on brand websites.

Web analytics tools have come a long way since their early logfile analysis days and now offer an advanced suite of measurement and analytics features, including the following, among many others:

- **Custom dashboards:** Leading platforms offer the ability to create custom dashboards, personalized to your site, and conversion events, including threshold notifications for key events and custom key performance indicators (KPIs)/goal definition.

- **Advanced segmentation:** Modern web analytics platforms such as Adobe Analytics or Google Analytics offer segmentation capabilities that let you build, manage, and apply powerful custom segments to all of your reports. Do you want to understand the differences in behavior among visitors from Facebook versus Twitter versus email lists? This is no problem with segments. Segments are an incredibly powerful tool that enables you to drill down and ask very specific questions about a specific group of visitors rather than always looking at traffic in the aggregate.

    In addition, these platforms also offer A/B testing, multivariate testing capabilities for experimentation. This feature gives you the ability to test variations of content and user experience on your website pages to determine which specific permutations yield the most conversions and highest user satisfaction.

- **Mobile analytics:** The mobile web has exploded, despite consumers spending more time in apps than with the mobile web. Mobile analytics is no longer only a nice-to-have feature. In fact, in late 2016, mobile Internet traffic surpassed desktop Internet traffic for the first time ever. It's a mobile first, desktop second world we live in now. That said, everything is dependent on your unique audience so be sure to validate your audiences' device preference and behaviors while planning. That said, generally speaking, mobile is a core requirement to provide a positive and effective brand experience, whether through a mobile-optimized site or mobile application. Web analytics tools have incorporated mobile support, and they offer a robust set of features to measure content across any mobile device. Mobile analytics provides answers to common questions such as these:

  - Where is my mobile traffic coming from?

  - What content are mobile users most interested in?

  - How is my mobile app being used? What's working? What isn't?

  - Which mobile platforms (and versions) work best with my site?

  - How does mobile visitors' engagement with my site compare to traditional and/or desktop visitors' engagement?

It's important to note that the mobile reporting features of web analytics platforms are vastly limited when compared to mobile app analytics, which give app developers or brands that have apps near real-time and detailed views into how consumers are engaging with their apps. The landscape of mobile app analytics tools is crowded, but some to consider and take a look at are Flurry analytics, Localytics, and Mixpanel. Many more exist, and you should evaluate them all to identify which one best suits your needs, but these three have the features and capabilities to support most needs, if not all.

Conversion Analytics

Your website exists for a reason. More specifically, it likely exists for a set of specific conversion events, whether that's directly selling product, capturing a lead, or driving a specific user action like downloading a whitepaper. Leading web analytics platforms provide insights regarding this key area and answer questions about how onsite user behaviors lead to conversions (regardless of what those may be—sales, registrations, leads, and so on).

One of the most advanced capabilities offered in the area of conversion analytics has to do with multichannel funnel attribution. You're no longer limited by the "last click" attribution problem. You can now gain insight into how each digital marketing or advertising channel is contributing to specific conversion goals, including paid search, paid display, social marketing, email marketing, and more.

Another useful feature is user experience path visualization, which enables you to determine the highest-performing visitor conversion paths. What are the most common and highest-performing entry points to your website? Where are users experiencing friction or disappointment along the path? What step in the user experience journey causes the most abandonment? These are all key questions involved in optimizing the user experience of your website.

Finally, some leading vendors, such as Analytic Partners, offer multitouch attribution measurement and modeling. Do you want to build predictive models to attribute conversions to specific channels to better gauge your channel mix and investment? No problem; these vendors can help.

Custom Segmentation

Custom segmentation enables you to personalize your web analytics in the way that's most relevant to your business. It allows you to define custom variables and classify individual user segments or groups.

Analyzing your traffic in aggregate might be interesting, but it isn't advised. As Avinash Kaushik—one of the foremost experts on all things web analytics—has repeated over the years, data in the aggregate is useless. You must segment or die. This has never been truer than it is today. It's one of the biggest issues we currently face with social platforms and the data they generate. Most social platforms provide vast amounts of data, but in the aggregate, which is not terribly useful. Facebook, for example, provides basic segmentation by certain demographics, such as age, gender, location, and a few others.

Visual Overlays

Visual overlays are a nice-to-have but also useful method for viewing web analytics data in a visual format. This typically includes overlays in the form of heat maps, click maps, activity maps, and geolocation maps that show physical locations of website visitors.

Social Media Reporting

Some people like to categorize any social profile in the earned category, but we disagree. A difference exists between real "earned media" through word of mouth, buzz, and so on and direct investment in maintaining a brand presence on a social platform. Maintaining a brand presence requires investing time and money on behalf of a brand, which is why we include social reporting in the owned media category.

Many web analytics tools now provide varying degrees of social analytics reports. These channels do not exist in silos but must work together. Converged media is the new standard. In an effort to measure the specific effect that social activities have on the metrics and goals that matter, we see these tools in the early stages of social attribution. There are indeed limitations now, but they offer the ability to

- Identify which social referral sources send the most engaged visitors to your site.

- Learn which brand content social visitors engaged with most and what visitors are sharing most.

- Learn how users engage with your brand content offsite, on websites that are not your own.

- Segment and measure the performance of individual social media campaigns.

- Create custom segments for users on individual social networks, such as Facebook and Twitter. This feature is useful because segmentation enables you to truly understand the differences between your user groups and provides you with insight to optimize and personalize the user experience.

- Identify which user-generated content is responsible for amplifying brand content; this contributes to true "earned media."

These social report integrations for web analytics tools do have some shortcomings. Data quality concerns, reporting inconsistencies (especially Facebook's track record here), and overall data coverage across markets and geographies are issues. For example, Google Analytics currently supports some major social platforms in its tracking, but it excludes others. This creates blind spots and can lead to questionable analyses and decision making, based on a false view of user behavior and the digital landscape.

Although an integrated solution containing both web analytics and social analytics is ideal, at this point you are better served by using best-of-breed tools for each. The social analytics landscape is crowded and specialized. There are many choices, and there are many redundant tools with little to no differentiation that have created an incredibly frustrating and difficult experience for buyers. Some consolidation has occurred via mergers and acquisitions to reduce these problems, much as it did in the early days of digital marketing with the early web analytics vendors, but it's not entirely over yet. Multiple options still exist for third-party social platform analytics to confuse buyers.

User Experience Feedback

Tools are available that enable you to gather very specific qualitative user feedback through onsite surveys. Some call this "voice of the customer," and others call it "visitor feedback." All of these tools share a common functionality, which is a continuous and consistent measurement of the user's website experience.

Clickstream analysis can provide insight into the volume of activity by page and conversions. It's a starting point, but it provides an incomplete picture of overall site activity, and it's why companies try to collect specific feedback. User experience feedback can be crucial for answering the following questions and determining how users feel about the overall website experience:

- How would you rate your overall website experience?

- What was the primary purpose of your visit?

- Were you able to complete your primary task?

- Could anything about your website experience be improved?

Site-survey solutions, such as those from iPerceptions and ForeSee Results, provide additional benefits, such as web analytics integration, threshold-based alerts to notify you about significant changes, and benchmarks in vertical industries for comparisons.

The combination of quantitative clickstream analysis to determine what is happening onsite and qualitative user experience feedback can answer many questions about what is working with an owned media asset and what needs improvement.

Real-Time Site Analytics

Real-time analytics overlaps with traditional web analytics in terms of technical capabilities, but real-time analytics run at hyperspeed. Real-time analytics is all about what's happening on your website *right now*.

Real-time solutions from companies such as Chartbeat and Parse.ly were created to solve problems for those on the frontlines who are responsible for managing publishing and media sites, but they're useful for just about any company. The assumption is that the end users are in sales, marketing, or content roles and aren't looking to immerse themselves in data and reports. They're focused on optimizing the user experience for each audience segment in real-time.

Real-time analytics tools provide analysis and reporting of what users on your site are doing on a second-by-second basis. You can use these tools to determine how active your users are on a page; what page interactions they are most engaged in; and what content topics and types are most consumed, shared, and ignored. Whereas web analytics focuses on clickstream analysis, real-time site analytics focuses on everything else that happens between clicks.

References

1.   "Ad Trackers Are On More than 75% of Websites;" Rahul Chadha, eMarketer, January 8, 2018. https://www.emarketer.com/content/ad-trackers-are-on-more-than-75-of-web-pages

2.   "eMarketer Scales Back Estimates of Ad Blocking in the US, eMarketer, February 15, 2017. https://www.emarketer.com/Article/eMarketer-Scales-Back-Estimates-of-Ad-Blocking-US/1015243

3.   "Audience Data: Where Marketers Are Investing Their Spending," Rahul Chadha, eMarketer, December 11, 2017. https://www.emarketer.com/content/this-is-where-marketers-are-spending-on-us-audience-data

Understanding Digital Analytics Concepts

Data and digital analytics have accelerated the pace of marketing unlike ever before, pulling analytics experts into the spotlight. The explosion of data-driven decision making has shifted marketing strategies and analyst tools in big ways. In this chapter, we examine the digital analytics concepts that continue to be essential in defining what marketers and communicators need to understand to compete.

Further, the massive insurgence of digital media has pushed the shift in marketer opportunities from messaging campaigns to defining relevant and personalized consumer experiences. So, not only have digital data and analytics further accelerated available data with which to plan better campaigns, more effectively optimized campaigns in flight, and measured performance in a more robust way, but they have also redefined marketing and media products for the industry.

One of the biggest detriments to this accelerated environment is a lack of familiarity with key terminology. A lack of clarity exists around the language and vocabulary surrounding digital data and analytics, what each of the metrics means, which metrics are most important, how each of the metrics is collected, how to develop goals, and which metrics fit those goals. Let's dig into how to set proper goals and objectives, what the key metrics are for digital analytics, and how to align these metrics with traditional tactics.

Starting at the Top

Before digging into specific metrics, understanding how to determine the right metrics for your campaign is important. Marketing and public relations textbooks have been teaching students for years how to set measurable goals and objectives, but the media and marketing communications landscape continues to change at a rapid pace. Marketing professionals have new channels, platforms, and tactics for reaching customers that might not be covered in a textbook.

However, just because the channels are new does not mean the way we arrive at meaningful and relevant metrics should change. What are the components of a measurable goal? Every practitioner—digital or otherwise—should know three things:

- **Behavior**—This is the most critical component of goal setting. Are you trying to increase awareness with your target audience, or are you trying to get your target audience to take some sort of action? Take a moment to sit down and write out what your desired behaviors are from the program.

- **Amount of change**—Identifying how much you want the behavior to change is important. It can be expressed as a raw number (for example, the number of new people entering a store is expected to go up by 5,000 customers) or as a percentage (for example, the number of new people entering a store is expected to increase by 10%).

- **Time**—Every goal should have a time element. Whether it is a year, a month, or a week, professionals should be looking to identify how long the program or campaign will last.

Many metrics are available to you, but the metrics that you actually use to gauge the success of a program should flow from the behavior(s) that you are trying to affect. For example, if you are trying to raise awareness, an appropriate metric might be impressions, page views, or reach. Similarly, if you are trying to drive consumers to a website, then tracking the number of conversions to clicks and visits would be most appropriate.

Spending the time to map out the specific behaviors you are looking to change, how much you want to change them, and how long it will take you to potentially change them is critical. Without that grounding, a very good chance exists that you will be analyzing too many data points, analyzing the wrong data points, and, most importantly, not truly understanding how your program is performing.

Applying a Measurement Framework

Data can be correlated to tell nearly any story—and nearly any campaign can be reframed to sound like a "win." This is why fully understanding how to give context to what they measure and report is critical for marketers and those using analytics. Establishing a measurement framework creates that accountability to what a *true*, shared vision of success looks like.

A measurement framework works by laddering up metrics to business or brand objectives. It is often used to help teams work together and speak the same language when communicating how to coordinate a complex set of marketing activities across multiple channels and platforms.

Figure 2.1 shows a sample using a simple framework that aligns metrics with KPIs with objectives.

	Create Awareness	Build Brand Opinion	Establish Brand For Me
Objectives	↑	↑	↑
KPIs	Reach Impressions Recall Share of Voice	Sentiment Conversation Lift Content Consumption	Relevance Familiarity Engagement
	↓	↓	↓
Metrics	Views Impressions Unique Views Screenshots	Shares or Repins Engagement Rate Comments Favorites	Likes/Dislikes Click/View Through Subscribers Sign ups

Figure 2.1 *Sample Scorecard Format.*

Frameworks can be done at a big picture level, substituting sample metrics for unknown ecosystems, or at the specific investment level for channels or platforms. In either instance, they must be customized specific to what organizational success looks like. They also must ladder up and down to demonstrate support of key objectives.

Objectives are generally set by CMOs, directors, or managers who are responsible for the overall strategy and performance of marketing investments. These objectives should guide decision making for all investments and approaches.

Key Performance Indicators (KPIs) are often a collaboration between measurement teams and strategy. These are the cross-ecosystem indicators that summarize how marketing is doing relative to specific objectives and desired outcomes. The common language of KPIs enables diverse marketing ecosystems to work together to accomplish a shared objective and creates accountability in what metrics are used to tell that story.

Metrics are where channel and/or platform expertise is required and are most often directed by analytics teams. These critical data points inform performance shifts at the channel and platform level.

We'll dive deeper into ROI and KPI frameworks in later chapter, but keep these terms in mind as you consider which metrics are most relevant for reporting.

Determining Your Owned and Earned Social Metrics

Social metrics are likely to be the most familiar metrics to communicators because these days very few programs are executed without a social component. An abundance of metrics are available to professionals, which makes landing on the "right" metrics all the more challenging. Unfortunately, this complexity is perpetuated by the major social platforms, each adding its own custom metrics to the mix, which makes some side-by-side comparisons across platforms difficult. To try to simplify this, we think social metrics can be broken down into two different groups:

- **Owned social metrics**—These metrics are related to the social channels (Facebook page, Twitter account, YouTube channel, and so on) that you are currently maintaining.

- **Earned social metrics**—When communications programs are developed, professionals design them in the hope that conversation will take place outside owned social channels. Every conversation about the program or the brand that you did not directly "pitch" would be considered earned. Earned media has enormous potential to help bands achieve their objectives, and it should be comprehended in any measurement strategy you develop.

The following sections dive into the specific metrics for the owned and earned categories. Keep in the back of your mind that the metrics described here are the most common metrics. The metrics that you pick for your program must align with the behaviors you are trying to change. Examining other metrics can be interesting, but might be a waste of effort. Relevance beats interesting in regard to metrics. Ensure the metrics are relevant to and aligned with the behaviors and outcomes that you're focused on changing.

Owned Social Metrics

If you are a communicator who is currently developing a program for your company or client and are not including a social media component, you are most likely in the minority. That is not to say that social media belongs in every program, just that in the majority of cases, some sort of social activation makes sense.

A number of ways exist to approach this topic, but we thought breaking down the top metrics by social platform that communications professionals are using today would be most helpful. Please note that these are only the metrics for the top social media platforms and not an exhaustive list across the entire social platform ecosystem. We do not explore a number of fringe social media platforms here.

> ✉ *Note*
>
> The following sections describe the key owned social media metrics across the bigger social media networks. Obviously, others are available to you, and you should always be looking to tie your metrics choices to the behaviors you are trying to change, but these are a good place to start.

Facebook

Facebook is the most popular social network and boasts more than two billion users. There is a pretty good chance that if you are reading this book, you maintain a page for a brand or client, and you have a personal page that you use to share photos, favorite articles, and news about yourself. If you are managing a Facebook brand page, you have access to Facebook Insights. Facebook Insights is Facebook's free, native analytics platform that enables page owners to see metrics on how their pages are performing and insights into their audience.

If you have logged into Facebook Insights recently, you know how daunting it can be. There are a lot of possible metrics, and it is not completely clear how you decide which ones you should be using. The answer to which metrics you should pay attention to depends on the behavior you are trying to change. However, there are popular metrics that almost every communications professional looks at when evaluating the page's performance. Here are the most popular:

- **Total likes**—Probably the most common and easiest to understand, total likes is the number of people who have "liked" your page.

- **Reach**—Facebook reach is the number of unique people who saw your content. It can affect every other metric you can pick: engagement, likes, comments, and clicks. Facebook breaks down reach into subcategories: organic reach, paid reach, viral reach, page reach, and post reach.

Organic reach is the total number of unique people who were shown your post through unpaid distribution. *Paid reach* is the number of unique people who were shown your post as a result of ads on Facebook. *Viral reach* is the number of unique people who have seen a story about a page published by a friend. *Page reach* is the number of unique people who have seen your brand page. Finally, *post reach* is the number of unique people who have seen an individual piece of content that you have posted.

- **Impressions**—Impressions are the number of times a post from your page is displayed, whether the post is clicked or not. Impressions can be seen by people that have either liked or not liked your page. People may see multiple impressions of the same post.

- **Engaged users**—This is the number of people who have clicked on one of your posts during a given time. It provides a good benchmark for how many people are actually reading your Facebook page's content.

- **Engagement rate**—Engagement rate is the percentage of people who saw a post and reacted to, shared, clicked, or commented on it divided by how many people see your post. Please note that some organizations have modified engagement rate to include or exclude specific metrics, and that is okay. Our goal here is to give you the standard definition that you can then use for your business however you see fit.

- **Video metrics**—An increasingly large number of posts on Facebook are in a video format. Facebook offers users a number of different video metrics but we tend to favor three specific metrics. The first is video *views*, which is the number of times your page's videos have been viewed for three seconds or more. The second is video *view rate*, which is the number of video views divided by the number of people who saw that piece of content. Lastly, we tend to favor looking at a video's *quartiles* as a measure of the quality of the engagement. By quartiles we mean measuring how far an individual user gets into a video, typically represented as 25%, 50%, 75%, and 100%.

- **Efficiency metrics**—If you have been following the marketing and communications trade publications you know that a dwindling amount of reach on Facebook comes from organic activity. Because of that, measuring how efficiently we are reaching people with our content is growing in importance. What are some key metrics that you should look at when measuring efficiency? The first is *cost per mention* (CPM). CPM measures the total amount spent on an ad campaign, divided by impressions, and then multiplied by 1,000. The second measure is *cost per engagement* (CPE). CPE is calculated as total amount spent divided by post engagement. We understand that post engagement is a vague term, but that is intentional. Facebook has a number of different post engagement metrics, but you should select the ones most appropriate for your business. The last critical efficiency metric is *cost per view* (CPV). This metric is calculated as total amount spent divided by three-second video views.

- **Likes, comments, and shares by post**—The preceding metrics in this list are page-level metrics, but you should also watch some post-level metrics. *Likes* refers to the number of people who have clicked the Like button on a post, and *comments* refers to those who have contributed some opinion on a post. *Shares* refers to the number of people who have posted your content on their page, thus generating earned media activity for your brand.

Twitter

Twitter has significantly grown its data and analytics capabilities since we wrote the first version of this book. Now you can gain access to the normal things like followers, retweets, replies, and likes, as well as mentions, impressions, profile visits, along with a host of media metrics, directly through their native analytics platform. Like Facebook, an increasing amount of activity happening on Twitter is paid advertising as brands try to cut through what is a very busy news feed for most users. Here are some common metrics you can use to evaluate your performance on Twitter:

- **Followers**—Similar to likes on Facebook, this is the number of people who have decided to track your brand's account; it is a snapshot indicator of the size of your direct Twitter audience.

- **Retweets**—This is the number of people who have shared your content with their followers.

- **Mentions**—Mentions refers to how often someone has mentioned your brand directly on Twitter.

- **Video views and completion rate**—Like Facebook, a growing amount of the content published on Twitter is in a video format. Video views on Twitter are calculated as the total number of people who have viewed three seconds of a video. However, this approach has brought some criticism of Twitter, due to videos auto-starting when in view. This can artificially inflate the total video views metric versus the actual number of users who watched the video. It doesn't make the metric useless, but it's important to be aware Twitter video views might be significantly higher than other social platforms when comparing video engagement.

Completion rate is exactly as it sounds, and is calculated as the number of people who have completed a video that has been distributed.

- **Efficiency metrics**—Much of what gets distributed by brands on Twitter today is in the form of paid media. Because of that, also measuring how efficiently you are reaching your target audience is important. There are three important efficiency metrics to measure on Twitter. The first is *cost per engagement* (CPE). CPE on Twitter is measured in a similar way as Facebook by looking at the total engagement divided by the total impressions. The second measure is *cost per view* (CPV). CPV is calculated as the total amount spent divided by the number of three-second video views. Lastly, is *cost per click* (CPC), calculated as the total amount spent divided by the number of clicks generated. Which one of these three efficiency metrics you select should be driven by your objectives. For example, if you're trying to drive clicks to another digital property, then CPC will be more important to you than if you're trying to maximize video content consumption to both your current audience and potential new followers, where CPV is much more relevant.

- **Clicks and click-through rate (CTR)**—Clicks refers to the number of times people have clicked a link that you shared, and the CTR is the number of clicks divided by the number of people who had an opportunity to click, typically expressed as a percentage. It is important to note that without the use of a link-shortening service, such as Bitly, tracking clicks is not possible. Posting directly to Twitter or Facebook does not allow you to track the number of clicks on a post. URL shorteners like Bitly provide the missing tracking and tell the whole story. We recommend combining whichever URL shortener you prefer within your linking and posting to avoid gaps in measurement and reporting.

✉ *Note*

Link-shortening services take an extremely long web address and shorten it to fit within the context of a character limited tweet or Facebook post. They also allow for custom or branded shortened URLs.

- **Impressions**—Impressions refers to the number of times someone viewed or had the opportunity to view your content. Impressions on Twitter are somewhat controversial as some analytics tools calculate impressions by including replies. If you reply to someone on Twitter, the only people who see it are you, the recipient, and the followers who overlap. If you are using a social media management tool, you should ask to see how it is calculating impressions. If you are calculating impressions manually, you should exclude replies from your analysis to get the most accurate count.

YouTube

Like Facebook, YouTube offers channel owners a robust native analytics platform for tracking performance and reporting. It offers metrics related to how the channel itself is performing, as well as how specific videos are resonating with your target audience. A lot of data is available to channel owners; these are the most popular metrics:

- **Views**—Views on YouTube can be broken down into how many times someone saw a video or the YouTube channel itself. A view is counted when the video has been viewed for 30 seconds or more.

- **Subscribers**—This is the number of people who have signed up to receive your content since you posted it.

- **Likes/dislikes**—This is the number of times a viewer had selected whether they like or dislike a video. This is typically expressed as a raw number, but it can be aggregated to show a ratio of likes to dislikes over the span of several videos.

- **Comments**—This is the number of times someone has offered an opinion on a video or your channel.

- **Favorites**—This is the number of times viewers have clicked on the Favorite link to show how much they like a particular video.

- **Sharing**—This is the number of times your video has been posted on another social network. YouTube aggregates sharing into a single metric.

- **Video view rate**—A view-through rate on YouTube is the number of times your video has been viewed, divided by the number of impressions that were served.

- **Efficiency metrics**—The most common measure of media efficiency on YouTube is cost per view (CPV). Cost per view is measured in a similar way as on Twitter and Facebook and is calculated as the total amount spent divided by the number of 30-second video views.

One important note about YouTube is that in many instances, the engagement numbers can be combined into one number. So, for example, if you are the channel owner, you can combine likes, comments, and favorites into one number that shows engagement overall. Or, similarly, you can combine the numbers and divide by the total number of videos to achieve an engagement rate.

SlideShare

One doesn't normally think of SlideShare as a popular social network, but following its acquisition by LinkedIn in 2012 it became even more popular. It is one of the top 100 most-visited websites in the world with more than 18 million uploads in 40 different content categories. The site also has more than 70 million monthly users and receives several hundred million page views per month. It is a valuable place to provide thought leadership and, if you are managing the communications for a public company, it's a place to share earnings announcements, investor presentations, and other documents of interest to key stakeholders. Not a lot of data is available, but channel owners can find some metrics:

- **Followers**—This is the equivalent of a like on Facebook or an account follower on Twitter. When you decide to follow someone or a brand on SlideShare, you receive notifications when new content has been posted without having to manually check like you would on Facebook or Twitter.

- **Views**—This is the number of times someone has seen something you have uploaded to your channel (documents and presentations).

- **Comments**—Viewers of your content have the opportunity to add to the discussion by contributing their point of view. This metric measures the number of such comments.

- **Downloads**—The number of people who have taken action and literally clicked Download to save a copy of the presentation that you have uploaded.

- **Shares**—Every piece of content that you upload can be shared to multiple social channels. Tracking how often your content is "picked up" and "placed" elsewhere is important, because it provides a strong barometer for how well it is resonating. This earned media activity should be captured and reported on as well to give you a sense of the virality of individual content you publish and promote.

Pinterest

When we wrote the first edition of this book, Pinterest had approximately 12 million users. With the explosion of the visual web and related social platforms, Pinterest now boasts more than 175 million monthly active users worldwide. Pinterest offers users space to create virtual pinboards for images of interest across the Internet.

Companies, particularly in retail and consumer categories, are creating branded channels on Pinterest, and the amount of data has been growing accordingly. The native analytics platform within Pinterest has thankfully improved as well since 2014. Pinterest has built out a robust analytics and advertising platform that gives its users a window into how your boards and content is performing. The following are some of the key metrics available to users:

- **Followers**—As with the other social networks listed earlier, followers on Pinterest are the number of people who have elected to view your content.

- **Number of boards**—This is the number of separate pinboards you have created for your account. Companies that are currently using Pinterest typically create pinboards based on product categories.

- **Number of pins**—This is simply the number of images or videos that have been "pinned" to a board you own.

- **Likes**—As is the case with the other channels, users can click the Like button for individual pieces of content. This metric counts those clicks.

- **Repins**—If you like something that another user has pinned, you have to click the Save button to share it with your Pinterest followers. This metric counts the number of repins.

- **Comments**—As with the other channels, users have a chance to offer their own perspective on a piece of content. This metric counts those comments.

- **Impressions**—Impressions are the number of times a Pin from your profile has appeared on Pinterest home feeds, category feeds, and search. Average monthly viewers include anyone who sees a Pin from your profile on their feeds.

- **Clicks**—Clicks are literally what you are probably guessing they are, which is the number of clicks on Pins from your profile.

- **Engagement rate**—This is calculated as the total number of people who have seen a Pin divided by the total number of actions.

- **Efficiency measures**—Pinterest's advertising platform has been growing since we published the first version of this book, and therefore it is important to look at two efficiency metrics. The first is *cost per mentions* (CPM). CPM is calculated in a similar way as on Facebook. The second key efficiency measure is *cost per engagement* (CPE). CPE is calculated as the total number of impressions divided by the total number of actions.

Instagram

Most, if not all, of you who are reading this book are likely actively engaged on Instagram. The popular photo sharing application has exploded since the first version of this book was published, driven largely by being acquired by Facebook. Instagram now has more than 800 million monthly active users and 500 million daily active users. More than 30% of Internet users in the United States are now on Instagram, and the platform has more than one million advertisers. As more of the Internet moves from text-based to image-based communication, it is safe to assume that Instagram will only to continue to grow. More brands will continue to use the platform to reach its key audiences through interactive and visually appealing advertising units. A number of metrics are available to brands and are broken into three different categories:

- **Overall metrics**—Brands can capture four key metrics in this bucket. The first is *impressions*, which is the number of times your ads were on the screen. The second metric is *reach*, which is the number of unique accounts who viewed your posts and stories. The third is *website clicks*, which is the number of clicks to links you've included in your business profile description. The last metric is *profile views*, which is the number of unique accounts who've visited your business profile.

- **Post metrics**—In addition to tracking likes and comments, which are self-explanatory, users can also track five other metrics: the *number of unique accounts* that saved your post; *impressions* per post; *reach* per post; and *engagement*, which is the number of unique people who have liked, commented, or saved a post. Like the other platforms outlined here, an increasingly large number of posts are in the format of a video. Because of that, users can track *video views*, which is the total number of times your video was viewed.

- **Stories**—Instagram stories are a way for users to capture real-time activity happening during the course of a 24-hour period. A number of metrics are available to brands using stories. *Impressions* are the number of times your story media was seen. Instagram stories also capture *reach*, which is the number of unique accounts who saw your story. Users can capture *taps forward* and *taps back*, which are the number of times someone taps to skip to the next piece of story media, or back, respectively. *Exits* is the number of times someone leaves the story viewer to return to their feed.

✉ *Note*

Instagram does offer the capability to capture live content, but no metrics are currently available to users of that capability. Expect analytics and metrics for "live" streaming on Instagram and other social platforms that offer it to evolve considerably and improve throughout 2018 and beyond.

Snapchat

For many of the same reasons that Instagram has grown, Snapchat has exploded on the scene since the first version of this book. Snapchat is a mobile photo messaging and multimedia sharing application that was released in September 2011. It was initially launched to share impermanent pictures via private message that could be viewed for a specified length of time. Despite its origins as an image-sharing application, video has become an important feature on the platform, with more than 10 billion mobile videos viewed per day. Over the last three to four years, Snapchat has really grown, now totaling more than 255 million monthly active users. However, with the rise of Instagram and Facebook stories, its user growth and usage has stagnated as of the publishing of this book. Although its long-term future is unclear, what is clear is that it will continue to be a way for certain audiences, particularly millennials and Gen Z audiences, to distribute video and image content for the foreseeable future. The five important metrics to track on Snapchat are :

- **Unique views**—This is the number of people who have opened the first video or image and viewed it for at least one second. Snapchat only counts each viewer once, thereby presenting an accurate metric of how many viewers each photo or video snagged.

- **Screenshots**—On other platforms like Twitter and Facebook, engagement is often tracked through reactions like likes, comments, and retweets. On Snapchat, engagement is captured by looking at the number of people who took a screenshot of a specific piece of video or imagery.

- **Completion rates**—This measures how many viewers watched your story through to completion.

- **Fall-off rate**—To calculate your fall-off rate, simply find the difference in views from one Snap to the next, divide the difference by the views on the first Snap, and multiply by 100.

- **Time-of-day activity**—Although Snapchat doesn't provide activity metrics, you can gain an understanding of your audience's key activity times by tracking the engagement associated with different posting times.

LinkedIn

LinkedIn, a social network aimed at professionals, allows members to contact past and current colleagues, look for a new job, uncover new business opportunities, and network with experts within a particular industry. Since the first version of this book was published, the platform has morphed into an effective way for brands to distribute content aimed at professional audiences through the news feed and company pages. With more than 500 million users as of April 2017, it is a hard platform to ignore for brands. The advertising side of the platform is a little bit of a black box to the outside world, but some metrics are available to page owners.

- **Visitor analytics**—This metric is broken down into traffic metrics and visitor demographics. LinkedIn gives users the opportunity to track page views, which is the number of times your page has been viewed. You can also track unique visitors, which is how many LinkedIn members visited your page, removing duplicate visits to a single page. The platform also offers robust demographic data on who these people are who have visited your page.

- **Content shares and likes**—This is exactly as it sounds, but is the total number of people who have shared or liked a piece of content that you have published.

- **Advertising metrics**—LinkedIn recommends a host of metrics to evaluate advertising performance—everything from impressions; to clicks; to total engagement; to cost per click, cost per mention, and social actions. Many of these metrics have been discussed at length throughout this chapter, and are not defined in unique ways by LinkedIn. If you are advertising on LinkedIn, remember to line up your metrics to your business objectives, as we outlined earlier in this chapter.

Earned Social Media Metrics

The best marketing programs have relevant tactics that resonate with the target audience using the appropriate channels, but the explosion of social media has created a second layer of performance that requires examination. This additional layer is described by many terms: earned media, earned coverage, or, in the case of social media, earned conversations. When marketing professionals create content to post on owned social media networks, they hope the content will spread and reach audiences beyond their direct fans, followers, or community. This dissemination could come in the form of sharing, which we covered earlier in this chapter, or it could come in the form of organic chatter in the broader community.

Communicators can track two different kinds of earned social media metrics:

- **Earned conversations**—These are social media conversations that are taking place outside the owned social media properties

- **In-network conversations**—Communicators should be looking to foster a sense of contribution in the online community. Tracking this kind of content separately is valuable in determining how well it does in driving action, typically additional engagement.

Much of this data is captured using social listening platforms, which is covered in the next chapter, but these are the primary data points most communicators gather when evaluating earned conversations:

- **Share of voice**—Most communicators are familiar with the concept of market share, and this is fairly similar. Share of voice tracks, typically in percentage form, how much conversation is happening about one brand versus another.

- **Share of conversation**—Share of conversation is often overlooked and, in our view, is a more detailed and accurate gauge of how aware people are of a product or campaign within a broader industry than share of voice. This metric tracks, typically in percentage form, how much conversation is happening versus the broader industry. Share of voice typically is a metric used to evaluate brand-level performance where share of conversation is used to evaluate specific product, service, or topic performance.

- **Sentiment**—The topic of sentiment is highly controversial. Simply put, it is the amount of positive, negative, or neutral (with gradations in between) conversation that is happening about a brand or product.

- **Message resonance**—Chances are good that your company, and in turn your communications program, is trying to advance some strategically important message or messages. Knowing how well (or not) a message is being received by the community is vital. This can be measured by how often keywords and phrases are being picked up in social conversations while being tied to the brand. Alternatively, many brands have taken to utilizing traditional survey research and asking questions of social audiences to determine message resonance.

- **Overall conversation volume**—Tracking the volume of conversation over time is critical in understanding how well a message has been received. Similarly, it is important in understanding how visible a brand is to the community. If your conversation volume trend line looks like a rollercoaster, then it is likely time to start revisiting your social media strategy. An important thing to keep in mind when evaluating the overall conversation is your search strings. You want to make sure the search string is as accurate as possible so that volumes aren't inflated.

The other element of earned social media metrics is in-network conversations. These are conversations, or content, that the community generates on its own and posts to owned properties. These are easier metrics to understand and gather because they are almost identical to the metrics outlined earlier in the section for specific social media channels. The only difference is that instead of looking at higher-level page performance (likes, followers, subscribers, and so on) communicators should be looking at post-level data (comments, likes per post, shares per post, and so on).

Social media data is abundant, and as it becomes more mainstream, more data will become available. Because of that abundance, it is easy to become distracted by all the potential data points. If you focus on the metrics we have listed and how they apply to your goals, you will not go wrong. That being said, social media data is only one piece of the puzzle. Communicators need to gather other digital components, as described in the remainder of this chapter.

Demystifying Web Data

Most communicators have had at least some exposure to web analytics tools, such as Google Analytics and Adobe Analytics. However, website data tends to be a confusing data source for many marketing and communications professionals.

The good news for marketers is that unlike the social platforms, website analytics have more standardization across tools and vendors, which means regardless of which tool you decide to use to gather website data, the outputs will look very similar. Page views, visits, unique visitors, or Average Time on Site are simple examples of standard metrics across web analytics tools. The bad news is that, as with social media, a lot of website data is available to collect and report.

Where should marketers begin? Whatever tool you select, the vendor will likely offer a training program, but regardless, the web metrics you decide to measure should line up with the behaviors you are trying to change. If you keep your eye on measurable goals, picking the right metrics in a sea of data should not be a challenge, as you've already done the preparation work to easily weed out the metrics that aren't relevant to your initiative. So, what are some metrics that communicators typically use? You can do a number of things to track the effectiveness of a website and how it interrelates with other channels. Suffice it to say, though, that the following metrics are the most popular metrics communicators are using today:

- **Visits**—Depending on the platform in question, visits is the number of times people have been on your site. Visits are considered to be unique in that if I come to your page, click a few links, and then leave, that is one visit. If I return to your site quickly, that is considered part of the same session.

- **Unique page views**—This is the number of visits during which a specified page(s) was viewed once.

- **Bounce rate**—Bounce rate is expressed as a percentage and is the number of visits in which a person left a site from the initial entry page.

- **Pages per visit**—This is probably the easiest metric to understand. It is simply the number of pages a person viewed during a single session. It is important to understand how many pages and which pages a person visited during a session to see which content resonated.

- **Traffic sources**—This is not one metric, per se, but knowing the traffic sources is helpful in matching up content from social channels to website presence.

- **Conversion**—Conversion is probably the most controversial metric because it is one that does not apply to all situations. In some cases, companies are using digital media channels to build awareness. In those instances, conversions in the traditional sense do not apply. If you are tracking conversion, it is the number of times someone has taken an action on your page—or a dollar figure expressing the amount spent on the page. If a visitor downloads a whitepaper, buys something from your site, or even signs up for coupons via email, the action is counted as a conversion. Whatever it is, conversion is an important metric for communicators to track. It is a clear way to demonstrate the value of a program. We recommend redefining *conversion* for your programs to mean any relevant outcome or behavior that a user takes through clicks on your website rather than a conversion being a click that directly correlates to a lead or a sale. In the earlier example, conversions of visitors who clicked and consumed a whitepaper would be highly relevant if you're a marketer trying to reach and inform a relevant B2B audience.

Digital Advertising Concepts

If you have explored digital advertising you are probably aware that getting started can be fairly overwhelming. To begin with, it is full of specialized terms that might be new to you. Second, the data sources, depending on the type of campaign you are running totals in the several hundred (if not thousands). Third, the types of advertising units that a brand can buy can also total in the hundreds (if not thousands). How does one distinguish between television advertising, online video (OLV), display advertising, and programmatic advertising? All of these platforms have their own unique creative applications and ability to target your core audience. Lastly, the number of metrics that you could use to gauge performance of your digital advertising campaign is huge.

We could write an entire book exclusively on digital and television advertising measurement, and such books do exist already in the marketplace. Alternatively, we could list all the metrics that you could use to measure digital advertising performance. However, for the purposes of this book we wanted to capture a series of definitions that you might run into when running digital advertising programs for your brand as a primer. Here are some of those key definitions:

- **A/B testing**—A method used to compare different versions of digital advertising or website landing pages to determine which one performs better.

- **Ad banner/digital display**—This is probably the most common form of digital advertising. These advertising units, which include static graphics, videos, and/or interactive rich media, display on a webpage or in an application.

- **Ad exchange**—A technology-facilitated marketplace that allows Internet publishers and advertisers to buy and sell advertising inventory in real-time auctions. Ad exchanges are a departure from the historical method of buying advertising inventory, where advertisers and publishers would enter price negotiations in order to show ads on a particular site.

- **Ad inventory**—Website publishers serve ads to visitors when they visit a web page. The number of potential ads that can be served is considered their ad inventory.

- **Ad serving**—The delivery of an ad from a web server to the end user's device, where the ads are displayed on a browser or an application.

- **Cookie**—Information stored on a website visitor's browser. A cookie tracks the visitor's movement on the website and is used to remember the visitor's behavior and preferences.

- **Demand-side platform (DSP)**—A system that allows advertisers to bid for and purchase inventory from multiple ad exchanges, through one single interface.

- **Display advertising**—A digital advertising format where graphic ads are shown on a web page. Display ads can be graphics, videos, interactive images, and expandable banners.

- **Data Management Platform (DMP)**—A data management platform pulls data from multiple different, potentially unrelated sources of data to define specific audience segments. Those audience segments are then often used to target groups through digital advertising.

- **Frequency**—The number of times an ad is served to the same consumer during a specific period of time.

- **Lookalike audiences**—A lookalike audience targets people who are similar to your existing customers, which helps improve conversion rates.

- **Native advertising**—Any form of paid advertising that is largely indistinguishable in form from the channel being used to present it.

- **Programmatic media buying**—An automated method of buying media, which ensures that advertisers are reaching the right person, at the right time, in the right place. The ads are bought on set parameters pre-defined by the company placing the ads. Programmatic advertising uses data to make decisions about which ads to buy in real-time.

- **Viewability**—This is an online advertising metric that aims to track only impressions that can actually be seen by users. For example, if an ad is loaded at the bottom of a web page but a user doesn't scroll down far enough to see it, that impression would not be deemed viewable.

We could list literally hundreds of terms here, but we did want to capture the most critical ones in case you run across them when executing a campaign.

Searching for the Right Metrics

Search analytics suffers a similar fate to web analytics, in that a lot of confusion surrounds what to measure and how to measure it. Some of that is due to the mysticism behind the search engine companies themselves, particularly Google's ranking algorithm, but the majority of it is due to search analytics being a relatively new field for many communicators because it's not something one can develop deep expertise on unless it's given a full-time focus.

For years, search analytics has been an area where specialists have come in and offered counsel to companies. Recently, a link has been created between social media and search analytics that makes it imperative for marketers of all disciplines to have at least a basic understanding of search data. This is imperative as search has only grown in significance. Since the original publication of this book in 2014, search queries on Google have only gotten longer and more specific as consumers refine their search intent. The data collection and metrics themselves are not so mysterious if you know how to break them down into manageable chunks. Search analytics is typically broken down into two categories.

- **Paid search**—A paid search is any form of online advertising that ties an ad to a specific keyword-based search request.

- **Organic search**—Organic search results are listings on search engine result pages that appear because of specific relevance to search terms.

Both types of search analytics have metrics tied to them. The following sections deal with each one individually.

Paid Search

As described earlier, a paid search is any form of advertising that ties an ad (creative and text) to specific keywords in order to appear more prominently in search results. It has often been the purview of search engine optimization (SEO) and search engine marketing (SEM) professionals. But now that the communications disciplines (such as public relations, marketing, digital media, and social media) have come together, it is important for all communications professionals to under-stand the various metrics that can be tracked when executing a paid search.

We are going to sound like a broken record throughout this book, but the paid search metrics (assuming that there is a paid search component to a program) should align with the behaviors you are trying to change. Here are some of the most popular paid search metrics:

- **Impressions**—An impression happens when a paid search ad appears on the search engine results page. This metric counts the number of such impressions.

- **Clicks**—This is probably the easiest metric to understand. It counts the number of times a user clicks on an ad and visits the predetermined landing page.

- **CTR**—The CTR is often expressed as a ratio, and it is the number of clicks an ad gets versus the number of impressions received.

- **Cost per click (CPC)**—CPC is the average amount an advertiser would pay for a click.

- **Impression share**—This is the ratio of the impressions your ad received to the possible impressions it could have received. This is similar to the share of conversation in social media analytics.

- **Sales or revenue per click**—Quite simply, this is the amount of money generated per click received on an ad.

- **Average position**—This metric measures where your advertisement appeared on the search engine results page.

You could use 10 to 20 additional metrics with paid searches, depending on your goals. However, the metrics listed here are the most popularly used and referenced. If your program has a paid search element, and you are not using one or more of those metrics, you should probably rethink your measurement plan of attack.

Organic Searches

Organic search results are listings on search engine pages that are tied to a specific keyword and are not being driven by an advertisement. The good part about organic search metrics is that even though users are not necessarily taking an action, through the use of tools, we can generally deduce what people are looking for by examining their search intent.

When a user visits a search engine and enters a word or phrase, there is likely someone on the other end analyzing that behavior. Understanding organic search behaviors is critical because some industries see very little volume of conversation online. The online community might not be participating, but they are most assuredly trying to learn something about the subject. That is where search analytics comes in.

Whether or not you have a paid search component to your program, you should be trying to understand the organic search landscape. What are the metrics that communicators can use? The following are a handful of the ones that are commonly used:

- **Known and unknown keywords**—How many keywords do you know that are driving people to your website? How many do you not know? Is there an opportunity to optimize your content based on those unknown keywords? It is very possible that your unknown keywords are also unknown to your competitors.

- **Known and unknown branded keywords**—Similar to the known and unknown keywords, communicators need to understand which words about their brand are being used most often.

- **Total visits**—Ideally, you are tracking total visits to your website in your web analytics platform, but this metric could also fall under the organic search bucket as well.

- **Total conversions from known keywords**—If you are properly optimizing your content based on known keywords people are using, then you should see an uptick in conversion. Again, in this case, conversions could be a dollar figure, downloads, signing up for a newsletter, and so on.

- **Average search position**—Yes, this metric overlaps with paid searches, but it is important to know where you rank in search engine results pages, based on your top known and unknown and branded or unbranded keywords.

The search analytics tools might be complicated, but the individual metrics are not. Social, web, and search metrics are the three primary buckets that communicators need to be familiar with. We have identified the most popular in each of those categories, but you should not feel constrained to these lists. If there are two or three in each category that make sense for your program, use them.

 Tip

Do not get stuck in the trap of trying to measure everything just because the data is available.

After you have picked your social, website, and search metrics, then what? If you have been paying attention throughout this chapter, you will probably realize that we have left out one very important piece of the puzzle: traditional analytics. The next sections tackle this subject.

Aligning Digital and Traditional Analytics

Just because digital media has exploded and subsequently created an abundance of data does not mean that traditional media and analytics are dead. In fact, when used together, digital data can strengthen traditional data and vice versa.

The best measurement approaches examine traditional media trends alongside digital media trends. Because consumers spend their time in and behave in an omni-channel, online and offline world, flowing across different devices and screens, marketers everywhere are attempting to come up with integrated programs and should therefore be developing integrated measurement strategies to more accurately gauge effectiveness of their programs.

At this point, marketers may be more familiar with traditional metrics than with digital metrics, so we have outlined what traditional research tactics you should continue to engage in even if you are gathering mountains of digital data.

Primary Research

The mainstream and digital trade press have published a number of articles arguing that surveys and other forms of primary research are dead. In fact, with rare exception, primary research is still a very important input for companies of all sizes.

 Note

When we say *primary research*, we mainly mean surveys and focus groups.

As abundant as digital data is, it cannot entirely answer certain things for communicators. Some of those measures include the following:

- **Brand perception**—We have seen a number of studies attempting to tie social presence to overall brand reputation, and, at least at this point, those studies are incomplete. Unless marketers ask very specific questions of the target audience, using online sentiment and volume to ascertain how a brand is currently perceived would be very difficult. Some decent assumptions can be made, but the story is incomplete.

- **Message resonance**—Message resonance is a metric included in the social analytics section, but it is still something that requires offline testing. Just because an online audience is picking up a key message does not mean it is because of the company's program. Plus, hard as it is to believe, some targets are still much more likely to engage offline than online.

- **Executive reputation**—Despite the growth in the number of brands engaging in social media activities, the corporate executives at those brands have not adopted social media at the same rate of speed. Those executives who do are genuinely embraced by the online community following the brand if they communicate authentically. When the communication is authentic, the brand does see a benefit. How much benefit? It is hard to tell without asking the online community following your brand, "Why?"

- **Advertising performance—Historically,** there has been very little experimentation in the testing of ads online. Typically, the ads were produced, run on traditional channels, and then posted to social networks. Not only is posting advertising verbatim to social networks not interesting, there is also a small chance it will not resonate if it contains no comedic value. This continues in 2018, but more and more brands are adopting best practices for developing the right content for the right channel. Quickly and efficiently testing advertising in small, highly targeted focus groups is still the most effective method. Many platforms allow for this and in 2018 there really isn't a compelling reason not to be doing so. Facebook is a good example here, giving you the option to run a variety of tests across ad groups and optimize in real-time based on the highest performer.

Traditional Media Monitoring

Social listening has made most of the traditional media monitoring platforms obsolete. However, traditional platforms still pick up plenty of publications that social ones do not. If you were to ask about building a list of reporters for a traditional media outreach, the first place to turn would not be a social listening platform.

We are not advocating that communicators should go out and spend big money on traditional media monitoring platforms. What we are advocating is that if you need to find recent articles in the mainstream press, you should pick the right tool for the job. In almost every case, the right tool for the job is a traditional monitoring platform.

Traditional CRM Data

The field of social customer relationship management (CRM) is growing, but it is still limited to a specific channel. There is still valuable intelligence on our customers that we need to be leveraging from traditional CRM databases. Brands aren't yet able to easily plug a CRM data source into all the social and digital platforms that they operate in. Today, it would require a custom, intensive effort for each specific social channel they would want to implement this on. Now, the goal here isn't to abuse the wealth of data that digital media creates on our customers by just dropping it into a database and forgetting about it. Rather, the goal is to look for trends we can identify from our traditional databases, look for the similarities and differences in online behavior, and try to understand how that information can be used to deliver relevant and personalized consumer experiences across all the digital touchpoints that they have with your brand.

Bringing It All Together

At this point, you should be more familiar with setting proper goals, using potential digital metrics and what they mean, and how you can continue leveraging traditional activities to help better inform digital ones. Assume for a moment that you have built your program, have begun executing your program, know which metrics you are going to use, and have begun collecting data. Now, what should you do? That is the million-dollar question, right? How often should you report? What should the reporting template look like? What should you report to your leadership versus to other internal stakeholders? The answer to all of those questions is, of course, "It depends on the company." However, communicators can follow some generally accepted practices that. Read on.

The Reporting Timeline

The frequency at which you report depends a lot on your leadership and how thirsty for data you are, as well as the time frame for your stated objectives. The best measurement programs utilize a combination of approaches. Those programs produce a monthly snapshot with a high-level synopsis of how core metrics are tracking. Then every quarter, those same companies produce a deeper dive that shows how the targeted behavior has changed. That said, for front-line managers or contributors focused on optimization at the channel or platform level, more frequent reporting will likely be necessary, whether that be daily, weekly, or monthly reports.

Tip

Arm yourself with the right data. The more relevant data you have, the better you can understand how behaviors have changed. Data eliminates anomalies and allows your communications to truly take hold with the target audience.

The Reporting Template

A number of templates are available to communicators, and oftentimes a simple email or Word document with key metrics tracked over time and an executive summary would suffice. However, most of the best-practice measurement programs create scorecards and build presentations based on those scorecards. The scorecards are typically integrated (traditional and digital together) and provide a snapshot and deep-dive into how the program performed.

🔍 *Tip*

Consider creating a simple matrix that shows the desired behavioral changes across the top and the channels used to affect those behaviors along the left-hand side.

Different Strokes for Different Folks

Not everyone within an organization needs to see a deep-dive report. Your manager probably wants to see it, but higher-lever stakeholders probably want a more condensed, executive-level snapshot. That can be as simple as a bulleted email with key highlights or as complicated as a truncated scorecard matrix. Figure out what your leadership would like to see and how often updates would be beneficial.

You now have a solid foundation for setting measurable goals, understanding what metrics matter and what the individual metrics mean, and knowing how the metrics can be utilized with traditional research techniques and how you bring it all together for either a monthly or quarterly (or both) report. Now, we will dive into each of these areas more deeply!

3

Choosing Your Analytics Tools

The practice of digital analytics involves both tools and the human analysts who use them. Tools make the data collection process easier and give an analyst a jumpstart on providing actionable insights. They also provide a way to scale data collection and insights across a large company.

The tools are critical, but so is the analyst. The analyst provides valuable context on the business, the goals of the data collection and research, the ability to cross-reference multiple data sets toward the solution of a business problem, and, most importantly, the selection of the tools themselves. A world of data is available to communicators and analysts alike, and many tools are available to collect that data.

In the first two chapters of this book, we have given you an overview of the synergetic media landscape and some background on the practice of digital analytics. In both of those chapters, we make reference to how the available data has exploded over the past several years as new channels have proliferated. In response to that explosion of data, hundreds, or maybe even thousands of tools that help companies collect data across a wide variety of channels have cropped up. In the first edition of this book, we spent a considerable amount of time going through tools for social media listening; search; and audience, content, engagement, and influencer analysis. While we think those chapters were helpful, we also realize that with the speed in which this industry moves, those chapters have a tendency to be out of date quickly. For this second edition, we instead focus our discussion about tools in one chapter, with some reference to specific tools in later chapters but only as examples for you to consider and evaluate on your own.

Over the course of the coming pages, we provide you a framework to manage your marketing capabilities. We discuss at length the process by which you can evaluate new capabilities that your organization may be exposed to, how your technology stack should be organized for maximum effectiveness, what tools you should consider as mandatory, and, critically, how to achieve adoption and usage of these tools. Let's start with a framework to evaluate new technologies.

Evaluating New Marketing Technologies

If you work in an agency or for a big company, you have likely been sent an email or some sort of correspondence through LinkedIn about some new-fangled marketing technology. Although it can be aggravating to be constantly inundated by these vendors, it shouldn't be surprising. Consider for a moment the growth of the marketing technology industry. According to ChiefMartec.com, the definitive source on the marketing technology industry, 5,381 marketing technology solutions are now available to consumers.[1] Of that number, 4,891 are unique companies. What does the growth rate look like? From 2016 to 2017, both numbers grew nearly 40%. Even more staggering, only 4.7% of the solutions from 2016 were removed from the consideration set, and another 3.5% changed in some fundamental way. These aren't just tools developed by a few developers in the basement of their parents' homes. Of the solutions available to consumers, 6.9% are enterprises with more than 1,000 employees or are public, 44.2% are private businesses with less than 1,000 employees, and 48.8% are investor-funded startups at any pre-exit stage. In most cases, these are well-funded organizations with something to offer to marketing organizations around the world. The long-tail of marketing technologies is significant, but shouldn't be dismissed completely out of hand.

Because of the growth of these solutions, doing the proper due diligence has become difficult because which tools should be evaluated isn't always clear.

In addition, a number of tools that have been developed are better for midsized businesses than for enterprise customers. Unfortunately, unless marketers spend a considerable amount of time using the tools themselves, they might not necessarily be able to make that distinction. With that being the case, how should you go about evaluating these solutions? First and foremost, let us make a plug for hiring a marketing technology leader. This is a growing field within marketing, driven largely by the explosion of tools. The individuals who fill these roles typically come from an information technology (IT) background or have a technical background as part of a marketing department. They play a critical role in bridging the divide between what the business requirements are and what the technological capabilities can deliver. They also can be a critical bridge between different departments within large companies who might be utilizing these solutions. If you can't hire a marketing technology specialist, the next best solution is to actively engage with your IT department to help with organization and evaluation. Do not be afraid of your IT department; it can be your best friend.

Whether you have a marketing technology department or not, what are some ways that you can effectively evaluate the tools you might be exposed to via email, LinkedIn, or at a conference? In our experience, a handful of criteria are the most effective for performing an evaluation:

- **Proprietary data sets**—You might be wondering how something is proprietary if it's clearly a marketing technology solution that's marketing itself to end consumers? The answer is actually quite simple. Almost every organization collects data on its key audiences, whether those are marketing audiences or customers. There will be data sets that you come across that provide more information on those audiences or customers, and when joined with your proprietary data, add significant value to the organization. If you come across a data set like this, consider it of maximum priority.

- **Audience data**—This should be fairly self-explanatory if you have been in the marketing or communications profession for almost any length of time, but any data set that allows you to understand your audiences more effectively should be prioritized. A number of solutions are on the market that can help, whether you work in pharmaceuticals, technology, or consumer industries. Again, consider whether or not this data set can be joined with proprietary data or if collecting this data set can give you a competitive advantage in your market.

- **Better measurement**—We talk throughout this book about the value of measuring bottom-line impact. It shouldn't be the only thing you measure, as we discuss later in Chapter 7, "Return on Investment," but understanding return on investment from your marketing programs is critical. If collecting a set of data helps you perform better measurement, prioritize it for evaluation.

- **Content performance**—Many of you have likely heard the expression, "content is king," and because of that a number of solutions are on the market that help you evaluate content engagement effectiveness. Similarly, a number of tools on the market can help you distribute content effectively to your target audience(s). If a marketing technology solution could help you understand content marketing performance or do better distribution, evaluate it.

- **Channel mix**—After audience and content, another critical evaluation criterion is understanding the right channel mix. We realize that this criterion could be broad. It could incorporate anything from social media listening vendors to syndicated research partners. This is where a marketing technology leader could be extremely effective for your business because it can understand the business requirements and the technological capabilities of the various vendors available. Our best advice, in the absence of a marketing technology leader, is to follow the business requirements. If the requirements take you toward a social media listening vendor for you to understand the right channel mix, follow it.

- **Ability to integrate and adopt**—One of the barriers to adoption, which we discuss toward the end of this chapter, is a marketing capability's inability to integrate with another data set. If you are exposed to a solution and you think it might be tough to achieve adoption or integrate with something else that might already be part of the stack, pass on the evaluation altogether.

- **Cost**—We list cost last in this list intentionally. In most cases, if you focus on the value a marketing capability could deliver to your organization first, then the cost will become easier to justify. Cost should not be the primary consideration when evaluating a marketing technology solution.

We do not foresee a scenario where the number of tools available to marketers will slow down any time soon. New requirements will continue to pop up as the field of digital marketing continues to evolve. With those new requirements will come new tools attempting to help those marketers scale whatever it is they are trying to execute on behalf of their company. We believe this evaluation framework should help you with the ongoing barrage of communications you are likely to receive from these vendors.

After you begin to evaluate new solutions and onboard them, organizing them in some sort of meaningful way that the business can understand is critical. We dive into that topic next.

Organizing Your Marketing Technology Stack

As mentioned earlier, literally thousands of marketing technology solutions are available to companies today. If a lack of understanding exists in the market about how to evaluate them, similar confusion exists about how to organize the technology stack after you have decided on a set of solutions. You might be wondering, "What does organization matter? Isn't it about identifying, evaluating, and then adopting the capability?" If you are someone who thinks that way, you are not totally incorrect. It is about identifying, evaluating, and adopting the solution(s) that help your business the most. From our perspective, there are three reasons why organization of your marketing technology stack is so critical:

- **Essential to adoption**—In most cases, when you are evaluating marketing technology solutions, you are doing so on behalf of other stakeholders within your organization. Given the wide range of tools available to you, it's likely clear that there isn't one solution that can do everything that your organization needs. If it isn't clear to those stakeholders how the tools are organized for their benefit, it's likely that they will not be adopted.

- **Continued investment**—Marketing technology solutions, particularly for large enterprises, are not cheap. The investment in them requires senior management approval, in many cases, before purchasing. It is also almost a given that you will need to continue justifying the investment as new solutions become available that can help your business. If the marketing stack isn't clearly organized, then the investment isn't likely to follow.

- **Success measurement**—We do not discuss it in significant detail in this chapter, but an important component of any marketing technology program is establishing clear key performance indicators (KPIs). Those KPIs could be anything from adoption, to return on marketing investment as a result of having the capability in-house, or delivering marketing programs more efficiently (cost savings). If the technology stack isn't organized well, properly evaluating effectiveness becomes hard.

Hopefully, you will agree that organization is critical to any marketing technology program, whether you currently access five tools or hundreds (hopefully not hundreds). Assuming you do agree, how should you go about organizing it to further adoption and demonstrate value to the business? In our experience two companies, Cisco and Intel, have pioneered the development and adoption of marketing technology. Over the course of the next few pages we dive into how each has organized its marketing technology stack, including a detailed case study from Intel. First, let's discuss how Cisco structures its marketing technology stack.

Cisco's Marketing Technology Stack

One of the earliest adopters and pioneers of marketing technology was Cisco. The company recognized early on that it was faced with a complex ecosystem of tools that required a significant amount of investment and organization. It also realized early on that the organization and adoption hinged on a dedicated team whose sole function was the management of the stack. The Cisco marketing technology stack is an excellent example of a well-organized, best-of-breed marketing stack. How it is organized and the level of adoption it has achieved organization-wide are truly masterful.

The marketing technology stack that Cisco deploys is customer-centric, with literally the customer at the center of every part of the diagram. Four concentric circles flow from the center of the diagram that represent the four stages of Cisco's buyer's journey:

1. I'm aware

2. I shop and buy

3. I install and use

4. I renew

Each of the solutions is identified by the stages of that journey in which it operates. Some are focused on one stage, whereas others provide service across all four as "systems of record."

The circles themselves are divided into four segments:

1. Customer

2. Partner

3. Seller

4. Data and operations

The first three are meant to service direct and indirect engagements with customers. The last segment is focused on internal marketing operations, including collaboration services, content management, and analytics. This particular view of the stack is helpful because Cisco is a company that employs direct and indirect methods of selling to its customers.

What we like most about the way the company has organized and explained its marketing technology stack is that it does not focus on the number of solutions. As we have hinted at throughout this chapter, the number of solutions is not relevant. But, in the event that you are wondering, Cisco's marketing technology stack features 39 different solutions. It has components of the largest marketing technology solutions offered by Google, Adobe, and Salesforce, as well as several from leading point solutions. In the next section of this chapter we discuss some of the specific tools that Cisco and Intel deploy that you should consider as essential parts of your technology stack.

Although we do not know for sure whether or not these solutions are well integrated or adopted, it is a fair to infer that they are given the nature of the solutions that Cisco is using. Most, if not all of them talk about integrating with other point solutions as part of their marketing materials. Also, having spoken to several members of the Cisco marketing team as part of events and conferences, we know that adoption is relatively high. We chalk that adoption up to its stellar organization.

Cisco isn't the only marketing technology stack that is extremely well organized. Intel is another. Let's dive into Intel's marketing stack next.

Intel's Marketing Technology Stack

The Cisco marketing technology stack is widely regarded as one of the best enterprise marketing stacks currently deployed. We would agree with that assessment but would stipulate that it is a close race between Cisco and Intel for best-in-class. Both brands started their marketing stacks around the same time, both deploy similar solutions to scale marketing programs, and both have dedicated teams whose sole focus is the development of the stack.

As part of the writing of this book, we solicited feedback from Geoff Ivey, Senior Director of Marketing Capabilities at Intel on how he has structured the company's marketing technology stack. He is a former colleague of Chuck Hemann, one of the co-authors of this book, and has spent a considerable amount of time in this industry. He is one of the foremost leaders in the area of marketing technology, so we thought his case study on how the company has organized its technology stack would be useful. Toward the end of this chapter, we also include another case study from Geoff on how the company has achieved adoption. First, though, here is Geoff's case study on organization.

"Organizing an ecosystem of tools in a large enterprise can be challenging but is actually pretty straightforward. The process of doing it requires structure. It starts with clarity around business priorities and goals and how we measure success. We draw this from our annual business planning processes. Then, we define the set of capabilities needed to support these business priorities. This collection of people-processes-systems defines your business capability. Inside of each capability zone, we then define a set of technology services, which becomes your service portfolio or what we refer to as our "gold stack." Finally, for that portfolio, we identify the discrete set of technologies (platforms, tools, vendors) that we will invest in, and then scan across our technology infrastructure to ensure our analysis is representative of what is actually deployed. In taking this approach, we start with what the business needs to accomplish, and end with the set of tools and vendors we intend to prioritize. This ensures that we have the right mix of tools and helps identify gaps and overlaps that we need to reconcile.

"The next major step in our process is to complete a maturity lifecycle assessment of each capability zone and the platforms and tools inside of them. By completing this exercise, we get a directional sense of how mature each capability is and ensure that the vendor and tool choices stay relevant to the needs of the business:

- "Where we need to consider piloting a new capability to advance innovation

- "Where we need to invest in scaling a capability more broadly for a stronger ROI

- "Where we have achieved maturity in a capability, but need to evolve certain features

- "Where our business needs have changed, and we have to course correct

- "And finally, where a capability has outlived its business need and is under consideration for an 'end of life'

"But, getting organized is generally the easy part. Staying organized is usually the challenge. Unfortunately, it is a little too easy for people within the organization to source their own capabilities. When this happens, you run into three risks:

- "Overinvesting in redundant capabilities and confusing users of the tools. "Which is the right tool to use?"

- "Fragmenting your customer journey. Your user experience becomes inconsistent, platforms lack integration, and your customer becomes lost down a dead end.

- "First-party data becomes siloed. You are unable to connect all the customer touchpoints, and lose the ability to yield end-to-end insights, as well as the ability to use that data to deliver a more relevant experience (through targeting and personalization).

"So, there are three things we do to try to maintain alignment and organization across our integrated stack of technology and tools. We're certainly not perfect, but we find that these three things allow us to spend far less time playing 'whack-a-mole' on the latest capability to sneak into the environment. It starts with clear ownership and decision making, requires good communication and education, and is followed up with a strong set of controls and governance:

- **"Decision making and ownership:** It is critical to have a defined process for bringing in a new technology, and have a documented view of ownership, both on the business and IT side, for each tool. Furthermore, have a well-established decision-making forum for technology decisions and be clear that this is a prerequisite for any onboarding of new tools. We use a forum, called our Digital MRC (for Management Review Committee), that chairs both business and IT decision makers.

- **"Communication and education:** The best way to stop new tools is to make sure the organization knows what is available. In my experience, people don't want the hassle of onboarding something new if we already have a good capability. Use the existing forums you have to share what you have, where you are evolving, and how the business can engage.

- **"Governance and controls:** In our world, this does 'take a village.' We partner with key business stakeholders, our IT organization, finance, and procurement. In doing so, we close the opportunity for someone to bring in a new technology unbeknownst to us and gives us sufficient opportunity to intercept before going too far down a path."

We hope you will agree that the way Geoff and his team at Intel have organized its marketing technology stack makes a lot of sense. While we recognize that not all readers of this book work for or represent companies the size of Intel and Cisco, we also recognize that the structures the two companies have set up are universally applicable. Whether you work for a small business or nonprofit, we think elements of each of these organizational structures offer some takeaways.

> ✉ *Note*
>
> You probably noticed as we walked through each of those organizational structures that we did not discuss tools in a lot of detail. In the next section we dive into specific marketing capabilities that your business can acquire and then organize like Cisco and Intel have organized their stacks.

Identifying Critical Marketing Technology Solutions

As we mentioned at the beginning of this chapter, the first edition of our book focused heavily on tools. That approach made sense in 2013 as many in the industry were just starting to get up to speed on an emerging marketing technology solution ecosystem. In the four years since that edition was published, the industry has matured significantly. We've documented already that the number of solutions continues to grow, and the end consumer of these solutions is more educated than ever.

Because of that, and because the industry changes so rapidly year after year (recall the statistic earlier in this chapter about the 40% turnover from 2016 to 2017) we have decided to focus much of this chapter on the frameworks you need to evaluate, organize, and adopt marketing solutions. That being said, we do feel that it is important to document some marketing technology solutions that are critical for you to have as part of your stack. The list that we are about to outline is not intended to be exhaustive. Rather, these are several solutions that we have worked with in the past and are known to deliver value to customers. They are also critical components of the Cisco and Intel marketing stacks, which we've previously identified as best-in-class. Here are some solutions that we consider to be critical:

- **BlueKai or similar data management platform (DMP)**—In Chapter 2, "Understanding Digital Analytics Concepts," we talked a little about what a data management platform is. As a refresh, a DMP is a way for companies to organize first-, second-, and third-party data that they can use to create strategies and tactics to reach core audiences more effectively. A number of DMPs are on the market today, but one that we consider to be best-in-class is BlueKai from Oracle. Google and Adobe both have competitive DMP solutions, and a number of smaller solutions are available to customers. Regardless, our view is that the DMP is the central component to any good marketing technology stack.

- **Social media listening vendors**—A number of social media listening vendors exist, as we make mention of throughout this book. However, our view is that one of the best-in-class solutions comes from Crimson Hexagon. Crimson's platform integrates with other content distribution platforms (more on this in a moment), offers sophisticated machine learning techniques to understand conversational trends, and has a robust capture of social media data. Regardless of the solution that you select, social media listening should be a part of your technology stack.

- **Sprinklr or Spredfast**—Over the last four years significant consolidation has occurred in the social media content distribution market. The two primary vendors today that most large companies turn to are Sprinklr and Spredfast. Both offer strong capabilities, rich data, and excellent customer support teams to manage the implementation. Before picking one or the other, please refer to the evaluation criteria that we outlined at the beginning of this chapter.

- **Google or Adobe Analytics**—While there are other web analytics vendors out there, most enterprises have standardized on either Google or Adobe. Both have benefits and drawbacks, but both offer users the ability to thoroughly understand how a consumer interacts with an owned property. The decision on which one of these platforms to go with is often dependent on your organization's ability to implement these new tools, and how often it integrates with existing tools. Again, please refer to the beginning of this chapter on how best to evaluate these solutions.

- **Eloqua**—A significant number of email marketing platforms are available to customers, but our preference is Eloqua. It provides rich data and the ability to segment a company's audience, but it also integrates well with BlueKai and other DMP solutions. As we mentioned earlier, the DMP is the most critical part of any marketing technology stack. The ability to integrate that comes inherent with Eloqua makes it a clear winner in our estimation.

- **Data visualization software**—This is a book on digital analytics, so you must have known that this would be a critical component of the marketing technology stack. A number of vendors are out there, but the two we prefer are Domo and Tableau. Domo is a cloud-based visualization platform that allows users to connect multiple data endpoints together in a seamless way. Domo is excellent for marketers who need a clean platform to understand marketing performance, whereas Tableau is better for analysts because it offers its users the ability to more easily manipulate data. Tableau is also a favorite of any IT department because it seamlessly integrates with internal data warehouses. For those organizations that have a smaller budget but still want great data visualization, Microsoft's PowerBI has a lot to offer in this area as well.

- **Tealium**—This platform offers many solutions to its customers, but its two primary benefits are in tag management and audience analysis. If you are managing a complex website with many different types of events that need to be tagged, having something like Tealium is essential to managing that process cost effectively. The company's AudienceStream product allows users to create a unified view of the customer's audience across channels. This is invaluable as you consider marketing to your audiences based on a customer journey as opposed to an individual channel.

- **Adobe Experience Manager**—Adobe Experience Manager doesn't receive the industry trade publicity that the DMPs do, but that does not mean it is any less important. AEM is critical to managing the deployment of content optimization on websites and communities. If your organization has a web footprint, AEM is an essential tool to consider.

While there are literally thousands more solutions for you to possibly select, we view these solutions as the starting place for your marketing technology stack. Before you start adding other point solutions, we recommend you properly evaluate the vendors listed, onboard them, and put together a plan for adoption. As you are identifying these tools, involving other parts of the organization in the process is important. Whether they are critical to the purchasing decision or not, they are essential to the adoption process.

Who Decides Which Tool to Buy?

Everybody wants to be the person who makes the final decision. In large companies with multiple decision makers, finding one person to make the call is likely going to be a challenge. However, the decision to buy a marketing technology solution is probably being led by someone in marketing or IT. That person, whoever he or she is, should be the final decision maker after consulting with a cross-functional team. The cross-functional team should include representatives from the following departments:

- **PR or marketing**—As mentioned earlier, one of these departments is likely driving the ship toward an eventual purchase. Someone from the other department should be on this team, as well.

- **Legal**—Someone needs to be there to negotiate the final contract terms.

- **Procurement**—Someone also needs to be there to write the check, of course.

- **Customer support**—Many digital marketing programs now have a dedicated customer support function. It is important that they be consulted on any specific needs related to both a listening tool and engagement software.

- **IT**—IT professionals have largely received a bad rap in digital media circles, but in this case, they serve a vital purpose. Having IT in the room early might mitigate challenges you might face technologically while adopting a marketing technology solution.

After a tool has been selected and the various parties have agreed to onboard it, the next critical step becomes adoption. A discussion about how companies achieve adoption of these marketing technology solutions is how we'll close this chapter.

Achieving Adoption of Marketing Technology Solutions

Your organization has gone through the evaluation process, an examination of how to organize your marketing technology stack, and has selected a handful of tools to get started from the list we shared earlier in the chapter. Now what do you do? The most obvious step is onboarding and start using the solutions, right? Wrong. In our experience most organizations buy, conduct some training, and then attempt to start using the platforms that have been selected. More often than not, this leads to momentary adoption of the technology. Just because there were a core group of individuals involved in the selection of the solution does not mean everyone will adopt it after it is onboarded. To steal and tweak a line from the movie *Field of Dreams*, just because you build it, doesn't mean they will come. There needs to be serious thought to the adoption plan for the solution(s) that you have selected.

One of the reasons that the Cisco and Intel marketing technology stacks have been held up as best-in-class is that adoption is extremely high. Is adoption 100%? No, and we would argue that should never be the goal. However, you can do some things within your organization to achieve adoption. We asked Geoff from Intel to provide a case study for how his organization achieves adoption. Here is that case study:

"In a large organization, it can be difficult to achieve strong adoption of capabilities and tools. Honestly, this has been my biggest challenge. Of the three parts of capabilities (people, process, systems), the people part always seems the hardest. Although there isn't a perfect solution to the adoption process—every organization is different—there are tactics you can take to increase your odds of success.

"The starting point for my team is to first understand the different types of roles you're trying to influence for adoption. People have different needs and have to apply what they know differently to get their jobs done. The least amount of success comes from a technology-first approach. You can't walk in a room and start to advocate the merits of a tool without understanding the needs of your stakeholders and how they will use the information in their decision making and activation. Believe me, I've tried it... We have to tune our education to meet the function or role. For example, in our marketing organization, we break our "users" into three roles. Some people will operate in multiple roles (wearing many hats), but we need to think about these roles distinctly:

- "**Marketing strategists:** This role's purpose is to understand the needs of our business and translate them into our strategies to reach intended audiences across their journeys to drive engagement and conversion. This group will likely never actually touch our MarTech tools. But they still need to understand them in three critical ways: First, how we use our MarTech stack to connect the customer journey to consistently reach our audiences in a relevant way; second, the insights we can generate to understand marketing effectiveness; and third, the data we have available to build audience segments for targeting and personalization.

- "**Marketing activators:** This role's purpose is to move strategies into "go-to-market" definition and execution. Marketing activators have similar needs to marketing strategists—connecting the customer journey and data for insights and activation—but also need much more detail on the process of using the MarTech stack for optimal delivery. In a large organization like mine, these roles may still be using agencies or contracted resources to execute, but need to understand how our tools can deliver the customer experience. They also want to understand how the technology and data can help them innovate and differentiate.

- "**Tool users:** This role is pretty self-explanatory. They are the fingers on the keys. This role is primarily concerned with what tools we have, how we have configured them with our processes, and what they need to do in the tools to deploy our marketing tactics. There is also training needed to drive an understanding of how we connect our data in order to measure attribution and marketing ROI.

"After we understand the roles and what their needs are, it simply involves defining and driving a structure for adoption that for us has four parts:

- "**Training/Education:** Framing the training against the backdrop of the business strategy and use cases is critical to success. Again, people need to *see* their role and responsibilities when using the MarTech stack. They also need the information when it is most useful. Doing a half-day immersion with teams around certain parts of the stack is great. But it can be even more effective to do a 30-minute refresher in a team's staff meeting prior to a critical stage in your business cadence (like right before annual campaign planning).

- "**Ongoing communication:** Keeping people updated on changes and innovation is important, but timeliness and effectiveness are necessary ingredients. We will communicate over email with some success. But we will proactively reach out directly to our key stakeholders (in person) with ideas and recommendations on how to take advantage of platform changes to make their marketing even better.

- "**Effective intake processes:** This is how we connect marketing strategists and marketing activators to production and tool users. Driving consistency with intake processes and forms, using a consistent taxonomy from top-funnel on down, and centralizing intake to make it easy to find and use are essential.

- "**Measuring and assessing adoption and maturity:** In our case, we have started using a maturity model survey that assesses our effectiveness across a number of business-led activities (analytics and use of data, content creation and management, user experience, optimization, and so on). This establishes a baseline for adoption and allows us to track our maturity over time."

It is our view that the approach Geoff has taken to achieving adoption of these solutions is excellent. Again, you might not be in an organization the size of Intel, but we think the suggestions he provides to achieve adoption are universally applicable to any business.

Conclusion

Over the course of this chapter, we outlined the criteria for successful tool evaluation, how you could organize your technology stack, identified some tools you can use to get started, and then provided some ideas on how to achieve adoption. Over the course of the next few chapters, we will go into greater detail on the use cases for digital analytics and its tools.

References

1. Marketing Technology Landscape Supergraphic (2017): Martech 5000, ChiefMartec.com, Scott Brinker, May 2017

4

Digital Analysis: Brand

At this point in the book, you have no doubt determined that there is an abundance of data available through digital marketing, social media, third-party data providers, and even the emerging universe of Internet of Things (IoT) devices. Fortunately, a growing number of tools are available on the market to help you diagnose your digital brand health and understand your total digital audience(s), and more clearly understand the consumer opinion of your brand through digital analytics tools.

Benefits of Digital Brand Analysis

Why consider doing a digital brand analysis? The old adage from management thinker and legend Peter Drucker, "You can't manage what you don't measure," is a classic reminder on why you need to regularly assess your brand's positioning across the synergetic digital ecosystem. Since the beginning of the consumer Internet in the mid-1990s, we've never seen a period like we are experiencing now in which so much change is occurring in experiences, tactics, and feature innovations across digital channels, social platforms, mobile apps, and IoT devices. In other words, things are in constant flux. A digital brand analysis can help you understand how discoverable your content is through search rankings, how engaging your content and experiences are across social platforms or brand websites, and how your brand compares to your closest competitors in these areas, as well as from the perspective of the consumer audiences you're trying to reach.

The impact of all of this on your digital marketing decisions is significant. It means that in order to stay consistently relevant, you must have your finger on the pulse of your digital brand health and your digital audience(s).

How often should you do a digital brand analysis? This is a question each brand must answer for itself. Doing a digital brand analysis requires time, money, and resources. That investment must be weighed against the value of the outputs, insights, and clarity you get from these analyses. Some companies use them only as an input to annual strategic planning initiatives, whereas we've seen other brands use them more regularly (that is, as the canary in the coal mine so to speak) as an early-warning detection system for shifts in the digital ecosystem or meaningful changes in audience attitudes, opinions, or behaviors.

Some additional reasons for doing a digital brand analysis include:

- It can help you better evaluate the effectiveness of your digital branding efforts as a whole.

- Getting sucked into a single digital channel and focusing on optimization tactics specific to that one channel, while getting further away from core brand positioning that you want to be consistent and seamless across the entire digital ecosystem is easy to do, and this analysis can help identify the strengths and weaknesses of your branding techniques and methods overall.

- This type of analysis can identify where the answer to any one of these questions is "no": Does the audience experience the same brand experience with our email marketing as they do if visiting us on Facebook? Is our YouTube channel brand experience consistent with the experience of videos on our brand website? Does the experience on our mobile app(s) consistently align with our mobile web experiences?

- Finally, while looking externally at all of these digital channels and platforms can tell you quite a bit, it cannot provide everything a brand needs to know about the digital ecosystem. Garnering objective feedback from the audience(s) you serve is a critical component of a digital brand analysis. You're able to capture highly relevant, qualitative responses from the consumer audiences that matter to you and use that, with your other findings, to triangulate any necessary course corrections to your digital marketing strategies and content marketing initiatives. That content could be for your brand website, Facebook page, Twitter account, LinkedIn page, YouTube channel, or even syndicated content via a partner. Your brand's content is the fuel for making your digital marketing program relevant and successful. Without content that truly resonates with your target audience, the chances of your program succeeding are quite small, regardless of the content format (text, audio, or video).

Brand Analysis in the Digital Age

This chapter walks through the approach and techniques for conducting a digital brand analysis, lightly touching on the tools that you can use to do so, but keep in mind our words from Chapter 3, "Choosing Your Analytics Tools," the tools in the digital medium change often, rapidly. We intentionally don't want to focus your time and attention on the content in this chapter, or any in this book, on tools that might not exist later this year or the next year, or at the very least do not function in the same ways, thus prohibiting you from using them as we describe.

That all said, what are the components of digital brand analysis? In this chapter, we break it into the following three components:

- **Brand share**—Marketers have long used the concept of market share for their own purposes as a proxy for measuring their impact on consumer attentions and brand preferences. It's a helpful way to gauge brand awareness, equity, and engagement. Establishing your digital brand market share covers several different dimensions, and we examine them in greater detail throughout the first section of this chapter.

- **Brand audience**—We're in the digital marketing age of audience, attention, and experience. So we need to rethink and realign how we go about gauging the pulse and perspective of the audiences we're trying to reach in digital format. This is an emerging area of measurement, with some straightforward and simple methods for calculating a brand's audience, but it can be negatively impacted due to the fragmentation of digital channels, platforms, and devices. That said, some useful ways still exist to quantify your audiences and use those findings as an indicator for the total number of people you're reaching, engaging with, and exposing your content and thought leadership to. We explore how to do this in the second part of this chapter.

- **Brand and consumer alignment**—Does this sound familiar? You've done your consumer research with focus groups and surveys, and you've analyzed all the digital data sources available to you from your web analytics, social analytics, and CRM tools. You've used all of those inputs to inform and craft your digital marketing strategy for your product or service and feel like you have a good handle on how you should market your brand positioning and content marketing efforts, only to be surprised (not in a good way) that after launching, you aren't seeing the expected outcomes or same responses your early research showed.

Believe it or not, the preceding situation is actually quite common, and one of the main reasons a digital brand audit is so important. It can identify where you and your target audiences are not aligned. Alignment is critically important for your content and experiences being relevant.

The last section of this chapter covers how to assess and identify whether your brand and consumers are misaligned, and how to go about fixing it. This primarily involves the use of specific and targeted social listening analyses of qualitative feedback by consumers rather than a quantitative exercise, but don't dismiss it for that reason. It can yield very powerful insights because it provides unique perspective that a brand won't get from some of the other digital analytics tools (search analytics, web analytics, and so on). Which social listening tool doesn't particularly matter as long as it has good data coverage across the digital properties relevant to your brand. That said, refer to Chapter 3 for details on our recommended social listening tools. All of them have their own individual nuances, and all are highly recommended.

Brand Share

What percentage of the category does my brand occupy? What percentage of the relevant audience for a category does my brand reach? Let's dive into how marketers answer these types of questions. We cover three dimensions (see Figure 4.1) of looking at brand share in digital marketing in this section. Let's examine them in greater detail.

Figure 4.1 *Brand share dimensions.*

Each of these dimensions can be valuable by itself but looking at all three, both independently and together, can yield interesting trends that you wouldn't see otherwise. For example, it's a commonly accepted belief that there aren't very stable links between what consumers say about a product or service versus what consumers mean (what they really think and believe) versus what they actually do. Consumers' behavior often doesn't match what they communicate or their feelings. This is why evaluating brand share with the three dimensions is so important. If we were only to consider one of them, we might have a real problem down the line because we based an important product decision or set of digital marketing decisions on a false belief or misleading consumer insight.

Share of Voice

Looking at share of voice, or "what people say," enables us to understand how much of the total conversation about a category a brand might occupy. In other words:

SOV = Discussions about Your Brand / Total Discussion in Your
     Category

What we mean by that is, if your brand is in the quick service restaurant (QSR) category, Subway, for example, what percentage of all consumer conversations in digital/social channels are about Subway? You then compare that against other QSR brands to understand where Subway stacks up against the competition (see Figure 4.2). This is a fairly common way that marketers currently measure trends in the overall health of their digital brands. Thanks to social listening tools, share of voice is relatively easy to calculate as well!

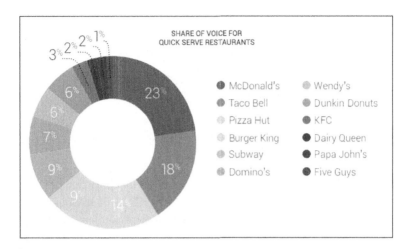

Figure 4.2 *QSR category share of voice by Brandwatch Analytics.*

As we briefly described earlier in the chapter, this can help you understand how successful your awareness efforts are within your marketing or advertising. At the macro-level, are they working? Is digital brand awareness for the brand increasing? If so, you should expect to see your SOV increase over time based on the fact that consumers are having more discussions about your brand, and more consumers are participating in those discussions as well.

Context is everything, so it's important to understand that any SOV analysis is only a snapshot in time for that category. Trending SOV over time will reveal the real insights that can lead you to action or a change. The snapshot is a good starting point, but the work doesn't end there. You can trend SOV manually, but thanks to social listening tools, the SOV trending process is pretty painless. With custom rules and filters, you can set up SOV dashboards that automatically update and show the trending over time, which allows you to monitor and dig into the details as needed if you spot shifts in either your brand's or a competitor's SOV. Including the competitive set in your SOV trending dashboard is a good way to identify the need to explore competitors in detail, because it's a high-level indicator that they might have made strategic changes to their digital marketing that are resonating with consumers and shifting the distribution of brand SOV within the category.

Share of Search

Looking at share of search, or "What people do," or put another way, "What people intend to do," helps us to understand how many of the total searches within a category are about brand's products or services. We say *What people intend to do,* because organic searches on Google or any other search engine are specific questions seeking a specific and relevant answer. In the last couple of years, the shift from simple keyword searches to intent-based searches has caused significant changes in how many marketers utilize paid and organic search marketing, as well as content optimization. Much like with CRM and direct response, marketers have long used lead-scoring methods to qualify and segment leads or opportunities; search marketers have begun to do the same. Is the keyword you're considering a "high-intent" or "low-intent" word? Matching your content and keywords to the high-intent keywords will correspond with an increased likelihood of being discovered or clicked on whether it's an organic search or a paid search. Leading paid search platforms such as Wordstream have developed features into their analytics that score keywords based on intent as we have described, with suggestions for your keywords based on the intent scores.

Back to calculating and using share of search (SOS):

SOS = Searches about Your Brand / Total Searches in Your Category

Sticking with our QSR example for this topic, if your brand is in the quick service restaurant category (QSR)—Subway, for example—what percentage of all consumer searches are about Subway? You then compare that against other QSR brands to understand where Subway stacks up against the competition, as shown in Figure 4.3. This is a fairly common way that marketers currently measure search trends and apply them to get a sense of the overall health of their digital brands based on consumer intent. Thanks to the plethora of search analytics tools available to you, share of search is also easy to calculate, just like SOV.

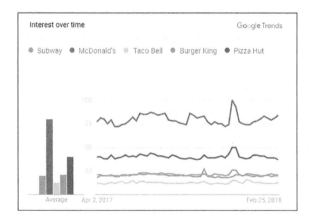

Figure 4.3 *QSR category share of search by Google Trends.*

SOS can be broken down further and filtered based on geography. This is important because we know consumer brand attitudes and preferences aren't universally true. Major differences exist based on different regions or locations. For example, let's look at the same SOS shown in Figure 4.3 but broken down by searches based on sub-region. Using Google Trends, we can quickly see that McDonald's and Pizza Hut dominate across all parts of the United States (see Figure 4.4). There may be pockets of micro-geographies where exceptions exist to this, but we're focused on understanding overall brand health using SOS, so we won't dig into the details here.

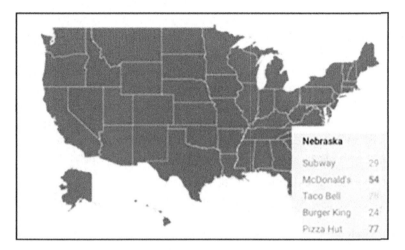

Figure 4.4 *QSR category share of search sub-region by Google Trends.*

As with share of voice, incorporating SOS into your brand share analysis can provide another data point to consider as you evaluate the success of your awareness efforts within your marketing or advertising.

Also, as with SOV, any SOS analysis is only a snapshot in time. Search trends change for many reasons and building a trended view of SOS for maximum benefit of this type of analysis is important.

Share of Audience

Share of audience is a relatively new concept for digital marketing analytics. It's borne out of marketers' need to understand their total audience in a number of ways. Traditionally speaking, and still very much true today, offline channels such as traditional broadcast media measurement used the reach and frequency of exposure to help answer questions such as:

- Who is my audience?

- How many people can I reach with my marketing or advertising efforts?

- Am I exposing more or less consumers to my content/message than my competitors?"

These are just examples, but the point is that the intent to understand a brand's audience has existed for some time. Digital analytics can play a big role in helping reframe marketers' view of audience. There isn't a single approach or way to do this, but we offer a simple and manageable approach that you can adopt, whether you're a marketer working at Coca-Cola or the local gourmet food market. This approach scales from small to big brands seamlessly:

Share of Audience (SOA) = Total Audience for Your Brand /
Total Audience Per Competitor within a
Category

Let's take a more detailed look in determining SOA because it is more complicated to get to than the other two dimensions of digital brand share. Here are the steps for each brand you want to include in the calculation.

1. **Inventory total audience across all relevant digital properties.** You need to decide where to draw the line because collecting audience data from every single digital touchpoint will be quite a burden and likely not worth the reward in terms of increasing the insights or value of this exercise. Remember, this is a high-level look at brand health with SOV, SOS, and SOA. None of these dimensions are meant to be used for detailed, tactical marketing decisions but rather as temperature checks for the strategic direction that a brand is headed to. You'll likely want to include all major social platforms you have a presence on, as well as any subscriber data you have for owned media properties such as your brand website or an email newsletter subscription, for example.

2. **Sum total all individual audiences you've collected.** This is obviously an easy calculation; the most difficult part is collecting them all first.

3. **Calculate the SOA for each competitor** by dividing your audience total with theirs, using the tool of your choice (although a simple spreadsheet will work).

Let's demonstrate these steps using only Facebook audiences. Figure 4.5 shows a simple view of each brand's Facebook audience.

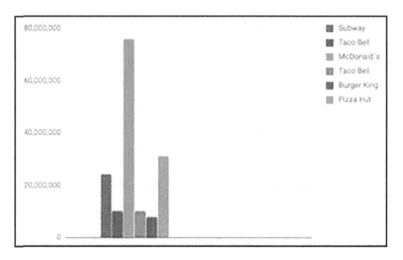

Figure 4.5 *QSR category share of audience—Facebook.*

Clearly, McDonald's has the greatest brand awareness and reach with the QSR audience. However, only a single social platform is represented, Facebook, so this illustration needs to have all the other data layered in to create the single audience view. Instead of illustrating this step for each platform, let's fast-forward to a point after doing this step for the other platforms; you'll have a brand's total audience represented in a single number. The SOA calculation comes next, as shown in Table 4.1. It represents your brand audience relative to the competitor's.

Table 4.1   QSR Category Share of Audience

	Subway	Taco Bell	McDonald's	Taco Bell	Burger King	Pizza Hut
Total Audience	75,123,452	53,871,621	112,098,773	23,000,222	24,018,862	44,000,123
Subway SOA		139.45%	67.02%	326.62%	312.77%	170.73%

In this SOA snapshot, Subway has a total audience of just over 75 million across the digital and social platforms we included in the scope of this example. For each of the competitors listed in Table 4.1, we divide the Subway audience by the competitor audience for a relative SOA metric. Subway's audience is ~140% of Taco Bell but only 67% of McDonald's total audience. Using this approach to assess SOA can help identify whether major differences exist between your brand's audience and your competitors'. Finding these differences can be a useful way to identify where you need to explore because a competitor has found an audience that is relevant to the category but isn't aware of or engaged with your brand. .

This approach has limitations and imperfections but has good value in illuminating dark spots in your digital ecosystem. One of the issues with SOA is that overlap exists in audiences across platforms. If you love the Subway brand and follow them on Facebook, you're likely to follow them on other social platforms that you also use, such as Twitter or Instagram, which creates a de-duplication issue for this type of calculation.

Brand Audience

When focusing on audience, you can do more work to effectively quantify and qualify a digital brand audience in other ways than SOA. Although marketers have many ways to describe audience sizes, reach, engagement, and health, we provide an approach that utilizes three different dimensions for total audience that marketers might want to consider, as shown in Figure 4.6. Questions like these are frequently asked by brand marketers:

- What is my total audience reach?

- How engaged is my audience?

- How much time and attention are my audiences spending with my content?

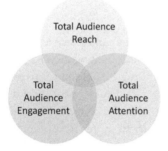

Figure 4.6 *Brand audience dimensions.*

Total Audience Reach

Understanding your brand audience in terms of total volume or followers or subscribers is one way to look at the health of your brand awareness and engagement efforts over time. However, it doesn't necessarily answer questions about how effectively you might be reaching your audience with your content marketing, advertising, or social engagement efforts. This is where thinking about total audience reach can play a role to identify answers. Using different data but from the same sources—your social platform analytics, website analytics, and email marketing analytics—you can piece together a total audience reach view that gives you not the maximum potential audience that you have, but the actual reach of your marketing and advertising activities to that audience over time. It's simply potential compared to actual. Both perspectives are useful but limiting if that is the only view. Total Audience Reach isn't a standard metric you will get from one analytics platform, but rather one you calculate by gathering reach metrics and performance from all of your analytics tools and combining them into a single view.

For example, you can do this in Facebook Insights by exporting the data for each post over a 30-day time period. Facebook provides detailed breakouts for organic reach versus paid reach as well, which means you're able to segment and calculate your brand's total audience reach for organic separately from paid reach. Warning—doing this task on Facebook, especially, might cause your blood pressure to rise because organic reach on Facebook has reached near mythical status. It's a pay-to-play world on major social platforms for most brands. That said, tracking both organic and paid total audience reach separately gives you the ability to detect and see whether, when, and where organic efforts broke through due to an unexpected success or engagement that might have generated significant earned media activities.

The remaining reach metrics are provided by the native analytics or insights platforms for each social platform (Twitter, YouTube, LinkedIn).

Total Audience Attention

Time is, arguably, the most precious and valuable commodity. We never have enough of it and brands are at war fighting for what little of it an audience is willing to give. Modern digital marketing and advertising has never faced greater challenges in terms of being successful. A whole host of battles exist that your brand and content are fighting to overcome and capture audience attention. *Attention*, by the way, continues to shrink. According to a Microsoft Corporation study in 2015, published on Time.com, researchers studied the brain activity of study participants and found that the average attention span was 8 seconds. This was a decline from 12 seconds, as recorded in 2000. They also noted these declines happened to coincide with the emergence of the mobile phone revolution. As a result, heavy multi-screen consumers' ability to concentrate and filter out distractions has worsened. Add to that worsening problem with ad blockers, device fragmentation, screen-shifting, and frequent social platform algorithm changes affecting your content's visibility, and you get the perfect storm of challenges for a brand trying to cut through all that noise and capture people's attention, even if for just 8 seconds.

Due to these trends, in recent years content marketers have begun to focus on a different way of understanding, measuring, and reporting on how their audience engages with them. Thus, "total time spent" or "total minutes spent" have been on the rise as a way to look at brand health in terms of total audience attention or top-of-mindedness.

Thankfully, calculating this metric is just as simple as the concept because nearly every one of your digital or social analytics tools collects data on time associated with the interactions or engagements with your audience. The data aren't collected or calculated the same way, but that's neither here nor there for our purposes of building a total audience attention measure. We'll forgo the debate between Facebook's definition of Time Spent versus Adobe Analytics definition of Time Spent on Site, versus YouTube's Watch Time Minutes.

Differences exist in how time metrics are calculated, and that is especially true across tool categories. Web analytics calculate average time spent on site very differently and with different levels of precision than a social platform or app such as YouTube or Snapchat. For simplicity's sake, let's just note that your digital platforms can all provide time metrics and use that to build up to the view that we're looking for.

After you've collected all the required time metrics, you can build a single view of total audience attention (or time spent if you prefer). You can then use this one metric to trend over time and monitor for any changes that might indicate your audience giving you less of their precious time and attention.

Total Audience Engagement

The last way for which we describe how to measure, trend, and monitor total audience is by their level of engagement. This is something you're likely measuring and reporting on already. A social marketing manager or a community manager is likely either providing reporting on your audience engagement already or working with an analyst on the team who develops these reports for you. In any case, the raw materials are there to put together a total audience engagement view. In fact, depending on the tools you're currently using, you might be able to construct this view right out of the box. Some of the social media management systems (SMMSs) we cover in this book such as Hootsuite or Spredfast have integrated analytics and reporting features that provide you with an overall engagement view. If you've done the work to get your social profiles integrated into an SMMS, then check there before attempting to build this feature yourself.

The most important step in an exercise to build a view of total audience engagement is to be specific and define what engagement means to you. This is a crucial step. Failure to do it will create issues for you down the line. First, you'll be chasing every social engagement metric known in the world, collecting everything because you can rather than because you should. What audience engagement matters is going to be unique depending on the brand. So think carefully about what meaningful engagements with your audience actually have the brand impact and start with those. Chasing irrelevant engagement metrics is a race to the bottom where you'll be lost, confused, and likely unsure why.

Brand and Consumer Alignment

Brand and consumer alignment is one of the most interesting areas and probably where brand marketers least focus on leveraging digital analytics to help shorten the distance between a brand and the consumer audience that they are trying to reach. In many cases, a large gap exists between a consumer and a brand because the brand isn't aligned with what consumers actually want/need/expect/believe. This happens, of course, very easily because of the weak links between "what people say" versus "what people do" versus "what people feel/believe," as we covered earlier in this chapter.

Good news for marketers! You can use a framework to solve this problem and identify alignment issues you might have with consumers or identify the ones that you didn't know you had. This framework is called the Brand Window (you'll see why shortly). It works by using social analytics tools (primarily social listening tools), to assess the impact of, and opportunities for, brand marketing and advertising by listening to what consumer audiences are saying and analyzing their relevant discussions across social platforms.

The Brand Window utilizes three unique views of consumer conversations (see Figure 4.7), broken down in a way to easily compare and contrast what consumers are actually talking about versus what the brand is talking about. If those two are not the same, you'll see the lack of alignment reflected in the results:

- **Consumer** perceptions—Additional stories that consumers are telling about the brand

- Brand **realities**—Brand stories that are being amplified by consumers

- Brand **aspirations**—Brand stories that are not being discussed by consumers

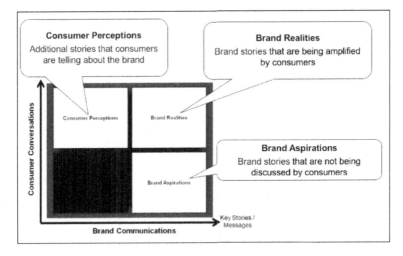

Figure 4.7 *Brand Window framework.*

The summary of steps for how to do this work is as follows:

1. Collect relevant data—use a social listening platform to identify the relevant conversations to your brand.

2. Export data for classification.

3. Classify posts or discussions based on theme or topic.

4. Populate each window pane of the Brand Window based on the classifications you've assigned to discussions (see Figure 4.8).

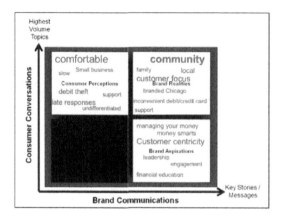

Figure 4.8 *Brand Window banking brand example output.*

5.   Analyze the results to identify meaningful differences or where a brand isn't aligned with consumer discussion or interests.

Brand Window analyses can be "quick and dirty" at a high level or very detailed if you have the time and sufficient data for analysis. Like we've said before, the value of an analysis is only as good as the analyst doing the work. Brand Windows can provide extraordinary insights if done well, or just an interesting but not all that useful output if not done well.

The key is to remember the strategic purpose that's driving the Brand Window analysis: to identify any misalignments between the brand and consumers. If you're able to do that, you've done a valuable service to your strategy and content marketing efforts because the marketers will be able to refine their targeting and approach to improve relevancy with the brand's audience.

The Future of Digital Brand Analysis

What possibilities the future holds for brands to use the spectrum of digital analytics tools is up in the air, but we think that tool usage certainly won't look like it has in the years past. In this chapter we provided some new and old-but-revised approaches to using digital analytics to provide the most accurate, reliable, updated view of brand health and trends impacting brand awareness and engagement. We expect to see more experimentation and blending of digital data sources in the future to provide marketers with what they need for high-level digital brand health judgements.

5

Digital Analysis: Audience

Audience insights have never been more valuable and critical to digital marketing and advertising success. Precision targeting across nearly all forms of paid media is now commonplace versus back in 2013. Even forms of traditional mass media such as broadcast television have evolved to a more personalized experience. Addressable TV advertising allows advertisers to show different, unique ads to different households to increase relevance and the effects of paid media.

None of this is possible without a better understanding of the audiences and individuals you're trying to reach. The first edition of this book described the early days of personalization, how we were beginning to have a digital experience uniquely our own due to creative cookie management, application of account preferences and other factors using data sets for geographic location, and browsing history. Fast forward just a few years, and these practices are no longer in the early stages of experimentation but are established norms for delivering relevance in marketing and advertising by leveraging rich audience insights.

The amount of audience data available to marketers has exploded. Using audience insights that are derived from analyses of various types of audience data is now a prerequisite for all forms of digital communications, and it doesn't stop there. The experience era that was ushered in around the 2015/2016 time frame places an even greater emphasis on audience insights because they became critical inputs for identifying what is necessary to design, create, and deliver hyper-personalized, relevant brand experiences regardless of where they occur. This matters more than ever because it's a win-win scenario—consumers win by receiving more relevant and personalized ads, content, and experience, and brands win because they are able to consistently meet consumer experience expectations across all of their digital and social channels and platforms. If your competitors are personalizing marketing and you're not, what compelling reason is there for a consumer to choose your brand over that competitor's? One feels known, comfortable, and relevant. The other feels familiar in a different way—disruptive, noisy, and out of context.

Consumers hold vastly more power now in regard to setting expectations for their content needs and experience preferences with the companies with which they do business. In 2018, consumers are incredibly well informed, technologically savvy (having spent enough time on digital and social platforms over many years that they are conditioned on how to navigate them effectively, thus very confident and comfortable), and bring with them the expectation of nearly instant gratification in regard to brands solving their problems or responding to their inquiries.

Numerous examples exist of how audience data is driving personalized content and experiences. One way that has taken hold is to use audience data to give back one of our most precious commodities, time. Personalization can remove friction from experiences, not adding worthless time to them, whether in the form of forcing consumers to watch an irrelevant ad, asking them to provide information about themselves that the company already has, or asking them what they want/need in that moment. Most of the data required to predict the answers to these questions and personalize the experience to deliver an expedited and relevant outcome has already been "set" in consumers' minds as the new gold standard for what they expect from the companies with which they interact, not just interactions with the Googles, Amazons, or Apples of the world.

Let's look at Google in more detail to understand the multiple ways it applies audience data to predict, deliver, and optimize the content, messaging, and experience people receive from them. For years, Google has gone to great lengths to understand users' mindsets and expectations. Google stockpiles vastly different types of data about users and their preferences across its portfolio of products and services, from Gmail to Google Search, even data from Android Phone usage.

Google knows all the basic demographic things that one might expect: name, gender and birthdate, location(s) (where you live, work, and commute). How about what you sound like? Your unique voice-print? Google has that, too, if you use Google Assistant on your phone or any one of its artificial intelligence–infused Internet of Things (IoTs) devices such as Google Home, Google Mini, or Google Max.

Don't forget Google's core product that we all use the most—Search. Google knows about your search history as well, what search results you've clicked on, what YouTube videos you've searched for and watched, liked, or shared. Tangentially related to the focus of this topic, if you're really interested in a deep dive on Google Search and big data and what researchers are learning about how people search versus what people say, we recommend reading Seth Stephens-Davidowitz's May 2017 book *Everybody Lies: Big Data, New Data, and What The Internet Can Tell Us About Who We Really Are*. It is informative and insightful, and he is one of the people leading the way with large-scale analyses of Google Search data to identify and map consumer behaviors in many key areas.

Back to Google data collection. It doesn't stop there! Google also develops detailed and sophisticated lists of what types of advertising it thinks you're most interested in receiving from it. Figure 5.1 is an example of an individual's Google Ad Topics matrix used to determine ads you like versus ads you won't like.

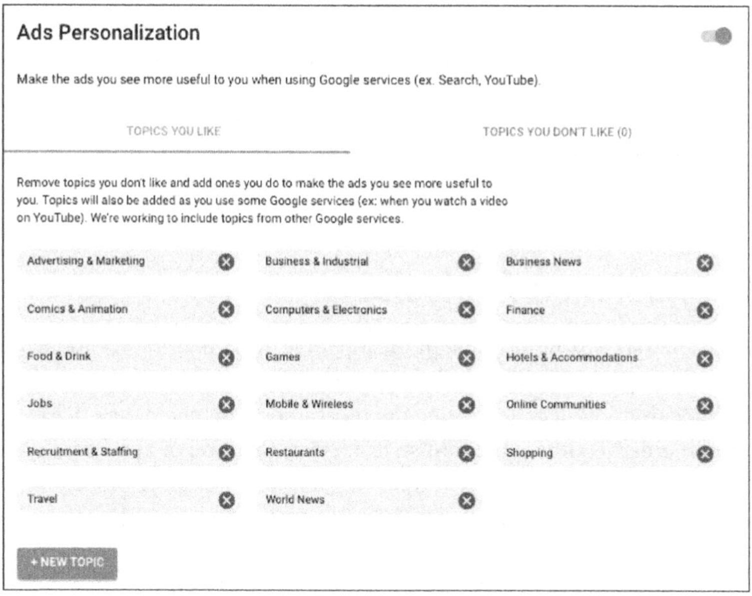

Figure 5.1 *Google Ads Personalization matrix example.*

To see this personalized view specific to your Google account, log in and click the Ad Settings link listed under the Personal Info and Privacy category, and click

Manage Ad Settings. The point isn't that Google is doing anything nefarious or wrong; it just shows how far companies' data collection efforts have come in just a few years.

Google is using all the data types and consumer information we've described (and most likely even more than we currently know) to make what it delivers to you as contextually relevant and timely as possible. Gone are the days where my search results look like yours. We likely won't see the same ads either, whether they are pay-per-click (PPC), display, or video format. Your results are never going to be the same as mine because Google has become more sophisticated at applying the data it captures about us in unique, personalized ways.

The collected data types described previously are many of the most common that we know of, but they're not the only ones. Many companies, like Google, also rely on proprietary first-party data to dictate a content, advertising, or experience decision.

It might not be obvious on the surface, but heavy lifting work behind the scenes is required for successful, personalized experiences. These can only happen with a keen understanding of the audience and their needs, expectations, and behaviors. As we've highlighted with Google, effective personalization requires pulling in digital data from a variety of sources and devices and performing rock-solid analyses. The end result is a clearer, less ambiguous picture about what makes an audience or individual tick, and it is something that you can begin to align your brand against as you develop your marketing and advertising plans. We called this process *audience analysis* in 2013, and it's an activity that has become very common among marketers and analytics tool providers since.

What Is Audience Analysis?

Audience analysis isn't new, although most people other than professional technical writers probably aren't familiar with it. Traditionally, *audience analysis* is the process by which technical writers determine the most important characteristics of their audience in order to choose the best style, format, and level of appropriate information when preparing a document or speaking. Basically, it's an approach to doing user research that will ensure you are delivering value to the target audience.

When done to support marketing efforts, audience analysis involves performing several different research activities that reveal key information about what matters most to the audience you're trying to reach, just like Google does. We've adopted this traditional concept because we believe so much potential exists for digital analytics to reveal audience insights. We have made some adaptations to reflect the specific needs of profiling the modern digital audience.

The term *audience* itself can be used as an acronym for remembering this technique:

Analysis—Who is the audience?

Understanding—What is the audience's knowledge and attitude toward the brand?

Demographics—What is the audience's age, gender, education, location, and so on?

Interest—Why is the audience reading, sharing, and interacting with your brand content?

Environment—Where does the audience spend time online?

Needs—What are the audience needs associated with your brand, product, or service?

Customization—What personalization and/or attributes of the experience should the brand address in order to add value for the audience?

Expectations—What are both the stated and unstated expectations that the audience has for their interactions with your brand?

Clearly, some of these activities aren't new to digital media; we've been capturing some of these types of data and using them to target users for years in digital marketing and advertising programs. What's new and different is the ability to go beyond basic demographic data and augment that data set with additional sources, such as psychographic, behavioral, and even user-interaction data based on social network activities.

Social networks are a rich source of these data types. Facebook's meteoric rise can largely be credited to the mountains of self-reported personal data its nearly 2 billion users have provided to the company. Facebook might very well be the largest source in the world of consumer activity, interest, opinion, attitude, and values data—second only perhaps to Google's goldmine of the global population's searches that they only reveal to Google, and no one else.

Audience analysis brings together several of the different concepts we've covered previously, adds some new ones that we discuss later in this chapter, and combines their outputs to formulate a holistic view of a particular audience or individual. You can apply techniques to data garnered from existing tools and combine the result with supplemental metadata to enhance your knowledge and understanding of the audience.

Audience Analysis Use Cases

The audience analysis approach is comprehensive, and if followed in its entirety, might require a significant amount of time and effort. That said, it doesn't mean you have to do every different analysis, every single time you are profiling an audience. As with most of the topics we talk about in other chapters, an analysis begins with goals and objectives. In this instance, it depends on the use case(s). Audience analysis can be quick and dirty or more rigorous and formal, depending on the use case and time available.

The following are some common use cases for audience analysis:

- Digital strategy development
- Content strategy development
- Engagement strategy development
- Search engine optimization
- Content optimization
- User experience design and optimization
- Audience segmentation

The following sections examine these use cases in more detail.

Digital Strategy Development

In addition to having clearly defined business objectives, developing a robust digital strategy requires having a clear understanding of the market, your competitors, and your audience. You'll be trying to find customers but first need to have identified their needs, wants, and expectations. If you identify those, you'll be successful. If you ignore them, your digital strategy will rest on delivering irrelevant content and experiences that offer little to no value. Getting clarity through audience analysis is the key to ensuring that you'll succeed through relevance. W2O's Gary Grates, architect of the agency's "Relevance Model" for audience communication, summed it up perfectly when he said, "relevance is the new reputation."

An audience analysis supporting a digital strategy initiative tends to be more comprehensive and lengthier than other strategies. This is due to the complexity of the digital landscape. We have moved far away from living in a digital world of "if you build it, they will come. "Social technologies and mobile devices have accelerated the fragmentation of the Internet. Your audience is scattered like bits and pieces across a vast network of sites and platforms. This means you have to source data from more platforms of several different types."

Content Strategy Development

Content marketing has grown substantially in recent years, with 76% of marketers in a September 2016 eMarketer survey indicating they planned to increase the amount of content they planned to create (see Figure 5.2).

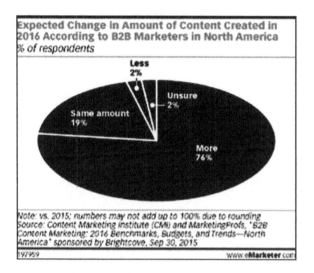

Figure 5.2 *Content marketing growth.*

Optimized content across channels and social platforms allows digital interactions to reach their greatest potential. Content strategists view content, regardless of type (text, images, audio, video, and so on) as products. They therefore plan, design, research, and test variations of content, just as you would a product, to ensure that content is relevant and valuable to the recipient. For content strategists to be effective, they require as much input about the audience as possible.

Content strategists work with many inputs to understand their audiences prior to moving forward. Audience research includes demographic, behavioral, and psychographic information, personas, and user experience flows, to name a few inputs. They also try to isolate and identify content consumption preferences and behaviors. Digital analytics provides these answers and audience insights.

Engagement Strategy

After your company has made a decision to utilize the appropriate and well-informed set of social platforms that matches your audience behaviors, engagement activity isn't far behind. Brands develop engagement strategies to maximize the number of desired outcomes produced on social platforms. However, even the best-laid plans can go awry and require course correction. Engagement analytics to the rescue!

Analyzing engagement activity reveals insights about what your audience likes, thinks, and needs. Nearly every major social platform has a native engagement analytics tool, with Snapchat being the only current exception. Facebook, Twitter, LinkedIn, Instagram, and YouTube all provide native analytics to anyone with a brand presence on their platforms. A diverse third-party engagement analytics ecosystem also exists. The problem is not lacking analytics tools to measure and optimize your engagement, but having too many tool choices.

Search Engine Optimization

Search engine optimization (SEO) is not new to digital marketers, although it may feel that way year over year because of how frequently factors that impact SEO change. Getting your content published and distributed has never been easier, but unfortunately that means it's also never been more difficult to be discovered through organic searches. Several additional factors affect SEO these days, one of which is the inclusion of social data signals into search engine algorithms.

Content Optimization

Optimizing your digital content to maximize discovery is not enough; you must also infuse the content distributed in your social status updates, tweets, blog posts, comments, and so on. This means the output of the SEO analysis has multiple uses, because content or links that are shared on social platforms are ranking signals for search engines such as Google. Exactly how much weighting gets put into these signals when calculating search rankings isn't clear, but Google has confirmed they are indeed factors. This means an irrevocable relationship exists between content and social planning, and publishing and linking efforts.

User Experience Design

The digital landscape is chock-full of complex systems. User experience design is important for simplifying things enough so that users can complete desired tasks and leave a digital experience satisfied. As we've already stated, audience analysis via digital analytics plays a big role in informing user experience designers about what the relevant steps are along a consumer journey, by providing what users need and expect, and alternatively, which steps are broken, causing dissatisfaction and abandonment. Web analytics, site surveys, and social analytics can reveal a combination of what people are doing and saying about their experience. Designers can incorporate these feedback mechanisms as input and optimize user flows accordingly.

Audience Segmentation

As described in Chapter 1, "Understanding the Synergetic Digital Ecosystem," segmentation is critical. Your audience is made up of unique segments, each with a specific set of online behaviors. Using a number of third-party digital analytics tools we've already covered and will expand on in later chapters, you can begin to build custom segments that reveal key behaviors and activities for you to align your marketing campaigns against. A good example of this is Forrester's Technographics, which handles segmentation and how consumers behave online. Forrester's Consumer Technographics study was most recently updated in 2017 and now includes survey topics that provide insights into digital behaviors across categories such as social media behaviors, digital commerce and spending, smartphone and Internet of Things (IoT) device ownership, digital payment methods, preferences, attitudes, and more!

Audience Analysis Tool Types

We have provided a high-level description of the uses for audience analysis. Now let's dig into the tools you can use to execute with. The landscape for these tools has evolved in both sophistication and number of tools available in recent years. Audience insight features and capabilities have been integrated into several digital analytics tools categories. As a result, selecting the right one can be daunting and time consuming if you were to examine every single digital or social analytics tool that can provide audience insights. Remember to follow the steps outlined in Chapter 3, "Choosing Your Analytics Tools" to ensure that selecting a toolset isn't a painful process and most importantly that you end up with a solution that meets your needs.

The digital analytics toolbox contains several categories of tools. Many different tools are available within each category, and overlap can also exist between tool categories based on specific features or capabilities, potentially making tool selection even more difficult. That said, here are the most common categories of tools available to you:

- **Search insights**—Search insights tools can be broken down into two distinct subcategories. The first provides insights into *search intent* based on actual consumer searches with Google or other search engines. These are useful for mining search engine volume patterns across geography, industry categories, brands, and competitors to identify actionable insights. Google Insights for Search, which has since been renamed to Google Trends, is still one of the more useful free solutions for this type of analysis. The second subcategory of Search insights is very much *keyword based*, with a focus on PPC/Paid Search activity and data. Google Ad Planner is a free option in this category, with premium offerings from many leading vendors such as Wordstream, Keyword Tool Pro, and KW Finder. These provide insights that have multiple use cases but are primarily aimed at supporting paid search advertising. If you're responsible for paid search, or PPC, you probably spending time in some of these tools every day. If you're not focused on paid search, you can still benefit from the insights these tools can offer because they give a window into the mindset and intent of consumers.

- **SEO**—You can still use SEO tools to monitor, track, and manage both your own and competitor keyword rankings. In fact, ensuring that you're organically "discoverable" by consumers is more important than ever. With attention scarce and paid media noise at an all-time high, marketers have come to realize that the simple formula of focusing on high-quality, relevant content and experiences is the path to success with owned media. Google has also increased the weighting of relevancy over time in regard to quality content on your site.

  So, because of this, there is a crowded marketplace for these types of tools, even more so than when we first wrote about it. Leading paid tool providers are familiar incumbents such as Moz Pro, SpyFu, and SEMRush. Although these tools are impressive, many free tools are available as well, such as Google Keyword Planner or Screaming Frog. This list doesn't even come close to scratching the surface of the universe of SEO tools in the marketplace. There are too many paid, free, and premium tools to cover in depth. Depending on your level of expertise and willingness to do the work, you can opt for completely outsourcing the work or doing it yourself. There is an SEO tool that will meet everyone's needs.

- **User surveys**—Voice of the customer (VOC) surveys capture answers from website visitors to custom and very specific questions that the brand wants insight into. They offer advanced features such as skip logic, randomization, website integration, reporting, and analytics. Surveys are a valuable source of qualitative feedback that you can tie to web analytics data to connect what an audience says with what it actually does. This type of VOC feedback can also be paired with offline qualitative feedback to either validate findings or identify where further work is needed to clarify what customers are telling you versus how they are behaving. Options such as SurveyMonkey, Google Forms, and LimeSurvey offer low-cost solutions, and premium solutions from companies such as ForeSee or OpinionLabs offer custom variable capture, advanced segmentation (very important to deliver relevant questions to different visitor segments to your website), and filtering as well as professional services support to aid you with execution.

- **Website profiling**—Website profiling services do exactly what the name suggests: You can enter a website URL and get back a snapshot in time profile of a website based on panel data from that service that reveals website traffic statistics, search volume, referring traffic sources, demographic data on visitors, related sites, and more. The landscape of leaders in this category has changed rather dramatically in recent years. Similar-Web, Alexa (acquired by Amazon), and Follow.net are some of the leaders in this space and offer both free and premium versions of their tools.

- **Web analytics**—Traditional web analytics tools are the grandfather of digital analytics tools but despite their age are the core on which a digital intelligence foundation is built. They have some of the most advanced capabilities for collecting, analyzing, and reporting on data to understand audiences and optimize website experiences. As recently as Forrester's Global Digital Intelligence Platforms Wave survey conducted in Q2 2017, nearly three-quarters of marketers cited web analytics tools as the number one technology for gathering digital intelligence (see Figure 5.3).

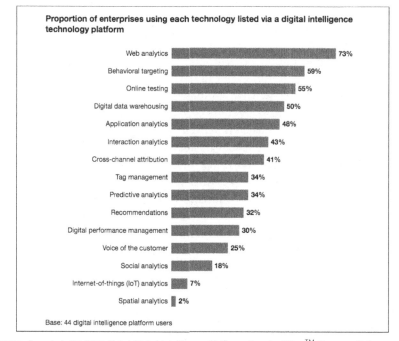

Source: Forrester's Q2 2017 Global Digital Intelligence Platforms Forrester Wave™ Customer Reference Online Survey

Figure 5.3 *Digital intelligence technologies marketers use most.*

These tools are primarily used to understand traffic behaviors, website experience pathing, content engagement trends, content virality, and sharing trends, and, of course, they are still a rich source of behavioral data. Analyzing clicks can still provide incredible insight and value, but there are limitations. A lot of critical actions happen between clicks, due to how consumers now engage with content and the types of devices used now that don't require clicks, but rather taps or voice instructions. As a result, an entirely new category of tool has emerged that focuses on answering the question, "What happens between clicks?" The days of living in an era that required you to count clicks in the aggregate and call it a day are well behind us and never returning.

Web analytics can reveal behavior patterns that tie back to several of the use cases referenced earlier, particularly user experience design. (Optimized user experience design = less friction = a happy audience = win-win scenario!). Many web analytics tools allow for custom segmentation, multivariate testing, and a wide variety of data ingestion and data source integration features. These features are important as they enable you to experiment with blending different data sets, and understanding which specific content types (text, image, video) an audience most desires by testing different variations. The campaign tracking and management features alone in the market leaders such as Adobe Analytics and AT Internet Web Analytics Solution are worth the cost, as they enable you to easily connect your paid media campaigns to specific content and actions taken on your website, thus easily answering the inevitable questions about campaign performance and engagement. Defining and planning efforts like these, as well as what behavioral tests you want to execute, takes time upfront, but it's time well spent because the results can reveal specific and valuable insights about audience intent, likes, and needs as well as content and creative assets (for example, video, image, link) on your website. Google Analytics (free version) is still an extremely powerful web analytics platform for those without the budget for a paid alternative.

- **Social listening**—At the time of the previous writing of this book, hundreds of social listening tools existed in the marketplace. How much has changed in a short time! The social listening marketplace has arguably undergone the most change and disruption in recent memory. Look no further than the Forrester Wave chart of leading social listening platforms over time. Beginning in 2012, Radian 6 and Visible Technologies were the clear leaders, with Radian6 commanding an unheard of ~90% share of the social listening market (https://www .forrester.com/report/The+Forrester+Wave+Enterprise+Listening+Plat forms+Q2+2012/-/E-RES61648).

Fast-forward a mere two years to 2014, and the market changed dramatically. Radian6 was removed from the market leader position as a result of its being acquired by SalesForce and integrated into their platform, ceding way to Synthesio and Sprinklr (newcomers), with Visible Technologies still in the leader category (https://www .forrester.com/report/The+Forrester+Wave+Enterprise+Listening +Platforms+Q1+2014/-/E-RES101261).

Despite all of these disruptions and changes in the social listening industry, more changes were ahead. By 2016, the category again looked different, with Synthesio, Brandwatch, and Sprinklr leading the way, followed closely by popular platforms such as Crimson Hexagon and Clarabridge.

Social listening tools and their roles in supporting an audience analysis are to identify the sources (both media type and individual URL) of relevant social conversation about your brand or product/service and to provide some audience insights in the form of demographic and psychographic profiles. Refer to Chapter 3 for details on how to select a listening tool and considerations for using social listening.

One aspect of social listening that is unique to audience analysis and that we cover in this chapter is how to utilize custom tagging and classification to better understand your audience opinions and likes, and how to deliberately apply sentiment analysis about specific brand, product, or services attributes in an actionable way.

- **Influence analysis**—Identifying individuals responsible for driving action among relevant members of your audience is important. This category is covered in greater detail in Chapter 8, "Understanding Digital Influence."

- **Sharing analysis**—Tools are available that are specifically dedicated to tracking share activity of content across digital platforms. These tools provide a window into the type of content that's most desirable and most interesting to your audience through URL-shortening services such as bitly and free sharing tools such as AddThis, ShareThis, or Gigya that provide share analytics reporting. For a more customized paid offering, you can try a tool such as Buffer.

- **Social profile and activity analysis**—Social brand profile and activity analysis is one of the features most commonly found in third-party social analytics tools currently on the market. Whether you're performing an analysis of your own brand or a competitor's social profile, these tools detail your engagement activity, friends/fans/followers, and published content to reveal insights and trends.

  For example, Socialbakers, a third-party tool designed to manage your social profiles on Facebook, Twitter, Instagram, and YouTube, provides the following type of analysis at the account level:

  - Followers by location

  - Followers by language

  - Page post trends

  - Audience engagement trends

  This information is more useful than previous outputs of these types of tools, as the trend analysis and engagement analysis provide more specific and actionable insights versus the early days of "counting" social activity because that's all you could really report on. Now we're taking steps in the right direction: actionable insights! You can also customize engagement toward reaching a specific audience and their interests by applying social analytics tools like this but at a narrower band of your followers, not in aggregate.

As social analytics tools have matured to provide these types of segmentation capabilities, their usefulness has markedly increased. This is the biggest advantage that web analytics, search analytics, and paid media analytics have over social analytics, even after many years of native and social analytics evolution and maturity of core features for these types of tools.

One final note about this category: As of this second writing, the social analytics category is still a wide spectrum of capability and specialization. On one of end of the spectrum exist specialized one-offs that focus narrowly on an individual social platform, such as Hashtracking for Twitter or Snaplytics for Instagram and Snapchat. At the other end of the spectrum live the social analytics dashboards. These solutions support and provide analytics for all major social networks. Some excellent tools you can explore in this area are SimplyMeasured, Spredfast, TalkerWalker, and Sprout Social.

Sprout Social (https://sproutsocial.com/) is an example of a social analytics dashboard. It provides intuitive and visual dashboards that give detailed reporting on the following:

- Twitter profiles analysis

- Twitter engagement analysis

- Twitter trends analysis

- Twitter feedback report

- Facebook pages analysis

- Facebook engagement analysis

- Facebook audience insights

- Instagram profiles analysis

- Instagram competitor analysis

- LinkedIn pages analysis

- Google Analytics reporting

Sprout Social is far from being the only full-spectrum dashboard provider. Several of the social media management system (SMMS) tools described in Chapter 3 also provide analytics dashboards for the social networks they support. Other market leaders such as Hootsuite and Sprinklr are good places to start if you have those needs. The SMMS marketplace has grown and evolved to the point that it's now regularly reviewed and included in the Forrester Wave research. Features, functionality and integrations with other data sources and systems are changing frequently, so keep an eye on future wave reports for the SMMS category.

Jeremiah Owyang, an industry analyst at Altimeter Research Group, has compiled a comprehensive SMMS list, which you can find online at http://www.web-strategist. com/blog/2010/03/19/list-of-social-media-management-systems-smms/.

Additional Audience Analysis Techniques

Much of this chapter has been dedicated to the specifics of what audience analysis is, why you perform it, and the specific uses for audience analysis output. In this section, we get into the specifics for some techniques that you can use to get more out of these tools than is provided out of the box.

Despite all of this focus and content on tools, it's an important reminder that the business of digital analytics isn't about tools. They are important, and give you the ability to answer many different types of questions but all of these tools are simply a means to an end. The quality of an analysis is directly tied to the quality of the human analyst and the analytical techniques the analyst applies to various digital data types. Tools can make an analyst more efficient, but they won't magically provide the answer by themselves.

Rightfully so, social data analysis is a big area of focus these days because of the potential insights that can be derived from it. Brands are trying to get answers to audience questions such as these:

- What conversations are taking place about my brand?

- What topics and/or themes are most talked about?

- Who is my audience?

- Where do they spend their digital time?

- What do we know about their content consumption habits, preferences and engagement behavior(s)?

- What are the affinities and related interests of my audience?

- What is my audience saying about their needs, both met and unmet?

- How does my audience feel about specific brand, product, or service attributes?

Social listening tools can partially give you answers to these questions, but not completely. Think of them as a starting point for your audience learning agenda and build from there using other data sources and tools. Let's break down where the job of social listening tools ends and the analyst's job begins. Given the questions we've offered, tools try to provide answers using word clouds, word frequency, or overall sentiment reporting. Although these provide stimulating eye candy, they are not in fact very useful at answering these types of questions, or at the very least are quite efficient at answering them. This is where custom tagging can create supplemental metadata that enhances your analysis and delivers actionable insights instead of only interesting information. Social listening tools (and some SMMSs) also offer insight into how your competitors are being talked about online.

Conversation Typing

To understand audience preferences and get answers, you need to apply custom *tagging*. Several of the leading listening platforms allow for this in their tools, but you need to plan for it up front to realize maximum value.

A common approach you can take that applies custom tagging is called *conversation typing*. At a high level, it is as simple as segmenting your conversations into the most common types. However, it's based on the specific conversation types that you care about and define up front.

As an example, owners of a larger brand might find thousands of relevant monthly conversations among their audience about one of their products or services. Those conversations share this common trait, but at the same time fall into very different groups, or types. Common conversation types such as complaints, compliments, or company announcements exist across all categories. There are also conversation types unique to a brand, product, or service. Adding these custom elements to your conversation analysis yields much greater understanding about what your audience is discussing and truly cares about.

For example, say that you're looking at a product review, or a conversation surrounding a specific event or conference. This type of custom tagging can be useful when applied at the next level down—product or service attributes. Instead of learning the number of conversations about a brand's latest new product—a new gaming console, for example—wouldn't it be even better to know specifically what percentage of your audience discussed product issues with accurate gameplay, skepticism about a particular product attribute, or commentary about the overall product experience? The overall list could look like this:

Standard/Custom Brand Response	Online Community Comment Type
Standard	Complaint
Standard	Compliment
Standard	Company announcement
Custom	Product attribute 1
Custom	Product attribute 2
Custom	Product experience feedback

There is no limit to what tagging you can create and apply, although the more granular you get, the more work you must do, but the more specific your analyses will become. The point here is that your analysis is now more relevant than ever before to your business. Instead of being brand relevant at a high level, the analysis now has laser-like precision to specific areas of your business, from marketing to customer service/support to product development. This is an approach for highly targeted social data analysis.

Classifying the standard data through human analysis and custom tagging turns interesting data into actionable data. For example, a brand could use the insights it uncovers to update product development efforts and fix bugs, alter the product development roadmap to reflect feedback about the audience experience, or even inform outbound marketing and advertising efforts based on the feedback learned from examining conversations about specific product attributes.

Event Triggers

It's one thing to understand the breakout of different conversation types that are being had about a brand, and another thing to understand a single, aggregate number of brand mentions. You can do more to understand what your audience is doing and what is driving those conversations so that you can optimize your media mix, content marketing, and engagement strategies based on a keen understanding of what events are triggering the conversation types that are most beneficial to you and your brand.

Event triggers analysis is something we first encountered while working on a large social listening program for a Fortune 50 brand. It was imperative for the company to understand the quantity and type of conversations about its product—and also what was causing the audience to have the conversations. So we developed a social listening analytical technique that we called *event triggers*.

The event triggers technique is essentially what the name implies, but you still won't find it in any social listening tool as an out-of-the-box feature. This technique comes after the conversation typing method described earlier has been completed. Event triggers analysis is a natural extension of that custom data enhancement. Building on the example previously used, the process is to examine all conversations of a particular type and to identify the root-cause event that sparked it in the first place. Although there are limitations to the technique and using it is not always possible, in many cases it doesn't require much more effort to identify and link the conversation back to a specific event.

Using our gaming console example, there could be any number of unique events responsible for triggering relevant conversations. Following a similar methodology to conversation typing, you might expect to find gaming shows or conventions, industry product reviews, PR announcements, competitor announcements, or consumer-generated product reviews as the events triggering relevant conversations.

The value in this technique is that it enables you to reveal enhanced insights that improve product attributes, make your marketing and/or advertising initiative more effective through optimization efforts, and reveal new opportunities that weren't previously identified.

In conclusion, you can use many different methods to gain valuable information about the audience(s) that you're trying to reach. There isn't a single, off-the-shelf tool that can give you a 360-degree profile of an audience that gives you everything needed to successfully deliver relevant content and experiences to them across all the digital touchpoints they have with your brand. However, using the AUDIENCE approach we've detailed, along with the tools from the categories covered in this chapter, will give you the best chance at understanding your target audience.

6

Digital Analysis: Ecosystem

Chapters 4 and 5 focused on how to conduct digital analysis to gauge your brand's health and how to leverage digital analytics tools to gain a rich and multifaceted understanding of your target audience. This chapter focuses on the complex and chaotic digital ecosystem in which your brand operates. The digital media and device fragmentation that has occurred over the past five years has exacerbated the complexity problem for marketers. As such, we need a way to bring clarity to a complex set of digital properties, platforms, and assets. Marketers will use the digital analytics tools available to help us understand the unique digital footprint for brands. You likely don't need to be everywhere in the synergetic digital ecosystem, nor should you try. That said, it doesn't stop many brand marketers from chasing the latest digital shiny object without a data-driven, evidence-based reason for doing so. In this chapter, we cover how and why you want to perform an ecosystem analysis.

Why consider doing a digital ecosystem analysis? Frankly, it can simplify things. It will also help you identify which digital properties and platforms are more important to you, your audience, your influencers, and even your competitors, than others. Digital ecosystem analysis is a hybrid of social listening analysis combined with techniques that user experience designers apply as part of their research for designing or optimizing customer journey paths. We can adapt some of their frameworks for our own purposes to bring a more logical, organized, and prioritized view of the synergetic digital ecosystem that your brand has to navigate.

The purpose of an ecosystem analysis is to answer the following questions for each digital property or platform:

- Why does this platform exist and what role does it play for my audience?

- Where is it and how does my audience discover it?

- What's the priority level for this platform? Is it an immediate near-term priority or a longer-term opportunity instead?

- Which audience segments use this platform? Why, and for what purpose?

- What is the benefit to the brand for being on this platform?

- What brand touchpoints does it have? Is it isolated by itself or integrated with others?

The digital ecosystem has grown to be too much for any one brand; instead of trying to figure out how many more digital platforms your brand needs, instead determine whether your digital pieces fit together. If they do not, what is the optimal combination of digital properties and platforms for the brand?

Each digital brand has its own unique composition of digital assets. Your audience and customers are unique to your brand. Sure, they might share commonalities with those of your competitors, but it's important to resist the urge to "clone" a competitor's digital ecosystem approach versus doing an analysis to determine what your own should be. This type of analysis is basically an audit, or inventory, of digital properties relevant to your brand and audience.

Ecosystem Analysis

The process for an ecosystem analysis begins with casting a wide net at digital properties. Thus far, most of the analysis chapters in this book have focused on well-known, large platforms and important owned media properties, such as a brand website. Here, however, we don't want to filter out anything as we're looking for not only the obvious big digital platforms but also the outliers, the edge cases that might be off of your radar currently, but not off the radar of your audience. With that, here are the major steps associated with the ecosystem analysis.

1. **Do a digital channel inventory.** Using a social listening tool, perform searches relevant to your brand, products/services, and audience. Unlike other social analyses, your focus here isn't just on finding volume of results with relevance; it's on uniqueness of results with relevance. Many social listening analyses overlook fringe properties that contain relevant conversation or results, only because in the search they are dwarfed by much large platforms with more volume of the same conversation, such as Twitter. The reason that's limiting in this exercise is that the focus is on relevance and quality, not audience size. Now that's not to say a third-party forum on a niche topic that happens to be a fit for your brand's product is equal to 10 times the volume of similar conversations on Twitter. Prioritizing them comes later. For now, you're in collection mode. Find as many brand- and audience-relevant properties as you can. Capture the details for each one that you'll need later to do a prioritization exercise. Be sure to gather additional metrics associated with each platform, as you'll need them to complete the prioritization part of this process.

2. **Identify the volume of conversations.** This step is straightforward to do, and your social listening tool should be able to easily isolate and identify the volume of relevant conversations happening on an individual property or platform basis.

3. **Determine volume of traffic.** This step isn't going to be as easy to determine but there are some methods for getting estimates of website traffic volume. Revisit the website profiling tools that were covered in Chapter 5, "Digital Analysis: Audience" for details on tools that you can use here. You're gathering website traffic volume information here in order to help you assess the size and scale of the opportunity for your brand. You might very well find an outlier with relevant audience and discussions only to discover it has very low traffic and a small audience. That doesn't mean it isn't potentially valuable to you, but it shouldn't be placed higher on the list than others with greater potential.

4. **Determine content relevance.** This step is critical because content relevance is one of the biggest factors that determine how likely a property or platform is going to play a role in your ecosystem. Determining how relevant the content and discussions are isn't too complex.

Create a simple scoring method that works for you without being too burdensome. Use it to assign each property in your inventory a content relevance score. This removes some of the subjectivity and is especially helpful if you have multiple people working together on an ecosystem analysis.

5. **Discover brand presence.** Determine whether your brand is already engaged with the audience on each property. Why would you want to include this in the inventory? Well, if someone from your brand is already engaging with your audience on the digital property you're assessing, you can learn a lot from that person about the role that property currently plays within your digital ecosystem. Another reason is to determine how "brand friendly" a particular platform might be. Consumers don't always want to cohabitate with brands on the digital platforms they spend a significant amount of time on. Now, you're probably saying but what about Facebook? Brands are all over it along with consumers. True, but there are relevant digital properties that are opportunities for brands where the opposite is the norm. Take Reddit, for example. Reddit has a thriving, extremely loyal audience but has not taken to allowing brands to invade their sub-Reddit communities. Brands and marketers to this day are still trying to crack the code in regard to Reddit community engagement. Because of this, Reddit isn't written off. Reddit provides enormous insights into audience opinions, attitudes, and preferences by analyzing Reddit community discussions.

6. **Prioritize platforms.** Now that you've collected a fair amount of ecosystem information and intelligence, it's time to make use of it and go through the process of organizing and scoring the digital properties and platforms that you discovered during the inventory. This is best done with a spreadsheet because you can automate the scoring through some creative formula wrangling, but you can do it manually all the same—we just don't like doing things manually if it can be avoided. It's more time consuming and increases the likelihood for errors, especially when working in a spreadsheet.

You're likely to have some surprises in the final results after you're done scoring each property. You might be surprised to see digital properties that weren't on your radar higher on the list than ones that you use frequently. Consequently, you might also find that well-known platforms with big audiences have a lower score and do not reflect the opportunity for you that their reputation carries. These are perfectly normal and common outcomes of an ecosystem analysis.

Ecosystem Analysis Outputs

We've saved the best for last. Working with the insights and information outputs of a digital ecosystem analysis is one of the best parts of this type of exercise. This type of information is best presented visually, with a before and after illustration to really make an impactful story about what your brand's digital ecosystem looks like. Let's take a look at some ecosystem maps, which are just examples of the data in an ecosystem analysis visualized in a simplified manner.

In this case, we're going to use EMC as our brand example (see Figure 6.1). EMC is a hardware and software technology manufacturer that sells to IT decision makers.

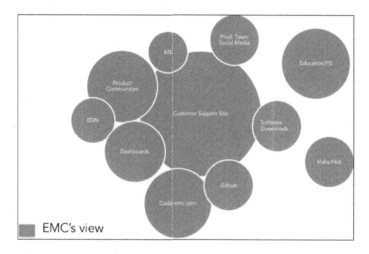

Figure 6.1 *EMC digital ecosystem map example.*

The visual in Figure 6.1 shows the EMC digital ecosystem but pre-analysis, before going through the steps we've walked through in this chapter. Look closely and nothing really jarring sticks out. It's fairly straightforward, a small combination of mostly EMC-owned media properties that the IT decision makers use to gather information, share, and ultimately decide on product purchases. Now, let's contrast that with a view of the EMC digital ecosystem based on a complete data set, via the inventory, and corresponding analysis as shown in Figure 6.2.

The lighter gray circles represent digital properties within the ecosystem that the EMC audience finds relevant and uses frequently, and that contain the type of content they are searching for. The dark gray circles are noticeably absent from the first map. This is a perfect example of what we described earlier in the chapter: identifying outliers or previously unknown digital properties that should be part of your digital ecosystem.

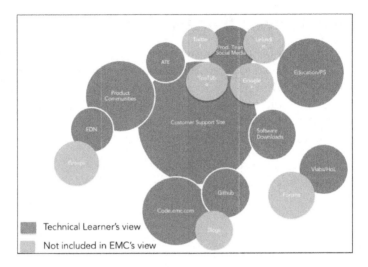

Figure 6.2 *EMC digital ecosystem analysis map example.*

Digital Ecosystem Maps

Spend some brief time searching on Google for *digital ecosystem map* and your head will spin. As with infographics, there aren't really standards for ecosystem maps at this time. It would be nice to see some de facto standards develop for creating easily communicated ecosystem maps and their relevant details across brands, but for now, this is the state of things. The upside is that you can get as creative as possible in regard to visually designing and communicating what your digital ecosystem map should entail. We think there is a world of possibilities and potential in the future around the data from this type of analysis and marrying it with some of the latest innovations in the data visualization space. Adding automation and integration between these two worlds would allow for ecosystem maps that can be reliably, efficiently updated and maintained over time. That's currently a manual process for most, but expect to see progress on this front, albeit slowly. Companies must first embrace ecosystem analysis and mapping more formally, and then the efficiency and automation will come.

The analysis of the digital channel ecosystem is a critical component to either launching a new marketing program or optimizing what the brand has been doing to date.

7

Return on Investment

Accurate understanding of effectiveness has never been more critical. Digital marketing has accelerated, jumping off of just platforms and into mixed reality. Organizations are pursuing digital transformation at an unprecedented rate. Shiny objects are everywhere and investments can often feel random. Budgets continue to climb. Forbes reports that the U.S. digital marketing spend will be close to $120 billion by 2021— comprising nearly half (46%) of all marketing spends. Further, organizations are re-examining their very structures based on how ROI is assessed. Now is our opportunity to level set these ROI measurement opportunities with accuracy and accountability.

The availability of data means marketers and communicators alike can no longer hide behind the lack of available information to prove whether a program was successful. It is all there; you just need to spend time creating your goals and setting up the mechanisms necessary to collect and analyze data. The problem is often determining what to track.

In Chapters 1, "Understanding the Synergetic Digital Ecosystem," and 2, "Understanding Digital Analytics Concepts," we described some of the foundational elements of digital analytics, including setting measurable goals. Without those measurable goals, the rest of the measurement process falls apart. If you set proper goals, you should have an abundance of potential metrics to choose from. One of those metrics is return on investment, (ROI).

ROI is the gain from any spending minus the cost of the investment divided by the cost. Dividing by the cost of the investment gives you a percentage gained or lost. It is really quite simple. Why then, according to many industry-wide studies, is there a struggle to measure ROI? Why are we still struggling to answer the questions of CMO's who want to invest more in digital marketing channels but are hesitant because we are not clear on what the contribution was to the business?

The reasons are many, and we examine them throughout this chapter. We'll talk about different approaches to measuring ROI, and then at the end of the chapter give you our recommended model for capturing digital marketing effectiveness that is a blend of ROI and other measures that help you tell a more well-rounded story of business impact.

Defining ROI

The concept of ROI is not a complicated one. To reiterate, *ROI* is the gain from any spending minus the cost of the investment divided by the cost. This calculation yields a percentage either gained or lost from your investment. This makes sense, right? Unfortunately, with the explosion of digital marketing channels, the process of calculating ROI has become more complicated. There are now so many additional touchpoints for marketers to engage their audience(s), and with that has come the challenge of isolating just how much that has contributed to the business. To combat the problem, the digital marketing industry has attempted to circumvent the need to calculate the financial return from a digital marketing program by creating different acronyms. Even with the passage of time since we wrote the first version of this book, we still see many of these acronyms pop up.

We do not mean to insinuate that the people who have come up with these acronyms have sinister intent. In fact, we think those who have created the acronyms are simply attempting to help those who struggle to capture digital marketing's value to the organization. Unfortunately, senior executives are not likely to understand or even accept any variation on ROI. Your immediate boss might accept some alternatives, but in our experience, senior leaders recognize ROI only as financial return on investment.

In the coming pages, we outline all the different variations on ROI so that you can understand what each of them means and why they are problematic.

Return on Engagement (ROE)

One of the variations on ROI is *return on engagement* (ROE), which measures the effect your organization's digital marketing activities have on engagement rates. It assumes that engagement with content leads to greater awareness, which then leads to higher likelihood of consideration, which then leads to greater likelihood to buy or increases in brand favorability. This has never mattered more to marketers than it does in 2018.

 Note

> **Reality check**: The value of attention has skyrocketed. Audiences have more options than ever, so time spent on your branded content or ads should be considered a gift. Brands need to remember this and respect it. Measure it. Optimize against it. But measure it the same way you measure love—not with money.

That said, the numbers matter. The math behind ROE tends to vary, even by social platform in some cases, which is one of its primary issues, but it is calculated primarily by understanding the effect a community manager or brand representative has on engaging with someone after that person has mentioned the brand online. For example, if your company's social media specialist or community manager reaches out to someone who has made a complaint about the brand and is able to rectify that complaint, then a potential ROE calculation might be the time it took to make the contact and resolve the issue.

Another way ROE can be calculated is by looking at the percentage of engaged users within a social media community. This calculation varies by social media network. Here is one approach for how it can be calculated for Facebook, Twitter, and YouTube:

- **Facebook**—The number of engaged users is calculated by adding the number of likes on a post, the number of comments on a post, and the number of shares on a post, and then dividing that sum by the number of fans (or likes).

- **Twitter**—The number of engaged Twitter users is calculated by adding the number of replies to the number of retweets and likes, and dividing it by the number of followers.

- **YouTube**—There are a couple ways to calculate engaged YouTube users. The first is to add the number of comments, the number of ratings, and the number of likes, and then divide that sum by the number of views of a particular video. Another variation is to add those same engagement metrics and divide the sum by the number of subscribers.

Knowing the number of engaged users and capturing the instances in which the community manager for your company improves or helps your customers are both valuable. However, some analytics teams have taken different routes you should be aware of that create inconsistencies and missteps for return on engagement:

- **Fuzzy math**—We have highlighted a couple different ways ROE can be calculated in this chapter, and there are likely many others that we have not covered here. When you are reporting results to upper management, ensuring that the math is clear and defendable is imperative. Although both of the methodologies we outline here are defendable, the effect on the organization is not clear.

- **Determining whether engaged users equal sales**—The fact that 25% of your fans on Facebook or followers on Twitter are engaged with your content does not necessarily translate into sales. To make that sort of correlation, you would need to do a lot of work on the back end to track your fans' or followers' activity. (We present more on this concept in the upcoming pages.)

- **Focusing on the wrong part of the funnel**—ROE is not a substitute for ROI because it isn't meant to capture sales. ROE could be an appropriate calculation if you are focusing on creating brand awareness, improving customer experience, and/or being more actively considered before a buyer makes a purchase.

Bottom line: ROE is a fine approach if you are trying to understand how an audience reacts to your digital content and experience initiatives. It is not, however, a method to track the financial performance of your social or digital media campaigns.

Return on Influence

Influence matters. Marketers spend a lot of time and money pursuing the pathways of influence on consumers. The complicated part is that it looks different for every brand and product. However, two attributes of influence are true for everyone:

Reach: Conversations or content with significant distribution or visibility

Resonance: Conversations or content that influences hearts and minds

This does not, however, mean return on influence is an easily composed measure. The fundamental issue with the notion of return on influence is that it is not necessarily tied to a sales behavior. Sure, digital marketers could design a program in order to engage influencers to ultimately result in an increase in the number of purchases, but that is not always done. Most often, digital marketers create influencer programs in order to grow volume of conversation and increase reach, or become exposed to an entirely new audience. A sale that results from that activity is great, but digital marketers often do not set up the mechanism to track that sort of behavior (that is, creating custom links to drive an influencer and his/her followers to a retail site).

A few key elements to keep in mind as you construct perspective on your organization's return on influence efforts:

- **Tweets, retweets, comments, and likes are not transactions**—Think about your own activity online for just a moment. When you click the Like button or retweet someone, is your next action to go and buy something from that brand? In most cases, the answer to that question is "no." How often have you retweeted or liked something because a friend of yours works for the brand? These activities *might* lead to a transaction, but they are not direct transactions.

- **The fan/follower value calculation is flawed**—Looking at the dollar amount spent on social activities and dividing it by the number of fans or followers acquired is inherently flawed. The primary reason it is flawed is that it does not take into account the way in which fans are acquired. Some fans are acquired organically, and some fans are acquired through the utilization of paid media or advertising. Each of those activities has different levels of return, depending on the organization. It is a big leap—one we are not comfortable making—to assume that a like equals increased likelihood to buy.

- **Not all fans are created equal**—Just because I like, retweet, or even comment on a post does not make me more likely to buy. In fact, I could be the exact opposite of the brand's target audience. Therefore, if I retweet or share a piece of information, have I helped the brand? Perhaps I have in terms of raising visibility or growing reach, but there is a very good chance that my "share" will not reach anyone who is a likely buyer of the product. Is that valuable to you as the brand manager?

- **Changing behavior is important but not inherently financial**—We take a very literal approach to ROI. ROI is, without doubt, a financial metric. Return on influence and the previously discussed ROE are not necessarily financial results. They do enable you to track the effect you are having on certain behaviors, which is great. However, causing people to retweet, share, or even speak more positively about a brand is not the equivalent to a sale.

As with calculating ROE, calculating return on influence can help you understand how you have affected behaviors. In fact, it can give you a long-term view of how brand opinion has shifted. It is not, however, helpful in determining how often your end consumer will eventually ring the register.

Return on Experience

Return on experience is gaining more and more attention as an interesting measure of success due to the emergence of mixed reality (digital + physical). Social media will also continue to be a contributing factor to this measurement approach. The foundational idea here is to quantify the brand interaction of an audience at scale. However, due to its relatively short existence, this approach is less mature, and currently return on experience as a success measure lacks specificity for both brand and audience that are included in alternative measurement approaches such as ROI. The primary issue is that the brand has no way to scale this sort of measurement. Surprising individual customers, who then in turn create positive word of mouth, is great. But accurately and reliably tracking this sort of activity simply is not feasible for many organizations that likely do not possess the necessary measurement and analytics resources. Frankly, if we adhere to the principles of coming up with measurable goals, "surprising" doesn't fit the bill.

The other difference with this approach is that it is inherently not a financial metric. If your team creates an amazing experience for your customer, it might lead to an additional sale or sales from that person's peers, but how do you know? You would need to set up the attribution mechanisms to track that person's activities, and if you did that, you would not be tracking return on experience. You would, in fact, be tracking return on investment.

Return on experience continues to evolve and will likely find its place in the measurement approaches toolbox, but it still has some maturation ahead of it. If this approach is a priority for your team, you might want to consider the value of "experience" in the long-term view. Experiences are indeed valuable to both brand and consumer. When executed with a considered, long-term approach, experience investments can improve key performance indicators (KPIs) that lead into net momentum. However, "long term" isn't used lightly. You must compare year-over-year growth over multiple years to truly understand the value of this perspective. Measurement must then be composed of metrics related to brand opinion, which often require consistent costly qualitative studies. One other way we've seen companies try to measure this is by measuring sentiment. Our issue with that approach is similar to the above in that it isn't a financial metric. The bottom line for experience ROI: Avoid this approach for campaign-based reporting.

Properly Tracking ROI

There are other non-financial variations to ROI that we are not dissecting here. Are they valuable to your brand? Potentially, but not as a way to track the direct effect your activities have had on the business. ROI in the truest sense of the word is an important metric for digital marketers to be tracking. At the end of the day, it's not the only measure of success; however, it is the metric your senior executives will care about the most. Because it matters to your senior executives, it should matter greatly to you. These are the people who control your budget and your career.

Before we get into the proper way to capture or calculate ROI, it is important to note that not every campaign requires calculating a financial impact. In fact, it's the impact of campaigns working together that proves a solid, sustainable ROI.

Recall the discussion in Chapter 2 about how important it is to set measurable goals. Sometimes increasing sales is the primary goal of a campaign, but not in every instance. Sometimes the goal of a campaign is to build awareness and brand affinity. Those two things might have some relationship to sales, but they aren't sales on their own.

Now that you know more about incorrect variations on ROI from social media activities, it is time to dig into how you can properly capture ROI. The tools required to properly capture the financial return of your programs will depend on your organization. A proficiency in Microsoft Excel or other statistical modeling software (for example, SPSS) might be required. This might necessitate bringing in outside support. Keep in the back of your mind that capturing ROI requires tools that not everyone within your organization may know how to utilize.

So what are some of the ways you can capture the ROI from your social media programs? Several years ago, the Altimeter Group, an organization that provides research on a variety of communications topics, released a paper titled "The Social Media ROI Cookbook." In this paper, Susan Etlinger and some others outlined six excellent approaches for measuring the revenue effect of social media. Those six approaches can be broken down into two categories: top-down and bottom-up. As an aside, although the subject of the paper was social media and it is a few years old at this point, we think its approaches do apply nicely to a broader set of current digital marketing activities. Over the course of the coming pages we'll capture what

Susan and the authors of this paper identified as ways to measure ROI, and then at the end of this chapter we'll capture a hybrid approach that you can take to your organization.

Understanding the Top-Down Revenue Measurement Approaches

"The Social Media ROI Cookbook" outlines three different ways brands can measure the top-down revenue effect of social media activities. It is important to note that these three approaches are typically the most popular with brands. They are often the easiest to capture, and they require the fewest number of internal resources. Unfortunately, they are often high level and difficult to scale. These are the three types of top-down revenue measurement approaches:

- **Anecdote**—This is probably the most common of the three, and it involves a verbal "share" of a relationship between a social media activity and a sale.

- **Correlation**—A correlation analysis takes a specific type of behavior and tries to establish a relationship between it and some other activity.

- **A/B, multivariate testing**—In this type of analysis, a marketer attempts to understand the effectiveness of two versions of some type of content (for example, a web page, a marketing email, or a social media advertisement) in order to determine which has the best response rate. You can think of multivariate testing as many different A/B tests happening simultaneously.

The following sections describe each of these three methods in a little more detail.

Anecdote Analysis

Anecdote analysis is likely to be the least concrete of the models we talk about here, but an anecdote is simply a verbally expressed relationship between digital, social, or media signals and sales. Altimeter indicates that this is likely to be seen in large, often B2B, companies with high consideration and long sales cycles, but visualizing a consumer example of this type of activity would not be hard.

An example of this sort of anecdotal relationship could be something like you tweeting that you're interested in buying a car. Let's say that the leader of social media for a large car manufacturer follows up on your comment with a reply directing you to the company's website. You might then reply to that person and indicate that you are now much more likely to buy a car, thanks to his or her outreach. Is it a direct sale? No. Did that person just create an opportunity for a sale to take place? Absolutely, and that kind of activity needs to be tracked whenever possible by an analytics or market research team.

You can probably see some potential issues with this approach, right? Although creating these kinds of opportunities for the brand is valuable for the company's social media leader, it is not practical for him or her to reach out to everyone who talks about buying a car. This approach is not scalable for most organizations, especially a big enterprise. The other issue is that the process of finding these conversations can be automated, but the outreach is still very manual. Such a manual process creates strain on existing resources. However, in some smaller companies, this sort of anecdotal feedback can help achieve buy-in for additional social media activities. At a bare minimum, it demonstrates that your customers are online and looking for information.

Correlation Analysis

A *correlation analysis* is simply an attempt to establish a relationship between two different variables. This type of analysis is used to identify patterns in behavior. It could be anything: comparing likes on Facebook to sales, the relationship between engagement on Twitter and in-store traffic, or even more advanced models that look at economic indicators and marketing activities.

The best thing about this type of analysis is that it can establish a relationship between specific digital marketing tactics and business outcomes. It's a well-established statistical approach, so unlike return on engagement or return on influence, you should not receive any pushback from internal stakeholders who are questioning the methodology.

However, the issue with this approach is that it is very manual. Each time you would like to understand the relationship between your digital marketing activities and some other behavior, the analysis has to be re-created. A trained analyst (another issue with this approach, by the way) needs to capture the relevant data for specific activity and the other variable you are testing it against. Furthermore, the analyst needs to spend time outlining all the other variables (and their data sources) needed to properly conduct the analysis. It is very rare to see a single digital marketing touchpoint contribute to a sale, though it can happen.

A number of tools make this process a little easier, but the primary tool of the trade is Microsoft Excel. The input might be a social media listening tool, or even an email service provider, but most of the work takes place in Microsoft Excel. Other tools, such as MarketShare, can help with even more advanced analysis. MarketShare can help you understand the consumer journey and what economic or environmental factors affect your marketing efforts.

A/B: Multivariate Testing Analysis

Multivariate testing is a method of testing a particular hypothesis using complex, multivariable systems. It is most commonly used to test market perceptions. Multivariate testing is a quickly growing area as it helps website owners ensure that they are getting the most from the visitors arriving at their site. Areas such as search engine optimization and pay-per-click advertising bring visitors to a site and have been extensively used by many organizations. Multivariate testing allows digital marketers to ensure that visitors are being shown the right offers, content, and layout.

This type of analysis is probably most familiar to digital marketers who have been engaging in this type of work for years. Those of you who are familiar with this type of approach have probably utilized this methodology in order to understand how a particular advertisement—traditional display or social media advertising—is resonating with your core audience. It can also be used to compare different tactics across multiple populations.

Like correlation analysis, A/B testing can provide strong insight into how digital marketing tactics affect business outcomes. That being said, the work to set up a proper A/B test has historically been somewhat manual. Tools such as Adobe Target have been developed to help digital marketers implement the test, but it still requires a human being to establish the variables of the test and then ultimately measure its impact.

The three top-down revenue-tracking approaches discussed here offer marketers insight into how social media programs are performing. They are not, however, without issues. The primary issue is that these methods are not very scalable. They require the presence of human beings who have deep knowledge of tools and statistics. Even through the math behind these analyses is solid, an element of uncertainty might still exist about how a campaign performed. With correlation and multivariate analysis, several variables in between the social activities and the business outcomes must be tested to truly establish a relationship. The bottom-up approaches described in the next section provide more granularity.

Utilizing Bottom-Up Measurement Models

The bottom-up measurement models offer a bit more detail than the top-down approaches. This does not make them better than top-down approaches, because each organization needs to consider its goals before picking an approach. The reality is that both types of approaches need to be utilized in some form to tell a complete story.

"The Social Media ROI Cookbook" describes three primary methods of tracking revenue impact using bottom-up techniques:

- **Linking and tagging**—Probably the most familiar method for seasoned digital marketers, linking and tagging uses a series of codes to track how a person comes to purchase your product.

- **Integrated**—Just as the name implies, integrated measurement utilizes multiple techniques to gather information about how a particular person makes a purchase.

- **Direct commerce**—This is probably the first "no duh" approach that we have outlined, but the direct commerce route utilizes some sort of selling functionality within the social network your brand is utilizing.

Let us dig into each of these in more detail.

Linking and Tagging Approach

Simply put, the linking and tagging approach enables marketers to apply a short link, ROI tag, or cookie to a site to track the source of a conversion. A short link is simply a long URL that has been shortened using one of a number of link-shortening services (such as bitly or tinyurl). Marketers can use a shortened URL to easily track clicks to a web property or an ecommerce site where the end user might make a purchase.

A cookie is usually a small piece of data sent from a website and stored in a user's web browser while the user is browsing a website. When the user browses the same website in the future, the data stored in the cookie can be retrieved by the website to notify the website of the user's previous activity. This allows a marketer to follow a particular person's path to purchase as she lands on the page and eventually surfs around it before buying.

A linking and tagging approach is widely applicable to any setting where a good or service is being sold online. It can be applied to the actual consumption of content on a website (such as whitepaper downloads or application submissions) that the brand could consider to be conversions. The good news is that it is also the industry standard for conversion attribution and allows for deep understanding of consumer behaviors online.

The bad news with a linking and tagging approach is that it does not account for any macroeconomic trends. For example, if the economy is going through a recession, or even if more people have become predisposed to purchasing in brick-and-mortar stores, the linking and tagging approach will not suffice. The other concern is that links often break, which prevents tracking of the activities post-click. Lastly, the usage of cookies is being more regulated around the globe and users have an increasing ability to opt-out of being tracked by a brand.

What types of companies should be utilizing linking and tagging? The answer is every type, from startups to large enterprises: the need is no different. These methods are particularly important for brands that have an ecommerce presence, are selling a lower-consideration item (think cereal and pet food), or have a longer sales cycle and want to optimize for conversions. In some cases, you might want to think about conversion a little differently. You can set up a tagging structure that enables you to track things such as whitepaper downloads as conversions or as leads generated. Those generated leads are just as valuable in the short term in industries that see longer sales cycles.

Integrated Approach

The integrated measurement approach utilizes an application, typically installed on a social property (most often Facebook) to track the user's activity. This application can be a way to serve up special content to users or direct them toward a place where they can either receive a coupon or make a purchase directly.

The best part about an integrated approach is that it tends to be very data rich. Here's what this means for communicators:

- **Understanding consumer behavior**—If you build an application that serves multiple types of content, these apps can help you understand what consumers want to see based on what they interact with the most.

- **Gathering consumer data**—Most of these applications "force" users to enter a name and an email address. The email address can be valuable when it is cross-referenced against an existing email database. However, the best applications gather that information as well as other demographic characteristics that can be very valuable for future testing.

- **Coupon redemptions**—For many B2C companies, these applications can offer the ability to serve up multiple types of coupons and track redemptions. While not a sale, per se, the download of a coupon is a pretty good indicator of a sale.

Other types of integrated measurement approaches exist. The most popular, and the one that seems to be growing rapidly these days, is the utilization of digital focus groups. The concept is similar to the concept of a traditional focus group, in that a small group of people are brought together in order to learn something about how consumers are behaving.

Digital focus groups differ from traditional focus groups in that they are online (obviously) and often are served up questions at varying intervals. For example, say that you are the head of marketing for a major technology company that recently launched a new smartphone device. You have a group of influencers who drive awareness of the product, and you would like to ask them a few questions. As the marketer, you could invite them to the digital focus group and ask questions about upcoming content, new product features, existing product features, and the competition to better understand their behaviors. It does not need to be a group comprised only of influencers, obviously, but you can see how you can use this method to test the effectiveness of content and even see how certain features might be driving sales. When you know what those features are, you can create content around those ideas to drive additional purchases.

The primary challenge with this type of integrated measurement approach is that the metrics are very siloed. Building a Facebook application is great and can be a source of great information about your customers, but it is limited to only people who are existing fans. What about the effect paid media has on your fans? The data is available, but it's not conveniently presented side by side with other Facebook data very often. With silos can come confusion about what the data actually means.

Direct (Social) Commerce Approach

One of the easiest ways to know whether your social media activities have driven sales is to sell directly through a particular channel. The most common method of doing this today is by creating a storefront on a social platform, such as Facebook, and selling your products directly from there. Tools such as 8thBridge, Moontoast, and Spiceworks enable users to create this sort of environment.

The direct (social) commerce route is the newest and has the most potential for direct correlation to sales. It is not something that very many have undertaken so far, and it probably will evolve to something well beyond a Facebook storefront. Bob Pearson, Chief Innovation Officer of W2O, an integrated communications agency based in San Francisco, talks about the birth of social commerce in seven different dimensions:

- **Multichannel marketing**—This represents the shift from two marketing channels to five pillars (.com, brick-and-mortar, partners, employees, and customers).

- **New media networks**—Individual communities are forming across a variety of social media channels.

- **Customers reached through search**—Many of your customers might turn to a search engine before they ever look to you for information.

- **A new content model**—This should go without saying, but customer-driven content drives the highest conversion.

- **A new approach for retail**—By understanding the effectiveness of each partner or OEM, you know how to build the right retail mix by brand, geography, and topic.

- **More effective media planning**—Using data, we can become even smarter about how we target different types of paid, owned, earned, or shared media activities.

- **New demand**—Creating new demand requires a focus on the broader community and not the influencers in order to drive sales

These are all really interesting approaches to measuring return on investment, but all have significant challenges in order to scale or implement them across large organizations. Additionally, while ROI is extremely important to measure for the sake of your senior executives, it isn't the only metric that matters. Different views for different roles at different levels in an organization will have unique reporting requirements. Living in a world where one metric rules them all is an uncomfortable place, and frankly not a fair judge of overall campaign effectiveness. Over the last four years since we wrote the first version of this book we've adapted from the singular focus on ROI into a three-tiered model that we'll discuss to close this chapter.

Three-Tiered Approach to Measuring Digital Marketing Effectiveness

Before we go any further, you might be flipping back to the beginning of this chapter where we said measuring ROI is critical and wondering why we're expanding beyond ROI. The reason is actually a very simple one, and that is because ROI alone does not help digital marketers plan future campaigns or optimize the campaigns that are currently in-flight. ROI can help plan, but the analysis showing return on investment often comes much later after the next campaign is already planned.

Instead of approaching everything solely through the lens of ROI, we prefer to take a blended approach with the digital marketing stakeholders that we work with on a daily basis. The three prongs to this approach are measuring effectiveness, measuring efficiency, and measuring impact. Let's discuss each of these in a little more detail:

- **Measuring effectiveness**—We just mentioned just that measuring ROI doesn't necessarily help a channel owner plan or optimize the program in-flight. This is where measuring effectiveness comes into play. Measuring effectiveness most often means understanding the individual impact that a certain channel (or channels) have against a previously identified KPI. For example, measuring effectiveness might mean the number of people the company has reached with a banner advertising campaign. Or, similarly, it might mean the rate in which our social media audience engages with the content that we have posted for that campaign. The important thing to keep in mind is that there does not need to be one metric you capture to measure effectiveness. In fact, there should be multiple effectiveness measures across the channels you are using for your campaign.

- **Measuring efficiency**—Anyone familiar with social media programs today knows organic reach doesn't really exist anymore (for example, organic reach percentage has been consistently sitting in the low single-digit percentage on Facebook). Almost every activation that we do digitally nowadays requires some level of paid media promotion. However, just because we need to use paid media to effectively reach our audiences does not mean that we should spend the money inefficiently. By measuring efficiency we simply mean identifying the cost to reach or have the intended audience engage with the brand in a certain way. Some of the common efficiency measures include cost per engagement (CPE), cost per view (CPV), and cost per acquisition (CPA). Achieving the intended goal of a digital marketing campaign is great, but doing so efficiently is the path to securing even more budget.

- **Measuring effect**—In case you were wondering where the concept of ROI might fit in, this is the place. Measuring impact includes taking all the various actions across the campaign and evaluating their contribution to the business (ROI). There is more than one way to do this type of approach. W2O (the company that Chuck Hemann currently works for) implements a model called return on media investment (ROMI). The ROMI model takes into account several variables—reach, website traffic, engagement, and search activity, among others—and tries to back into what those activities will contribute to the bottom line. It provides an excellent foundation in which to plan digital marketing and media activities, but it also provides a set of goals that the campaign activities need to achieve. Lastly, the ROMI model also provides a framework to introduce actual numbers at the end of the campaign to truly evaluate how close we were to our benchmarks and what we need to change in the future.

Before closing this chapter, we want to offer one relatively large statement: Engaging in digital marketing activities is not entirely about the sale. Sure, in cases where we can track a direct business outcome, we should be doing it. However, digital marketing can create greater brand awareness and stronger engagement with the brand and do so in a comparatively cost-effective manner. We do not recommend only looking at ROI. We do recommend you use the framework we've just outlined—effectiveness, efficiency, and effect—so that you can tell a more complete story about the performance of your campaign. The topic of digital marketing measurement and reliably and accurately measuring impact will continue to be a challenge, and one we as an analytics industry need to solve quickly.

Whether you like the top-down, bottom-up, or effectiveness, efficiency, and effect model we've shared here, do not be caught flat footed when your CMO asks you how your digital marketing program performed. Adopt an approach and consistently use it to measure, analyze, and report on the performance of your programs.

8

Understanding Digital Influence

In this world of converged digital ecosystems and mixed reality, digital influence can inform every step of developing consumer relationships through the purchasing lifecycle unlike ever before. It's a knowledge accelerator, replicating what consumers would do with friends and family offline. Simply put, digital influence is composed of data points indicating how and why attitudes are formed and decisions are made.

It is gold to CMOs.

We have talked at length through the first seven chapters about the abundance of customer data available to marketers. That data can be used for planning or optimizing campaigns, personalizing content and experiences, or measuring performance. Alternatively, that data can be used to develop lists of people who might be influential in shaping a brand's online identity. Note that we were very careful to qualify *online identity* versus *offline identity*. We elaborate on that idea when we discuss some of the failings of online influence analysis later in this chapter.

Not only is influence mining a gold-rush topic that could have multiple data inputs, it is also a topic that can be sliced and diced into many different pieces. For the purposes of this book, we look at five core elements of digital influence:

- **The reality of digital influence**—Some argue that digital influence, or the presence of influencers, is misguided. The argument is that what really takes place is that large groups move topics forward.

- **Modern-day media lists**—For many in public relations fields, working from a predetermined list of targeted media is commonplace. That kind of thinking is not only antiquated but will likely also lead to less-than-desirable outcomes.

- **Tools of the trade**—As is the case with social listening and search, a number of tools are available to marketers to measure influence. Those tools have pros and cons, both of which are discussed in this chapter.

- **Online versus offline influence**—A distinct difference exists between someone who moves conversation online and someone who causes behavior change offline. There is a link between the two, but right now tools are not tapping offline influence. Particularly, online influence tools do not tap into word-of-mouth suggestions between friends and family. This is an issue that continues to persist four years after we wrote the first version of this book. We investigate this phenomenon further in this chapter.

- **Using the influencer list**—It is not enough to just create a list of influencers. You have to create strategies to use the list.

Fundamentally, the influence question is one of measuring and analyzing human behavior. Why does someone decide to create an abundance of content about a particular topic? Why does someone gather content from a particular source? Why does an influencer's content "move" more than someone else's? These are all questions we ask when trying to determine someone's influence on a particular topic or idea. Will we ever land on a common point of view regarding online influence? Before answering this question, let us discuss the five elements of digital influence.

Understanding the Reality of Digital Influence

Think about how you make decisions in your everyday life. Where do you turn for information? Who do you ask for advice? What sources do you trust to give you accurate information? Is this group of people and sources a large crowd or a very small one? If it is the former, how large is that group? If it is the latter, is it the same four or five people every time?

These are questions consumers of goods and services (and information) do not even think about. If you need to buy a new television, for example, you instinctively know how you have done that in the past and then take action. If your source has been Amazon.com, you sit down at the computer or pull out your smartphone and start looking at the options. You do not necessarily think about what sources you turned to previously, or even who you might have asked. You know you need to take some sort of action.

Part of what makes the topic of digital influence so challenging is that there is not a "why" button associated with any of the influence tools discussed in this chapter. Or, in the case of analyzing social conversations, not every consumer explains why he took the action that he took. Similarly, when you analyze the traffic patterns of a website, there is not an explanation provided for why someone clicked on a particular link. You can speculate based on informed opinion, but that is all you can do.

The good news is that there is informed, academic debate on both sides of the digital influence question. There are basically two camps on the digital influence question: those who say that a small group of people can move a topic, and those who say that a larger community drives a topic forward. Both sides have really strong points of view that require some further examination.

The "Tipping Point" Phenomenon

Let's bring the conversation back into the communications realm and a little out of the social science discussion. How often have you watched a news cycle for your company or client following an announcement? Have you ever paid attention to how much volume of conversation there is or how long it lasts? Have you looked at who was driving that particular news cycle? In our experience, the answer to the latter question is often a limited number of people. Whether it is one person or five is irrelevant. Usually a single source picks up the story first, and a wave of "copycats" follows or syndicates the news.

How does a news cycle begin or spread? Obviously, it is started by an idea or, in the case of communications, a piece of content. That piece of content could be in the form of a press release, an interview, or even a statement posted on a website. Whatever form it takes, someone will find it and write about it. How much attention it gets overall is a function of a lot of things—and beyond the scope of this discussion. What's important to know, though, is that a single person finds it and spreads the idea. This is an example, albeit rudimentary, of the idea Malcolm Gladwell wrote about in his book *The Tipping Point*.

In the book, Gladwell argues that ideas and behaviors often spread like infectious diseases. He says that these ideas and behaviors often start with one "carrier" and then make their way into the entire ecosystem. Although Gladwell was not talking about digital influence, per se, you can see how his ideas could be applied to this area. An idea or a statement, in the case of a brand, is created and posted online. That is followed by an enterprising blogger or mainstream news source picking up the idea and writing about it. After the blogger or mainstream news source picks it up, other bloggers, news sources, and interested parties begin to syndicate the idea. Eventually, you reach a place where a lot of people are talking about the idea (with the volume depending on how interesting the idea is), which was started with a small group of interested individuals.

We are aware that we just took a pretty complicated psychological concept and broke it down into a handful of small tidbits, but that's the idea, in principle. In the case of communications, a small group of individuals create the news. As Gladwell would say, these individuals create the "tipping point" whereby the rest of the community pays attention.

One of the criticisms of this approach is that a brand does not have, in most cases, a single consumer, and by identifying individuals, you ignore the rest of the people who buy your product. We dive into this in more detail later in this chapter, when we talk about using an influencer list, but the truth of the matter is that not every consumer is a content creator. If we are talking about furthering a message online, we certainly care most about the content creators. In the case of the online world, the number of content creators is actually a very small group.

What are the other criticisms of the influencer model? Who is arguing the other side of this debate?

The Community Rules Phenomenon

On the other side of the digital influence debate are those who believe that the community, or a larger group of individuals, drives a topic or an idea forward. This group does not believe that one influencer, or a small set of influencers, drives an idea forward. It believes in the power of the community at large to drive an idea forward.

This theory gained traction thanks to Duncan Watts, then a researcher at Yahoo! and now the principal researcher at Microsoft. In a paper titled, "Influentials,

Networks, and Public Opinion Formation," Watts argued that ideas are driven by a critical mass of easily influenced individuals. He also argued that highly influential people do not drive large-scale changes in public opinion; instead, large-scale change is driven by easily influenced people who influence other easily influenced people. Essentially, Watts argues that it is better to reach a large group of people than a smaller group of people. By reaching a larger audience, he says, a brand (or person) can change public opinion more quickly.

Generally speaking, this model fits the mindset of the communicator who is looking to maximize reach as well as impact. We have all heard of a communicator who is trying to achieve as many impressions as possible, right? This approach has been around for many years, and there really is not anything wrong with it. It is the way most communicators have been measured and are continually measured. It isn't necessarily a good barometer to measure overall impact, but it is one measure in a set of many other metrics.

The bigger issue with this approach, especially in the context of digital media, is that trying to reach everyone in the intended audience is very difficult—and very expensive, and nearly out of reach most of the time. The majority of brands do not have enough staff members who can actively influence a large community. It is why many have taken to identifying influencers to help spread a particular message.

Whether you agree with the influencer model or the community model, the common thread is reaching a core group of people to spread an idea. That, at its heart, is influence. The only difference is the number of people you are trying to reach and how you are trying to reach them.

Developing a Modern-Day Media List

Those who have grown up in traditional public relations firms are no doubt intimately familiar with the media list concept. In case you do not come from that world, we take a moment to explain how these lists come together:

1. **Identify the pitch idea**—The first step is identifying what the pitch is going to be about. Essentially, you determine what message, or news event, you are trying to convey to the author.

2. **Determine the media type**—If you lump mainstream news and bloggers together when you are only trying to reach bloggers, you might confuse people who are trying to take action on it. Therefore, you need to determine the media type.

3. **Identify the "beat"**—Most likely there is a target beat that you will be looking for at the different media outlets.

4. **Select a tool**—Most corporations and agencies have access to media list generators, such as Cision, for downloading a list of media. When you have a tool, you can download your media list.

5. **Lightly scrub the list**—You need to identify the people you have a relationship with already and check to see whether any of those reporters have moved on.

6. **Begin pitching**—After you scrub the list, you can start pitching the reporters on your news idea.

Public relations professionals everywhere have replicated this approach for decades. The lists are constantly recycled, with notes being added periodically as people change beats or leave an outlet. It is not a bad concept, but it really is only a starting point. The problem with this approach is that the lists are static, and if you are at all familiar with the online world, you know that it moves very quickly. It is not enough to download a list and use it for months on end anymore. The other reality is that just because a list of reporters has been downloaded from a tool doesn't mean the people are influential. Additionally, the news landscape is constantly evolving (reporters leaving publications, going to new publications, retiring, and so on) so that lists are very hard to keep fresh.

So, how can you tweak this old-school media list approach to fit today's modern world? How do you create a list of influencers and not just a list of media everyone will know? Following these seven suggestions will help you create a more effective media list:

- **Use Google and blogrolls**—You do not need to come up with sophisticated Boolean queries. All you need to do is know how to properly format keyword strings based on your topics. After you have identified sources, check the sites they are linking to and reading. They are most likely good sources for content.

- **Think relevance first**—It isn't enough to just identify someone's beat. If you are targeting health care reporters, for example, you need to realize that a number of different subcategories exist within health care. Your job is to find the people who are the most relevant to the story you are trying to tell, not necessarily the person or outlet that reaches the most people. Relevance is greater than reputation in this circumstance.

- **Think syndication second**—Because this is a chapter on influence, it is important to bring up syndication. You do not want to target only people who write a lot. You want people who write a lot and have their writing shared by relevant people in large numbers.

- **Think post volume third**—If you have identified relevant people, chances are good that those people are also frequent writers on your subject. When people care deeply enough about a topic to write about it, quite often they also post frequently.

- **Think reach fourth**—There is a reason we have identified reach fourth. If you are identifying people who write a lot, are relevant, and receive widespread syndication, reach will take care of itself.

- **Tools still matter**—As much as it might have seemed like we were being negative about tools like Cision, they still do have their place as a starting point for research.

- **Refresh frequently**—Do not refresh your list only once per year, especially if you are in a tumultuous industry category. Communicators should refresh their influencer lists every quarter.

🔎 Tip

Do not fall into the same trap communicators have fallen into for years. Take the time to build a list that is relevant and full of people who are widely syndicated and reach a lot of people. If you do, your messages will resonate better.

Using the Tools of the Trade

If you are at all familiar with the concept of digital influence, you are probably wondering how we have gone this far without talking about tools. A number of tools are available on the market today, mostly web-based tools that offer users the ability to identify and rank influencers. Fundamentally, these tools enable social scoring. Marketers can use these tools to rank one person against another. So much change has occurred within the influencer identification and analysis space over the last four years that keeping pace is very challenging. For this version of the book, we trim down the discussion on tools significantly. Why? If you have been paying attention to the digital marketing tools landscape over the last four years, you know it has been plagued by expansion in some areas, and rapid consolidation in others. Our fear in writing too much about tools is that by the time this book is published either a tool might be gone or something else might have popped up to replace it. However, we will spend some time talking about some of the primary tools still involved in this ecosystem.

We focus some on Klout because it still exists and is used by the online community, but then address some of the tools in the market that help round out an influencer analysis toolkit.

Klout

Klout is one of the original tools in this industry, and continues to play a significant role in shaping the industry after it was acquired by Lithium Technologies in 2014. Klout continues to position itself as a tool that analyzes data across multiple social media channels in order to determine a person's collective influence. Ever since it broke onto the scene several years back, it has been the subject of much consternation, as individuals have struggled to understand how the scores are determined. At the outset, Klout was measuring online influence using data captured from only a handful of networks. However, over the past few years, it has expanded to include metrics from Instagram, Foursquare, YouTube, LinkedIn, Google+, Yammer, and so on. With the addition of new networks has come the addition of new metrics so that now the algorithm includes 400 metrics.

Entire books have been written about Klout. In February 2012, Mark Schaeffer released a book titled, *Return On Influence: The Revolutionary Power of Klout, Social Scoring, and Influence Marketing*, in which he details Klout's evolution, how brands are using it, and its effect on marketing as a whole. We are not going to get into that much detail here, but we do dissect a few elements of Klout's platform:

- **Scores**—The Klout scores are easily the most polarizing aspect of the platform. They're calculated in a way that is largely unclear to the marketing world.

- **Publishing and Topics**—Klout has recently added topics, which could be an interesting way to identify potential influencers.

- **Klout's future**—The Klout platform and algorithm are constantly changing. Later in this section, we predict what we expect Klout to do next.

Let us dig into the scores first, because they are probably what most marketers know about Klout.

Klout Scores

The way Klout comes up with an individual's score continues to be unclear to the outside world. We know that it is based on an indexed and weighted scale from 0 to 100. We also know, based on what has been published on Klout's website, that it includes up to 400+ metrics in the final calculation. The good news is that we know users have the ability to include multiple channels in their score. Users can include Facebook, Twitter, YouTube, LinkedIn, Flickr, Google+, Instagram, Foursquare,

Yammer, and Last.FM, among others, in their scores. At a minimum, the score has the ability to represent the entirety of someone's online presence.

Unfortunately, the positives do not outweigh the uncertain aspects of the scoring mechanism:

- **Algorithm ambiguity**—As noted earlier, about 400 metrics go into calculating the score. What those metrics are is a complete mystery. We can speculate based on channels analyzed (for example, number of followers on Twitter), but it would only be speculation.

- **Weighting uncertainty**—We know that Klout measures multiple channels, but which channels receive the most weight—Twitter, Facebook, other channels? How are the channels factored into the final analysis?

- **Score comparisons**—One of the favorite pastimes of marketers, done in a joking way or not, is to compare scores. However, it is not clear how Klout indexes people against each other. Is it based on work in similar industries? Is it based on the number of channels being analyzed? These are big questions if we are to take the scoring seriously.

- **Fluctuations in scores**—We respect Klout's desire to tweak the algorithm in order to make the scores as real as possible, but monthly, even daily, fluctuations are not realistic. A person's influence should not move two points or more in a given week. The counter to this that the platform might offer is that they are refreshing the score based on the last 90 days of activity, so that is why it fluctuates. Still, we should not see that much variation.

- **Post volume**—The assumption has always been that frequency of posts is a component of the score, but what is the ideal amount to be posting to boost your score?

In an ideal world, Klout would post the algorithm in its entirety for people to study, but we need to be realistic. The algorithm is part of Klout's intellectual property, and we respect the desire to protect it. However, a simple posting of metrics or a quick explanation on weighting could go a long way.

Publishing and Topics

Several years back, Klout rolled out topic pages that demonstrated what topics you, as an individual user, ranked on against the rest of the Klout community. Over the last several years the topics pages have morphed to show a user content about the subjects that he or she is influential on. Users have the ability to share content on their social networks straight from these topics pages.

The other new feature that Klout has unveiled over the last few years is the ability to publish your social media content through its platform. Users have the ability to identify content, schedule it for specific distribution, and then share it out with their social media users. From there users can measure the impact it has on their respective social media community.

Klout's Future

The future of Klout, and other influencer analysis tools like it, is just as unclear today as it was four years ago. A definitive need still exists inside of companies to have the ability to identify influencers in a scalable and cost-effective way. However, there are just as many questions today about how these platforms come up with their scoring and ranking as there were four years ago. Additionally, a number of platforms have been acquired or outright gone out of business because the technology they possessed was useful to a larger organization or the user base just wasn't there. Lastly, many of the social listening vendors have developed their own social influencer solutions to compete with the Klouts of the world. Social listening tools have achieved (and will continue to achieve) much wider adoption than the point solutions offering social influence scoring or ranking.

Other Important Influencer Analysis Tools

If you are going to go the route of a more manual approach to influencer identification, meaning not using a tool within your existing social listening suite or leveraging some other algorithm, you will want to take advantage of a few tools to make sure that your data is complete.

The first is a platform called BuzzSumo (http://buzzsumo.com/), which among other things, captures the most shared content among a group of people (or influencers). The platform also shows you the total reach of an individual, his or her domain authority, and how often the community engages with that person. Figure 8.1 shows an output from a BuzzSumo analysis for reference.

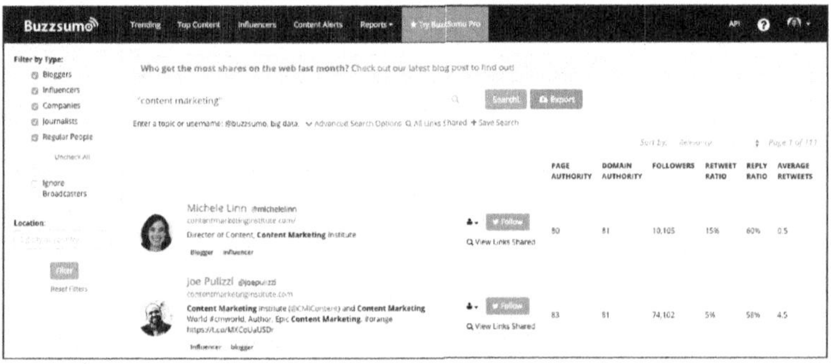

Figure 8.1 *Output from a BuzzSumo analysis.*

Another tool that is critical to rounding out your influencer analysis toolkit is MozBar. MozBar is simply a Google Chrome browser plugin that makes it easy to see SEO stats for websites as you're browsing. If you have the full bar displayed, it'll show you things like keyword difficulty score and backlink info for whatever page you're on. Looking at the rankings and authority of a potential influencer can tell you how well campaign activities on their website will increase your reach, as well.

Follower Wonk is another tool many marketers utilize to identify which influencers are already following your brand (see Figure 8.2). You can also use the platform to search Twitter. By using its Twitter search tool, you can easily search for users with a lot of followers (an indicator of influence), then compare different users or filter through potential influencers who are already following your brand.

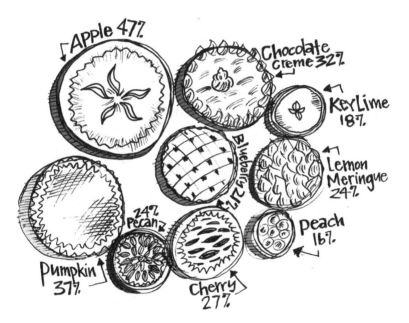

Figure 8.2 *A sample view from the Follower Wonk platform.*

The last tool that you will need is some sort of distribution or engagement platform. Note: You will only need to utilize this tool IF you do not currently utilize a social publishing platform like Sprinklr or Spredfast. If you do not have access to one of those platforms, you can always take advantage of a more cost-effective solution, such as InkyBee. The benefit of a platform like InkyBee is that not only can you engage with influencers, you can also use it for discovery.

We expect that the influencer tool landscape will continue to change. Social listening platforms will continue to either acquire existing solutions or build their own. Entrepreneurs with a data science or big data bent will continue to invent tools intended to measure online influence. As we mentioned earlier in this chapter, this remains a gold-rush topic and will continue to be so for the foreseeable future. Because of that, we want to turn our focus to how you could go about developing your own list, and then after you do, how you can use it.

Developing Your Own Influence Approach

Although the Klouts of the world do an excellent job of aggregating a large amount of data, they are still black boxes in many regards. If you do not feel comfortable defending the list that you have assembled and run through one of these tools, you should not use them. You can create your own approach just by taking a little bit of time to collect information. If you choose to develop your own approach, here are some things you should think about:

- **Platforms for analysis**—If you were developing a Twitter influencer approach, looking at blogs probably wouldn't make sense. But if you were trying to develop an online influence approach, you would probably want to look across multiple platforms.

- **Date range**—Our preference is always for a longer data capture period—preferably 12 months—but that kind of effort can be labor intensive. Narrowing the range to 6 months should eliminate any random anomalies that might skew data.

- **Weighting**—Think about what you are trying to achieve with your program. If it is maximum engagement, then you probably want to weight engagement metrics more highly. If it is reaching the most people, then you probably want to weight the reach metrics more highly.

After you have landed on answers to the preceding questions, the most critical thing to do before you begin your project is define the metrics that you will capture to actually rank the individuals in your list. Literally hundreds of metrics exist that you could possibly gather, so prioritizing is important. We are not going to share all of those metrics here, but rather give you a construct you can use to group the sets of metrics together for easier analysis. The three primary groups of metrics to identify your influencers are:

- **Outlet and individual relevant reach**—You'll notice a theme with the next two groups of metrics, and that is we think it's important to not just look at the outlet but also the individual. In the case of relevant reach, that could be the number of Twitter followers a reporter or blogger might have. If we're capturing the outlet, that could be the circulation or the number of relevant people visiting the publications' website.

- **Outlet and individual syndication**—This is a critical component and most often missed when determining online influence. Not only do you want to know how much reach a person gets when he publishes a piece of content, but you also want to know how much residual reach you get when his respective communities share that same article or post. Again, similar to reach, knowing just how much syndication an outlet and individual will get is important.

- **Outlet and individual relevance**—Likely the most obvious, most overlooked metric is relevance. Essentially, what we mean by *relevance* is the amount of on-topic content a user or outlet creates versus the amount of off-topic content. It's a simple ratio that allows us to determine whether this is an outlet or individual who genuinely shapes a community or just a random contributor. There isn't a specific ratio you should be shooting for when you are looking at their content, but in many cases influencers who contribute anywhere between 25 and 50% of their content to a topic are definitely shaping the conversation.

- **Likelihood to Engage:** A critical, more qualitative metric would be how likely the influencer is to engage with the brand. That doesn't mean your company shouldn't identify this person as influential, it just means that you would want to denote that monitoring that person's activity is far more likely.

How you weigh each of these metrics categories is entirely at your discretion; however, we tend to focus on relevance, syndication, and reach in that order when developing our own influencer lists.

Online Versus Offline Influence

One of the places where tools like Klout do not excel is measuring the effect of offline word-of-mouth influence. If you were to recommend a particular brand of television, for example, to a friend over dinner, the online influence tools would have no mechanism to capture that recommendation unless you voluntarily offered it up while making an online purchase. We have not yet encountered a tool that would serve as a good proximity for offline influence, but we should assume that it is coming.

On the surface, an influencer list is excellent for identifying who will drive reach and engagement simultaneously. It is less clear how it will cause offline behaviors to change unless we utilize primary research to test and ask the critical question, "Why?" A sensible approach to bridging the online and offline research gap would be asking simple questions in market research testing about how a certain purchase decision was made. For example, always asking how a person found out about a particular product or service would be wise. If it were online, then it would be worth asking an additional question of where, specifically, the person learned about it.

Using the Influencer List

Although this book and chapter focus mostly on the analytics behind influencer analysis, we would be remiss if we didn't spend some time talking about how brands can utilize influencer lists. What good is an influencer list that you have spent a considerable amount of time creating if you don't use it? If you don't develop an activation plan, the list becomes merely a fancy dust collector.

It isn't enough anymore to think about using the development time needed to build a list as a pitch-only investment. The reality is that a list has applications that stretch well beyond earned media. The list has paid, earned, and shared media applications as well. See Figure 8.3 for a detailed outline of this model.

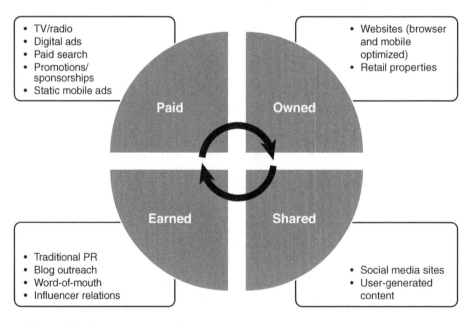

- TV/radio
- Digital ads
- Paid search
- Promotions/ sponsorships
- Static mobile ads

Paid

Owned

- Websites (browser and mobile optimized)
- Retail properties

Earned

Shared

- Traditional PR
- Blog outreach
- Word-of-mouth
- Influencer relations

- Social media sites
- User-generated content

Figure 8.3 *An integrated media mix for influencer lists.*

Let us take a moment to dive into each of these elements:

- **Paid media**—Because we have taken the time to identify people and outlets that are offering the most relevant content, we can assume that these sites might also be quality locations for banner advertising.

Similarly, these influencers can be excellent test subjects for television and radio advertising.

- **Owned media**—Aggregating influencer content on your owned properties can be a valuable approach. Instead of consumers being inundated with your static marketing copy, bringing in relevant influencer content (assuming that it is not bashing the brand) can offer website visitors valuable information.

- **Shared media**—As with owned media, sharing influencer content on shared media properties (for example, your Facebook brand page) can be a useful way to supplement content development and generation, and it also offers people a unique voice.

- **Earned media**—This is the most obvious application for influencer lists, and it mirrors very well traditional public relations activities. Fundamentally, it involves using the influencer list in the manner described earlier in this chapter, in the section "Developing a Modern-Day Media List." You have, in theory, developed a fluid media list that is highly relevant to your topic, and it should be a constant source for pitching ideas.

There are additional ways to segment the earned media targets from your influencer analysis. If you have done your homework, you will have identified people who are clearly influential but not the best outreach (earned media) targets. Specifically, there are four ways to break down the earned media targets (see Figure 8.4):

- **VIPs**—These are the people you would bring to corporate headquarters or to whom you would give special access to company personnel and products, when available.

- **Exclusive access**—You want to build a good relationship with these people because they generate a lot of conversation. They should also be receiving special content and first looks on new products.

- **Pitch list**—If you are announcing a piece of news, these are the people to whom you would send the press release. They drive conversation, but they aren't necessarily your most vocal brand advocates. This group is much less likely to write about you than the VIPs or exclusive access crowd.

- **Listening only**—This is where most of the negative influencers reside. They drive conversation, but they would never be invited to headquarters or given access to company executives. Keeping tabs on them is important because they might be the likely source of an online crisis.

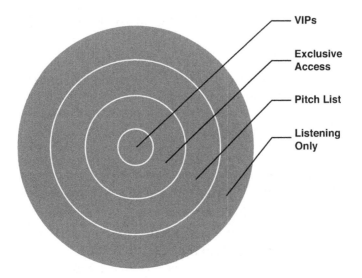

Figure 8.4 *VIPs, exclusive access, pitch list, and listening-only earned media targets.*

The development and use of influencer lists is a growing field. Public relations professionals have been reaching out to influencers for years. Now you have access to more data you can use to determine whether, for example, a mainstream news reporter is *actually* an influencer. What data you collect to ascertain influence is also evolving, as is how you crunch it. As Jay Baer has said, this is a gold-rush topic that has a lot of people trying to solve the issues identified here. Who knows? Perhaps two years from now, all these issues will have been solved, and communicators will have a concrete approach. Until then, consider the advice we have given you throughout this chapter. It will help make your influencer analyses more accurate and effective.

9

How to Use Digital Analytics to Inform Marketing Programs

Thus far, we have spent time talking about how the media landscape has evolved, grounding you in the basic digital analytics concepts, and detailing how to use digital analytics to understand a brand, audience, and ecosystem. With these basics in mind, we now pivot toward use cases. The most common use case for digital data is, of course, to support the development of marketing programs—whether it involves understanding the audience, how that audience engages with content, or where the audience tends to spend their time online. The possibilities for the data are endless, especially as the tools themselves evolve to meet customer needs. It is important to note that other use cases could exist in addition to the ones we present. What we offer are the use cases most commonly used by organizations of all sizes.

The most common use case for social and digital data is marketing. That is, you take the data points created by your customers' online activities, develop insights from them, and then use those insights to alter or create marketing strategies and tactics. Most companies begin their journey toward using digital data by using it to inform marketing programs. As organizations mature other use cases such as using data to anticipate a crisis or inform product development (use cases discussed in upcoming chapters) become more prevalent.

Where should you get started using digital data to inform marketing programs? The first step is to refer to the first two chapters of this book on the converged media landscape and the basic digital analytics concepts. The second step is to read the remainder of this chapter. For the purposes of this chapter, we focus mostly on using digital data to inform marketing program planning.

Based on our experience, the following handful of elements are important to understand when you are using digital data to inform marketing programs:

- **Audience**—Likely the most important, and likely the thing marketers take for granted the most. Marketers often assume that their traditional segmentation models are the ones they should use to target through external outreach. That's exactly the wrong approach, and one we consider to be lazy.

- **Content**—The amount of data available to us about content performance is staggering. Not only do we know whether a member of our target audience likes videos over images, but we can get as granular as the video format, length, subject matter, and distribution. For any marketing program, that level of granularity is critical.

- **Channels**—Said simply, a critical marketing planning input is where our audience tends to spend the majority of their time online. Without this knowledge it is entirely likely that we will try to engage our target audiences in all the wrong places.

- **Previous campaign performance**—It was George Santayana who said, "Those who cannot learn from history are doomed to repeat it." That couldn't be truer about marketing programs.

Within each of these four categories are a number of data points that you could gather to effectively answer them.

Throughout the rest of this chapter we highlight three different types of digital analytics projects you can undertake to understand audience, content, and channels.

We assume that you know where to go to assess the performance of previous campaigns:

- **Social media landscape analysis**—A landscape analysis can afford marketing organizations many things. It can tell you where the audience congregates and shares content, tell you what the key conversation themes might be, give you a window on who the audience is, and begin to give you a sense of how media is consumed. Importantly, this data is applicable for not only your brand but your competitors as well.

- **Search and owned analysis**—When you are conducting a search and owned analysis, it is important to understand the keywords and phrases that people use, those keywords and phrases that bring people to your website, how people engage on your website, and how people feel about the experience.

- **Media analysis**—The media analysis is one part understanding past performance, and one part conducting research through the use of third-party research tools.

The following sections talk about how each of these different analyses is conducted and what you should expect to get out of them.

Understanding the Social Media Landscape Analysis

Believe it or not, when we wrote the first version of this book, social media was still fairly experimental for large organizations. The early adopters at the enterprise level were working under the belief that launching a presence in social media would offer a closer connection to customers. Although that proved to be the case, some of those early brands were placing "bets" on channels that could have failed just as easily as they succeeded. We realize that pointing out social media success stories as possible failures probably is a little confusing but hear us out.

If you are managing the digital marketing, traditional marketing, or public relations for your company, or if you are working for an agency, wouldn't you like to have access to data about how your customers (current or potential) are behaving online? Wouldn't you like to know the kinds of words they are using to converse? Wouldn't you like to know their preferred channel for conversing? These are just a handful of things you could learn from a landscape audit.

The social media landscape audit has become a critical input into the marketing planning process. It is not that the days of social media experimentation are over. Quite a bit of experimentation still takes place. However, the difference today versus five years ago is that experimentation is now done more thoughtfully and is only a small slice of the marketing budget. Today, marketers of all kinds are looking for data and justification for launching a particular online strategy or tactic.

✉ *Note*

Although in most cases a landscape audit is done at the start of a program, it can often be done after social strategies and tactics have already been implemented. The audit can also follow any other preliminary listening efforts that might have taken place.

The following sections describe the steps needed to complete a landscape audit.

Scoping the Landscape Audit

The possibilities with a landscape audit are endless. If you are working for or representing a large brand (such as Disney, Dell, Pepsi, Coca-Cola, or Cisco) you are likely faced with a diverse business with multiple products or business units or both. Because of that diversity, a landscape audit could easily go from being a very good idea with strong insights to be a really bad idea with hundreds of slides of data telling no real story. How do you avoid the second scenario? As with any other project, developing the proper scope helps mitigate the possibility of receiving a data dump at the end of the project. Developing a proper scope involves six key steps:

1. **Outline the brand objectives**—Whatever the marketing program, clearly defining the business objectives is imperative. Without those brand or business objectives in mind, the insights delivered from the research are likely to be flawed.

2. **Determine an area of focus**—A landscape audit is meant to be comprehensive. However, *comprehensive* can be a bad word when it leads to a mountain of data and very little insight. Defining what you are going to be searching for when conducting the analysis is important.

3. **Develop a set of keywords**—After determining the scope, creating a set of keywords is essential. It cannot be a random set of media monitoring keywords that have been used forever, though you could make such a set as one input. There are often several different inputs to a set of keywords. We offer more detail on this in a moment.

4. **Understand data inputs**—While using the term *landscape audit* might signify only the use of a social media listening tool (see Chapter 3, "Choosing Your Analytics Tools"), in reality it could be much more comprehensive and include other data inputs.

5. **Define the research question(s)**—Outlining the question(s) you are trying to answer with your research is critical to an excellent end product. In Chapter 13, "Building Your Research Plan," we talk about developing your research plan and hypothesis.

6. **Build a time line**—The research you are going to conduct cannot go on forever. When does the project begin and end? When are the interim check-ins for the project? How much data will you be collecting for the project? A typical landscape audit encompasses about 12 months' worth of data. It is worth noting that not every social media listening solution comes with 12 months of data automatically. Oftentimes you need to request the additional data, and might have to pay an additional charge

If you walk through all the steps in this list, your landscape audit scope should be good, and your resulting research report will be very insightful. There still remains the problem of needing all the information in one place; this is critical because we are all busy and attend too many meetings. If a critical project partner misses a meeting about a landscape audit, that person needs to know where to find the documentation. The scoping document helps ensure that knowledge transfer is seamless. This document should be broken up into the following sections:

- **Details of the project**—This could be something as simple as the owner of the project within your organization, the original requester, and the amount of budget being allocated for the project.

- **Project scope**—This part of the document contains the brands to be included in the analysis, and the products, regions, languages, and time frame for the analysis.

- **Situation overview**—This part of the document states why your organization is conducting this research. This is essentially the same as the brand objectives step outlined earlier in this chapter.

- **Research objectives**—Who is talking about the brand online? What are the key topics of conversation? Where do the majority of conversations take place? These are just a few of the sample research objectives or questions you could ask.

- **Existing data**—There may be data that the team needs to reference as part of the landscape audit. This data could include existing market research, search analyses, web traffic data, or any brand plans. This section of the document can include links to those documents or, at minimum, the key takeaways from each of those other pieces of research.

- **Type of deliverable**—In most instances, the type of deliverable will be outlined as a presentation with key insights. However, people in your organization might want multiple formats (for example, a Microsoft Word document, PowerPoint presentation, or Keynote presentation) for delivering the data. Ensure that you know all the format types needed before getting to the end of your project.

- **Desired delivery date**—Again, these projects cannot go on forever, but they can be labor intensive. Give your team some time to produce the report but be clear in the scoping document what your expectations are for the date of delivery.

When your scoping document is created, you can actually begin the landscape audit. The next section outlines all the elements of a best-practice landscape audit.

 Note

Many of these foundational elements that make landscape audits successful are applicable to the two other types of analysis—search and owned, and media analysis—that we discuss later in this chapter. Keep them in mind as we reach those sections.

Elements of a Landscape Audit

When your scoping document has been created, it is time to start conducting your research for the landscape audit. By this point, you should have decided on your social media listening tool and have developed a set of research questions you want to answer with your research. You should also have a firm understanding of the topics you are researching, the brands you are including from an internal perspective, and the competitors (or peers) you are using for comparison.

Even when you have a well-crafted scoping document, a very real possibility still exists that you are infected with analysis paralysis, and you can download hundreds of thousands (if not millions) of conversations, analyze them, and put them in a slide deck that lacks any insight to help the business. The reality of social media data is that it is plentiful, and analyzing it can often be daunting. A scoping document helps, but some guideposts about what should be in the report are even more helpful.

Our best suggestion is to ask around before trying to determine where those guideposts truly lie. Ask other divisions within your company if they have conducted this type of research. Ask your peers at other companies if they have done a landscape audit. Heck, ask an open-ended question about landscape audits on social media channels if you think you would get a good response.

You might be hoping that we'll provide you with those guideposts. We can give you some ideas, but keep in mind that they are general suggestions. What we suggest is generic help that comes from our experience doing hundreds of such audits for brands of all sizes. The following list addresses several things you should be trying to answer with a landscape audit. What you pick from this list needs to be based on your brand's objectives and the research questions you are trying to answer:

- **Current share of voice**—Share of voice is the percentage of conversation happening about your brand versus about competitor brands. Those competitor brands should have been identified in your scoping document.

- **Current share of conversation**—Share of conversation is the percentage of conversation happening about your brand versus about the entire category. For example, if you are conducting a landscape audit for Dell, one of your measures could be looking at the volume of conversation about Dell versus about personal computers. The share of conversation would be calculated by dividing the volume of conversation about Dell by the volume of conversation happening about personal computing. In our experience, this number almost never exceeds 5%.

- **Location of conversations**—Your landscape audit should identify which channels contain the most conversation. That could be Twitter or news, as is typically the case if you are conducting a landscape audit at the corporate level. It could also be blogs and forums, as is often the case with brand-level analyses. Wherever those conversations take place, you need to know about them.

- **Key conversation themes**—A critical input to developing content on any channel is understanding what the online communities already talk about. This could be themes that mention your brand, only the competitors, or only the industry. A landscape audit should help you identify what people are passionate about when mentioning you and also where the opportunity lies when your competitors are mentioned.

- **Individuals or outlets driving conversation**—The landscape audit should begin to identify which people are mentioning the brand, competitors, or the industry most often. We talk more about influencer analyses in Chapter 8, "Understanding Digital Influence."

- **Keywords people are using online**—Much like identifying the themes, the landscape audit is meant to identify what words people use when mentioning your brand, competitors, or the industry. The goal of identifying the keywords people are using is to ensure that your content also uses those words. This helps you speak the community's language, and it also helps with natural and paid searching.

- **When conversations take place**—If you have conducted any landscape audits in the past, you have likely seen a volume line graph with spikes showing peaks in conversations. You should be looking for when people are doing the most talking about your brand or the industry in order to properly sync your content with that trend. This part of the analysis should also help you understand which conversation themes have really resonated.

These are the high-level elements of the landscape audit. Obviously, the amount of research you do against any one of these points can be quite extensive, based on the volume of activity and your overall goals for the project. However, every one of these elements should be included in your landscape audit at some level. If you do not include one of them, you will leave a gaping hole in the finished product that might result in missing a key insight that could help the business.

Fitting the Landscape Audit into the Program Planning Continuum

It should be relatively obvious that a landscape audit is most useful when it is completed before you create digital strategies or tactics. A landscape audit is a rich source of intelligence about your customers, the industry, and your competitors. It's so rich that coming up with a digital strategy, or even developing content without conducting the audit, would be terribly shortsighted. If you move ahead with the development of a strategy and tactics before conducting a landscape audit, you could enter the community talking about something completely different from what the community actually wants to hear. Trust us when we tell you that doing that is far worse than spending four to six weeks conducting a landscape audit and determining what people would like to hear.

All this being said, a landscape audit could be conducted at the end of a program to either change the course or gauge the effectiveness of your program. Yes, it is a measurement tool as much as it is a planning tool. A company that conducts a landscape audit at the end of a program or while a program is currently underway typically does it to inform the future state. That is a perfectly acceptable use for an audit, but it's important to know that it might result in the revelation that your current program strategies and tactics are flawed based on the research.

▶ *Caution*

Before moving on to talk about search and owned analysis and its role in informing marketing programs, we should note that the landscape audit is not a be-all, end-all solution. Sure, it has tremendous value and gives us great intelligence on our industry and customer. However, it should never be assumed that what is unearthed in the landscape audit is the entire story. Tom Webster, vice president of strategy and marketing for Edison Research—an organization that conducts market research and exit polling worldwide—is fond of saying that social media research (or, in particular, landscape audits) can allow us to ask better questions as marketers. We completely agree with this sentiment. A landscape audit is only one piece of the marketing planning process.

Search and Owned Analysis

As we discussed in Chapter 1, "Understanding the Synergetic Digital Ecosystem," the various online channels available to marketers today are colliding. How people interact with your brand in search is likely going to lead them to an interaction in social media, which may lead them to an interaction on an owned property. Before we go any further it might be helpful to define what we mean by an owned property. By *owned property* we simply mean a method of content distribution that is entirely owned by someone within your organization. Very specifically, in this case, we mean your website. Now, returning to the point of this section, while understanding the landscape audit outputs as we previously discussed will give you a lot of invaluable data about who your audience is, what they like (and don't like), and where they interact, it isn't everything you need to know.

Search analysis represents an excellent data source to inform your marketing programs. Why do we say that? Simply put, while the landscape analysis helps to really identify the content creators, not everyone in digital marketing is a creator. A much larger number of people engage in online activities to learn about a brand, product, industry, or group of companies. This more passive behavior about our audience provides a window into how they might like to be reached in the future, assuming direct outreach isn't appropriate. We talk about search and keyword analysis tools as part of several chapters throughout the book so they are not the focus in this section.

Instead of focusing on the tools, we want to point you to a series of *search* data points you might find useful for planning marketing programs. We think there are several:

- **Keyword and key phrase volume**—Every brand that we have ever worked with is interested in ranking highly for specific keywords in search engine results pages (SERPs). The keywords and phrases that your company might rank highly for today aren't necessarily the ones you want to rank highly for in the future. To truly optimize and build the right content for maximum search visibility it is important to understand what words and phrases are searched for most often.

- **Device type**—If you believe like we do that delivering the right content at the right time with the right message to the right audience is the most critical mission marketing has, then you will likely agree that understanding the right distribution vehicle is almost as important. We are going to assume that you are aware mobile searches are trending higher than desktop searches these days, so understanding what device people use to search using those critical keywords and phrases related to your brand is critical.

- **Page depth/time on site**—Search tactics are most often employed to improve visibility and drive the desired audience to an owned property. Therefore, understanding how deep people get within your owned property and how much time they spend on your site after arriving from search is critical.

- **Time series analysis**—Similar to the phenomenon we discussed in relation to a landscape audit, trending how people are searching is important. If there are matching trends between the social conversations and the search trends (and there often are) then you have a window into when and how you should engage with your audience

- **Search gap analysis**—A step not often taken when conducting a search analysis to inform marketing programs is looking at the keywords utilized on your owned properties and aligning them with the words most often used in search. This gives you a ready-made way to optimize existing or develop new content. It also helps to improve visibility and engage with your audience most effectively. Think about your own web browsing behaviors. When you search for something, land on a brand's website, and find what you want, how happy do you feel? Please take the steps to identify this gap.

Many, many more data points come from analyzing search behaviors but those are the most important in our estimation. You probably noticed some of the analyses listed sound an awful lot like owned channel analysis, and you would be correct. Again, the converged media landscape is the order of the day. It's impossible to study one channel without studying your entire ecosystem.

With that in mind, we want to similarly outline the data points you could be looking at from your *owned* properties to inform marketing programs. Again, several possibilities include:

- **Visitors**—Yes, this should be an obvious one, but we don't just mean looking at the number of people who come to your owned property. Just as important is the "who," meaning the characteristics of the people who come to your website. While the two largest web analytics platforms, Adobe and Google, give you some out-of-the-box information about your audience, supplementing that data using first-party information collected via your data management platform (DMP) will be important. If you need a refresher on what a DMP is and can do, please refer to Chapter 2, "Understanding Digital Analytics Concepts."

- **Device type**—Yes, this is a duplicate from the preceding search analysis section, but it is equally as important here. Understanding what devices people use to visit your owned property can give you a good idea on what type of experience to build or what types of content would be most effective. Again, out-of-the-box solutions like Adobe Analytics and Google Analytics offer users the ability to ascertain this level of detail.

- **Video performance**—Forgive the somewhat vague, "video performance" description, but it is critical. More companies than ever before are hosting videos on their websites. It is important for you to know how many video plays have occurred, what the play rate was and how often those video views were complete.

- **Time on site**—This is another carryover analysis from the preceding search section, but important to call out here as well. Be aware, time on site could be a false indicator if people come to your site and leave the browser window open for an extended period of time. Because of that possibility, we like to overlay time on site with number of pages visited to get a true sense of engagement.

- **User experience surveys**—Most large companies conduct focus groups and/or surveys to better understand what people like and don't like about their owned properties. If you have this data already about your website, that's great. If you don't, consider engaging a company such as OnResearch, which specializes in these sorts of user experience tests. You would be surprised at the level of audience and content insight you will be able to glean from this work.

- **Social and web content gap**—Do you utilize your social channels to drive audiences to an owned property? Do the words you utilize in your social content align with what a member of your target audience would see on your website? If so, that's great. If you think there's a chance that the answer is no to these questions, go ahead and conduct the assessment.

At the end of the search and owned analyses you should have an even better sense for who the audience is (whether they engage or not), what types of content people are interested in, and where your audience is spending the majority of their time. There is one last step that you should consider taking when planning your marketing program, and that is conducting a media analysis. Let's dive into that next.

Conducting Media Analysis

The last phase of your research to inform a marketing program is conducting a media analysis. You might be asking, "Weren't we looking at media as part of the landscape audit, and search and owned analyses?" You would be correct, but what we mean by *media analysis* is looking very specifically at the performance of your previous media efforts through display, online video, and television tactics coupled with primary research. We mentioned earlier that this section is a mixture of understanding past performance with doing new and unique forms of research.

Let's start with the former—understanding previous media efforts. For the sake of the rest of this section, we are assuming that your marketing program will be executing some form of media. It's growing increasingly impossible to avoid it, even if your intention is to execute almost exclusively through social media channels. From our perspective, there are two things you should try to understand about previous media performance:

- **Partner and publisher performance**—Every media campaign has a key performance indicator (KPI), or a set of KPIs. We talk about many of the possibilities throughout this book. Regardless of your organization's KPIs for media, it will be important for you to understand which of your previous partners or publishers (for example, the *New York Times*) contributed to achieving those goals most effectively. This isn't to say that you should optimize 100% of your media spend to those publishers that contributed, but seeing how each of them performed uniquely can help you study why certain partners and publishers were more effective than others. The data for such an assessment will likely come from your media agency or some other in-house resource if you are executing media entirely inside your company.

- **Asset performance**—For your media campaign did you see videos contribute to your organization's goals? Maybe display banners proved to be most effective based on your analysis. Was there a certain banner size that was most effective? Again, these sorts of questions aren't meant to guide your creative team to only create videos, or only create banners of a certain size. Answering these questions, though, can help you optimize your spend most effectively.

If your organization is more advanced from a digital analytics perspective, the next logical step would be for you to overlay the performance of partners and publishers with the asset type to get a more well-rounded view. It is not necessarily critical, but if you were looking to see whether it was media or content that drove performance, this would be one method.

The second part of a media analysis is using third-party data sources to understand a host of things from media consumption behaviors, to audience demographics and psychographics, to offline purchasing behavior, to whether or not a physician wrote a prescription for the drug you are currently marketing. As you might have guessed after reading Chapter 3, literally hundreds of third-party data sources are available to leverage. Our intention here isn't to highlight them all, but rather highlight some of the more effective data sources for your consideration.

Here are some third-party data sources that you might consider utilizing as you plan your marketing program:

- **Forrester Technographics Surveys**—If you are not already familiar with this organization, Forrester Research conducts a number of surveys throughout the year to understand audience behaviors far more deeply. What do we mean by audience behaviors? Simply put, this refers to possibilities such as what types of devices they use, where they turn for content, what some of their primary demographics are, and what motivates them to make a purchase. If you are marketing for consumer and/or technology brands, you should consider investing in Forrester Technographics research as it is a rich data source for planning purposes.

- **Kantar Media**—Kantar Media has a number of media intelligence tools for brands to take advantage of, but specifically in this context we recommend investing in Kantar's SRDS Media Planning Platform. Specifically, SRDS identifies which outlets reach your target audience most effectively and gives campaign metrics that help make your partner and publisher decision easier.

- **comScore's Media Metrix**—If you have spent any time in the media planning and buying world, you no doubt are familiar with comScore's tools. Media Metrix provides a relatively complete view of consumption habits of your audience and its competitors, along with demographics and how your audience travels from one media platform to another. It also, as you might suspect, can help you understand the total size of your target audience.

Many other possibilities are out there for you to explore, and you should pick the tools that make the most sense for your business. These are just a few we would highly recommend you have as part of your digital analytics toolbelt.

In this chapter we gave you three different types of analysis to more effectively plan a marketing program. It is important to conduct as much as what we've outlined as possible so you get a clear understanding of your audience, what types of content you need to create to reach them, where you need to reach them, and how you can leverage past performance for your upcoming campaign. Although it might look like a lot of research to conduct, our belief is that your marketing programs will be better off for doing the work.

10

Improving Customer Service

We are living in an exciting and transformative business environment. Innovations in technology, such as digital media and mobility, and connectivity speeds have permanently changed (and continue to change) consumer behavior. These technological innovations have influenced consumer expectations in irrevocable ways as well. These are not trivial changes; the changes define the specifics for how companies market and sell products and services, how customers are serviced and supported, the timely responsiveness of brands, and more importantly, the myriad channels/ methods available to a customer to choose to engage with brands they do business with. The evolution of social platforms from a place to connect and communicate to a platform for connecting, commerce, and problem resolution has accelerated these changes like no other development seen in the history of the Internet.

Customer Expectations

Digital-only businesses, such as Zappos, have completely changed the game and raised the bar for customer experience and support. These expectations are not limited to Zappos or the category it does business in but rather have leaked into all industries.

Consumers now expect companies to meet their needs in a much more sophisticated manner than brands have historically done. Now, it's on the customer's terms, not the company's. Leveraging the robust universe of data available to a brand, customers expect a personalized and contextually relevant experience at every touchpoint with a brand, regardless of the division or group within a company that they are dealing with. "Know me, understand me, predict my needs, and deliver" sums up the modern consumer attitude toward brand customer experience.

As a result, you have to provide customer service and support in places where it might not already exist. Doing that on major social media platforms such as Twitter or Facebook is table stakes in 2018. To stand out, progressive brands such as American Express, Food Network, and Amazon have extended their customer service and support offerings beyond social platforms and into the AI (artificial intelligence)-driven world of home products such as Alexa and Google Home, as well as major messaging platforms such as Facebook Messenger, Kik, and WeChat in the form of AI-driven chatbots that work seamlessly across desktop, mobile, and tablet devices. The biggest difference between now and 5 years ago is that back then, if a company thought it could simply build out a call center to handle customer service via a toll-free number and effectively keep customers satisfied, it could still survive, albeit on a declining trend line. In the experience era of 2018, that simply won't do. Consumer expectations are far greater in the areas of personalization, speed of responsiveness, and convenience. The trend of "on customers' terms" was beginning when we wrote the first edition of this book, and it has only accelerated exponentially since then. We live in an omni-channel customer experience world, which for brands means a customer service and support program that comprehensively includes assistance via live agents on a brand website, email, social media, apps, chatbots, FAQ resources, customer communities, and credible and trusted partners as well as third-party subject matter experts.

Why does this matter? It matters for many reasons, and we'll look at several of the most important ones. First, according to a Forrester Research report in November 2017 focused on 2018 predictions, consumer trust in institutions and companies is at an all-time low. As a result, they project a customer reckoning in 2018 with potential mass defections from brands by dissatisfied customers (Forbes, 2017).[1] Second, the frequency of interactions between customers and brands has increased since 2014. This is simultaneously both good and bad for brands. It gives brands the opportunity to deliver positive customer experience more often, thus increasing loyalty and customer satisfaction. The other side of that coin is that the potential for negative brand experiences and dissatisfied customers is also increased. Third, customers who have good customer service experiences are likely to purchase again regardless of the original channel in which they purchased, thus increasing revenue and customer loyalty according to an April 2017 study from eMarketer titled, "Customer Experience 2017: The Journey Toward Customer-Centricity Continues." [2] There is no rocket science here: If companies are able to meet customer expectations and provide satisfactory outcomes during customer service experiences, the customers remain loyal to the brand. However, it's much easier said than done today, given the expectations that customers have when engaging with brands. The good news for brands is that the technologies, data, and processes needed to meet those high expectations have never been more prevalent and available than they are today.

Another reason it's critical to deliver on customer expectations during a service experience is also nothing new: It impacts the holy grail of customer outcomes, which is word of mouth. Both satisfied and unsatisfied customers tell other people about their experiences, positive and negative. Unsurprisingly, customers who have negative experiences tell *more* people. According to the White House Office of Consumer Affairs, news of bad customer service reaches more than twice as many ears as praise for a good service experience. On a related note, and from the same source, for every customer who bothers to complain about your brand, 26 other customers remain silent. Most importantly, according to American Express, three in five Americans would try a new brand or company for a better service experience. That number has only grown since 2014. The combination of rising consumer expectations regarding positive brand outcomes with previously mentioned advances in connectivity, mobility, and personalization have created the perfect storm for companies striving to provide modern customer service and support. Combine those points with the fact that these consumers now live in a hyper-connected world with nearly infinite choice for products and services, and it's easy to see how delivering exceptional customer service has never been more important to keeping current customers and acquiring new ones.

In the first version of this book we talked at length about the shift away from established channels such as website live chat agents, interactive voice recognition, and self-service to emerging channels such as text/SMS messaging, social media, and mobile apps. Those trends have grown along the same trajectory since 2014, and they continue to gain traction because they allow customers to get answers quickly. They also allow customers to multitask and be efficient with their time. Despite advances in the former customer experience techniques, we don't expect this trend to slow down. Customer service and support on social networks and mobile technologies have been so broadly adopted, across all major age groups, particularly with Millennials and Gen Z, that it's altered customers' expectations for acceptable responses from the companies they do business with. Provide value in an instant gratification manner is the new mantra for brands seeking to deliver positive customer outcomes regardless of digital channel or platform. The bar has never been higher, which can easily be interpreted as a negative, but for brands seeking to differentiate themselves through consistent and exceptional customer experiences, this is the opportunity they have been waiting for to distance themselves from the competition.

Digital customers live in an always-on, instant-gratification world that provides practically unlimited choice. Catering to the customers' specific needs and channel preferences on how to best serve and support them is the only sustainable scenario. If companies don't remove barriers to efficient and effective customer service experiences, customers will abandon them for a competitor.

With some emerging channels, such as customer conversations and interactions on public social networks, data isn't locked in corporate databases behind a firewall but is freely available, both to a company and its competitors. Herein lies a unique opportunity to apply digital analytics to reveal hidden insights that you can use to improve customer service. Let's get into the details of what approaches are available to collect this information and look at some case studies of companies that have already extended their customer service initiatives into emerging media channels such as social networks.

The Social Customer Service Conflict

Despite the new normal of consumers desiring customer service and issue resolution across all digital channels, many companies have been slow to embrace the opportunity and implement the necessary changes within their own organizations. Social media platforms and mobile technologies have changed everything in regard to supporting customers. Customer service hours have evolved and are different from standard corporate hours. Customers need support when they need it, regardless of corporate schedules. When you add the expectations of the "instant gratification era," primarily on social media, to that mix, it creates an environment where customers rate an unsatisfactory experience unless they received support when and where (channel) they need it. You can call it *ad hoc support* or *customer service on demand*. Whatever the name, the expectation is there, thanks to companies like Dell and Comcast, early pioneers in the area of experimenting with social media to help customers.

A conflict exists, and several obstacles must be overcome. Although an organization might aspire to provide social service to customers, some companies don't have the internal resources to support it. According to research on social media and customer service conducted by SAP and Social Media Today, more than 77% of companies currently invest less than $50,000 in social customer care. To put that number in context, consider that Fortune 100 companies spend hundreds of millions, even billions, on traditional customer service and support programs. When we wrote the first version of this book, the lack of resources being dedicated to online customer service and support was considerable. Since then, we've seen an uptick in that spending, but not nearly to the degree that it needs to be for brands to meet customer service expectations, especially given how critical of a function it is to support the brand. A sizable gap exists between consumer time spent in digital channels for problem resolution and brands' spending on digital customer care. Four years later, this is still an area of opportunity for companies to differentiate and deliver value through compelling brand experiences to customers.

Another obstacle facing companies tackling social customer service is integration—or lack thereof—within the broader marketing organization. The proliferation of channels is exacerbating the silo problem that companies have. Customers don't want or need another digital silo. Companies bear the burden of integrating social service channels into traditional channels to ensure that customers are interacting with them using a single, continuous communications channel. For example, customers want to be able to start a conversation in one channel (such as Twitter) and have it seamlessly carry over to email or the brand website, without the need to start the conversation all over again. You've likely experienced this at one time or another, having been asked to provide your name, address, or account number redundantly after being transferred for the sixth time to a different department within the same company. This is a symptom of lack of integration among systems, departments, and processes.

There are two primary incentives for companies to integrate digital/social channels into their existing customer care programs. The first is simply about meeting consumer demand. According to a 2017 "State of Social Customer Service" study done by Conversocial, phone/voice is cited as the most frustrating channel for problem resolution. More consumers than ever are turning to digital channels, multiple in fact, to get their issues resolved by the companies that they do business with. In fact, 74% of consumers use three or more channels when trying to get help from big companies, according to *Jay Baer,* a customer service industry expert and author of *Hug Your Haters,*[3] a 2016 bestselling book about why and how customer service needs to change.

The second incentive is financial. Servicing and supporting customers via digital channels is simply more efficient than using traditional options such as a call center. From a cost perspective, the difference is not even close either. An Incite Group study found that supporting customers via social media interaction costs $1 compared to $6 for a call center interaction. Factor in the scalability of supporting customers with digital channels versus call centers, and the efficiency argument is even stronger. While it's easy to point to more mature and leading social service programs of companies such as American Express, T-Mobile, or Lenovo, many companies' social service programs are still in their infancy and thus immature, or non-existent at all. They struggle with meeting customer expectations for response times, providing appropriate coverage (responding to all inquiries), and finding appropriate answers.

According to data from Twitter, leading B2C companies are only responding to about 60% of tweets directed at their customer service accounts. Regardless of whether or not the tweet is directed to the customer support account, fast responses are an essential part of meeting customer expectations for social care. Forrester has found that 77% of U.S. online adults say (CX Social, 2017)[4] that valuing their time is the most important thing a company can do to provide them with good service. Why are companies still slow to respond? There are five primary reasons, based on our experience:

- Difficulty in finding the correct answer

- Waiting for guidance from other stakeholders on how to answer

- Challenges in locating the appropriate message to answer the issue at hand

- The tools for engaging customers are challenging to use

- Lack of resources to dedicate time and attention to monitoring and responding in relevant digital channels

In addition, meeting response time expectations isn't easy. Consumers have a nearly instant gratification attitude toward these digital interactions. Seven out of ten consumers now expect a company to respond to them within an hour of the original request if it was made through social media platforms, based on a survey by Lithium Technologies.

Stepping back, all the issues we've just covered point to process, education, and training/policy issues within a company, not problems inherent in any social platform or technology. These specific issues have been addressed with traditional customer service channels such as call centers and live agents, and it's a matter of formally extending those more mature business processes into new digital channels, such as social media platforms, mobile apps, messaging platforms, and chatbot technologies. Later in the chapter, we look at how some companies are doing that, but first, let's dig beyond the obvious answer to why you should support customers in digital channels. We look at the three main areas of opportunity to utilize digital analytics to identify insights and opportunities to improve customer service experiences.

Beyond issue resolution, why should you support customers in digital and social channels? What's in it for the company, other than just a new expense? The answers are simple but present an incredibly powerful opportunity to learn and then optimize the customer experience to improve brand loyalty. Responding in an hour or less, and at scale, is a daunting challenge for brands, but the rewards are worth it.

Companies that are able to meet expectations in digital customer service interactions stand to benefit in several ways through increased customer satisfaction, increased customer loyalty, and increased revenue. These factors also positively influence customer advocacy and word-of-mouth within your customer base. All of this leads to a result every company is interested in, which is a longer-term relationship with the customer. The following sections describe three ways you can do this.

Understanding the Customer

Who is your audience? What are their expectations for the experiences they have with your company? How do they behave on digital channels? What content types, topics, and formats do they prefer over another? These seemingly simple questions are difficult to answer if you don't have access to the relevant data sources and systems. The 2018 marketers or customer service representatives don't need to guess who the customer is; they know! The tools covered in previous chapters enable you to use the appropriate digital service points to collect data about the audiences that you're interacting with or targeting to reach. Finding this information is critical because segmentation plays as important a role in customer service as it does in marketing and sales. Customization and personalization of customer service experiences is arguably even more important than it is for acquisition of new customers.

We also know that as a general rule, channel preferences change across demographic groups. Data from a 2016 research study by Dimension Data[5] that was analyzed and presented on eMarketer.com demonstrates that demographics affect channel preferences for service and support. For example, younger age groups, filled with people who are digital natives, unsurprisingly skew higher toward using social media for customer service. In fact, consumers under 35 years old are actively using all digital channels for customer service, with particular emphasis on social media and email. In fact, nearly 39% of consumers under the age of 25 use social media as their primary means for customer service. Email sticks out as the primary means for consumers aged 25–54 years old. Above 35 years old, a dramatic decline exists in the use of social media and mobile apps for customer service, but the overall trend continues to grow upward as brands offering omni-channel customer service steadily becomes the new norm. Regardless of age group, consumers are becoming more and more comfortable relying on digital channels and technologies to resolve their issues or interact with brand representatives.

Because customers move between channels and/or apps seeking answers or customer service, it can cause confusion and uncertainty as to where to invest precious brand time, energy, and resources to offer customer service and support. Applying digital analytics to solve this problem and precisely identify which channels your customers want to use is critical. You can't, and don't, need to provide service on all the channels. Identify the ones that matter most to your audiences and then deploy them according to best practices for those channels.

Understanding Customer Intent

You don't need a sledgehammer to drive in a finishing nail. For customer service in digital channels, you need to use the right tool for the right job. You can use both social and web analytics to understand customer behavior on specific channels and digital properties, and you can make changes to guide customers to the appropriate channels, depending on their issue. Twitter and Facebook might be great for time-sensitive, lower-complexity requests where email wouldn't be nearly as effective. Conversely, time-intensive or complex customer requests are better suited for live agents or web chat. The nature of the specific problem has a big effect on what channel customers seek to resolve their problems.

Performing an inventory on existing customer service requests and mapping out their complexity to the channel that is likely to create resolutions can be a helpful exercise for prioritizing decisions on what problems to solve and where. Maximize the value of the channel to deliver a satisfactory experience. Knowing intent, what a customer came there for and wants to accomplish, is key in being able to not only to resolve the problem but also provide the most relevant and personalized customer experience.

Personalizing the Customer Experience

Customers seek personalized service. When we wrote the first edition of *Digital Marketing Analytics*, personalized service experiences were still optional for brands, a nice-to-have but not required nor expected as the norm by customers. Fast-forward only four years later and we're living in the "experience era." Providing exceptional customer experiences is no longer a choice for brands, but rather required to be relevant and considered by consumers. It's one of the few ways that a brand can differentiate itself from the competition. For example, knowing who the customer is and knowing her preferences (past purchase history, past service issues, communication needs, channel preferences) is easier if you're talking about a customer relationship management (CRM) database that supports a call center. What about personalization for a Twitter interaction? This requires a level of integration previously not asked of companies; it also requires connective tissue between many systems of record—customer databases, commerce platforms, product databases, recommendation engines, content management systems, and third-party social platforms. The list of data sources that companies must pull from and integrate continues to grow, with no end in sight for the time being.

Let's now dig into the models or approaches companies have taken to provide digital or social customer service and what aspects of those you might take for your own purposes to improve customer service for your organization.

Social Customer Service Models

It's appropriate here to introduce the idea of a maturity meter for customer service when describing the different approaches companies have taken to offer support in social media. A three-stage maturity model can be used to evaluate social service efforts. The three stages are ad hoc, limited, and formal. This section covers cases of different companies at each stage and describes the data and analytics available and how companies can utilize those to produce better customer service outcomes by understanding, more precisely, who their customers are and what they are trying to do.

The Ad Hoc Stage of Customer Service

Most companies take an ad hoc approach to social customer service at the onset. It often originates through the good intentions of a single individual within a company. In other cases, it starts for the opposite reason: The company is dragged into a social service interaction on Facebook by a vocal customer with immediate needs. The ad hoc stage is informal and inefficient in that it can't easily scale without major changes to address foundational gaps in the company. At this stage, companies do not have formal objectives, policies, and education internally. Data collection and analysis are minimal, if they exist at all. The priority is on handling frontline requests.

The Limited Stage of Customer Service

The limited stage of social customer service is more coordinated and organized than the ad hoc stage in that multiple individuals support the effort, and the company has a mechanism for more meaningful data collection and reporting. Some objectives have been set, and processes have been put in place, but this stage is still limited in that it lacks integration with the rest of the company, both culturally and systematically. The connective tissue described earlier, which is necessary to provide personalized customer service interactions between different data sources, is still missing at this stage. Data collection and analysis begin to emerge here, with an emphasis on counting activity—but that is not necessarily the most reliable indicator of customer satisfaction.

The Formal Stage of Customer Service

The formal stage of social customer service is full-scale support for all products and services across the company. It includes everything mentioned thus far, in addition to dedicated teams, governance, workflow, and crisis preparation. One of the most important distinctions between this and the other stages is the connection of different business units/groups within the company, which is an effort that directly increases coordination and efficiency and decreases duplication of efforts to resolve customer issues. This integration includes aggregation of data specific to customer satisfaction rather than social data and metrics associated with marketing or brand building.

The following section provides a specific example of a company that is serving and supporting customers in social environments.

Delta Air Lines

Airlines are easy targets for criticism about how they handle customer issues. However, Delta Air Lines deserves credit for embracing emerging trends and leveraging new communication channels (both social and mobile) to reduce customer issues and provide satisfactory responses more quickly and efficiently than it did in the past. Delta has been a pioneer in regard to social customer service. It was one of the first brands in the category to officially support customers on Twitter, and it was the first to implement a booking engine on Facebook as well. It has evolved its social customer service program over time as the company has learned what things work better than others. Like most other global brands, Delta is present on the social media outposts you would expect: Facebook, Twitter, YouTube, a corporate blog, and more. Delta has added other support options over time as customers' preferences shifted beyond the major social platforms. It has expanded customer service to platforms like WeChat, offered video-chat calls for certain types of customer service requests, and has also been experimenting with chatbots in innovative ways that enhance the travel experience and give more personalization and choice to customers. For example, one chatbot lets business class passengers choose their in-flight meals several days before their flights.

Delta took a strategic approach when considering how to solve customer needs via social channels, and it decided to create something entirely new, dedicated to assisting customers via social media. In May 2010, @DeltaAssist was born. It looks different now than it did back in 2010, but the primary charge remains the same: "Serve as a way to interact and engage with customers in a meaningful way." @DeltaAssist was originally staffed with four customer service agents, officially providing answers Monday through Friday from 8:00 a.m. to 6:00 p.m. EST. That didn't last long, as customer issues don't punch a clock. The program has evolved and is now staffed by 40 social media specialist agents who provide continuous coverage 24 hours a day, 7 days a week to resolve customer issues. The once standalone @DeltaAssist Twitter account has been merged with the primary account for the brand @delta.

Any successful initiative begins with clearly defined objectives, and Delta is very specific about what assistance this social service program will and will not provide to customers. The following services are offered, and for each we show an example of a customer request and @delta response:

- Answers to questions on policies and procedures.

- Travel help (for example, airport, online bookings, post-travel questions)

- Rebooking assistance, which is incredibly convenient and worth using if you fly Delta

- Complaint resolution

- Random/fun information and answers to questions

By funneling all customer service requests online to the @Delta handle, Delta has reduced response time considerably. A study done by WaveMetrix in September 2012 demonstrates just how much response time has been reduced. WaveMetrix compared Delta with four other airlines (see Figure 10.1) to determine which companies have the timeliest responses to tweets. Delta easily won on responsiveness. There is an added benefit to having the separate handles: Because all customer issues are directed to @DeltaAssist, the main social profiles for the Delta brand are not littered with customer posts about complaints or problems. This all but ensures that Delta will have the lowest response time unless a competitor copies Delta's approach and validates Delta's operational structure for having a dedicated team of agents supporting social media.

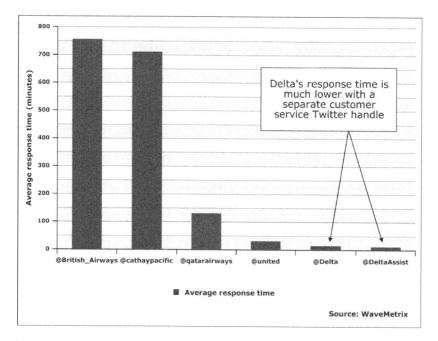

Figure 10.1 *WaveMetrix's comparison of airlines' tweet response times.*

As we've discussed throughout the book, aligning social goals to business goals is essential to enable the development of a relevant measurement strategy. Over time, Delta has matured and evolved its own social customer service measurement approach to be consistent with how the company measures customer service effectiveness. Instead of relying only on total volume of mentions, tweets, and followers, the health of the @Delta customer service initiative is viewed through the same lens as the traditional customer service channels in the company. Specific metrics such as resolution rate, response rate, and compliments are key performance indicators (KPIs) that are tracked each month. The volume of inbound requests is part of that, but it is not a true indicator of how @Delta contributes to keeping customers happy.

References

1.   Morgan, Blake. "Consumer Trust At An All-Time Low Says Forrester In Their Most Recent Report." "https://www.forbes.com/sites/blakemorgan/2017/11/14/consumer-trust-at-an-all-time-low-says-forrester-in-their-most-recent-report/#a3c75f91a198

2.   "Customer Experience 2017: The Journey Toward Customer-Centricity Continues," eMarketer, April 25, 2017. https://www.emarketer.com/Report/Customer-Experience-2017-Journey-Toward-Customer-Centricity-Continues/2002050

3.   Baer, Jay. *Hug Your Haters.* New York, New York: Portfolio/Penguin, March 2016.

4.   Sigler, Lisa. "Social Response Times: A Mark of Maturity." February 22, 2017. https://cxsocial.clarabridge.com/social-response-times-mark-maturity/#_ftnref1

5.   "Consumers Demand More Multichannel Customer Service," eMarketer, August 25, 2016. https://www.emarketer.com/Article/Consumers-Demand-More-Multichannel-Customer-Service/1014397

11

Using Digital Analytics to Anticipate a Crisis

Almost every company faces a crisis situation at some point. Whether that crisis is a plant closing, large-scale lay-offs, or executive management changes, a company's value is always under threat. Good marketing departments have developed crisis plans that account for these types of issues, and they are constantly tweaking those plans to match how the business is moving. Underperforming marketing departments are blindsided by issues and are usually inundated with press attention.Social media amplifies the flow and volume of news during a crisis. If the Wall Street Journal, New York Times, *or* Associated Press *pick up a story about your brand, you will likely face hundreds of additional articles and thousands of tweets. In addition, bloggers not necessarily friendly to your brand will pick up the story and offer their own slant. Those bloggers might have limited reach, but it takes only one with a network the size of the* Huffington Post *to help make a small crisis into a big one.*

Crisis does not just impact mainstream news, the blogosphere, or the Twittersphere; it can also affect searching. One of the stories we love to tell is that if you do a Google search for Exxon, you still see mentions in the first two results pages of the *Exxon Valdez* spill (oftentimes buried in other stories), which occurred more than two decades ago. Google indexes all the attention that Twitter, blogs, and news sources give to an event and makes it available for years after. Therefore, a crisis no longer lasts just a month or two. It has the potential to live on for years after the fact because of search engines.

There is good news in all of this for brands. Understanding that a crisis is always right around the corner is a good first step. In addition, taking the time to develop a crisis plan that includes social media is essential. One of the elements of crisis plan development is taking the time to document all potential issues. In our experience, brands are aware of at least 90% of issues that the company could face. These issues could come from operational challenges, customer service complaints, product disputes, and so on. Wherever the issues come from, the company has likely heard of them before. It is also our experience, however, that most brands do not document those issues correctly.

This chapter examines how brands can utilize social listening data to anticipate a crisis and, if a crisis does arise, how to ensure that mechanisms are in place to gather conversation data and react to it.

Developing a Modern-Day Issues Management Plan

As mentioned earlier, a brand is aware of approximately 90% of issues that arise. Unfortunately, most of the time those issues are not well documented in a communications crisis plan. The obvious question is "Why not?" The reality is that all it would take is for the corporate communications team to sit down with business unit leaders for a day and whiteboard all the potential scenarios. Everyone is busy, but we're talking about protecting the brand's value. But we digress.

W2O Group, a full-service marketing and communications consultancy based in San Francisco, and the firm that employs one of the authors of this book (Chuck), has developed an excellent model—the modern-day issues management plan—to tackle these issues (see Figure 11.1).

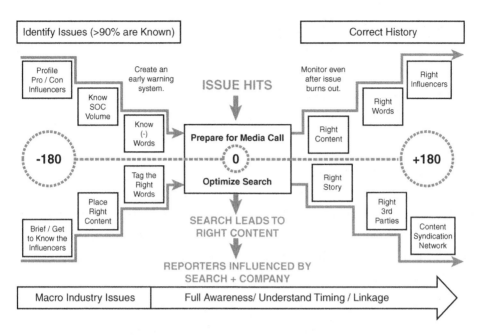

Figure 11.1 *W2O's approach to issues management.*

Although the model looks very complicated, it is in practice very simple. It relies on social media listening efforts to essentially create an early warning system for a crisis. It is based on the premise that a brand does not need to go on the defensive when a crisis strikes. In fact, it can go on the offensive to correct the record. The three distinct phases to this approach are:

- **Identify known issues**—This takes some diligence, but the known issues must be documented. Not only must the known issues be documented, but several other elements must be researched and outlined as well.

- **Face the crisis day**—If you currently work for a brand or an agency that represents a brand that has faced a crisis, you know what that day looks like. It's typically chaotic. However, if you have done the due diligence in the first phase, you might be able to reduce the crisis tidal wave.

- **Correct history**—After the issue hits, you can leverage the things you have learned in the first phase to help correct the record.

Let's dive into each of these issues in more detail.

Identifying Known Issues

Taking the time to identify known issues is a critical step in mitigating the damage that can be done in a crisis situation. Not only that, but this upfront work might also help prevent a crisis from ever seeing the light of day online. To identify the known issues and properly prepare for a crisis situation, you should do the following:

1. **List the known issues**—You should identify a core team of individuals to list all the known issues the team members could face in their parts of the business.

2. **Know the share of conversation volume**—How much conversation is taking place about your brand right now versus about the general industry? Do you know?

3. **Profile pro and con influencers**—Knowing who drives conversation for the brand, both positively and negatively, is key.

4. **Brief and get to know influencers**—The brand does not need to invite every one of the influencers to headquarters, especially if they are not friendly, but you should know everything you can about them ahead of time.

5. **Place the right content**—Based on what you know influencers are writing about, and what issues could arise, are you posting the right kinds of content online?

6. **Know the positive and negative words**—When people search for you, do you know what words they are using? Do you know if those words are positive or negative?

7. **Tag the right words**—Are you using the words people are using in conversations and in searches to appropriately tag content on social and web properties?

The next several sections cover these elements in more detail.

Listing the Known Issues

We have said it several times throughout this chapter so far: Making the effort to list your known issues is essential. You do not need a huge team of people to create the list, but the list needs to be comprehensive enough so that you are not surprised when an issue arises.

Also, in case you are concerned about adding another thing to your already over-flowing plate, the job of listing the issues is not the exclusive job of the marketing department. If you reside in the marketing department, you will likely be asked to lead the charge, but you are going to need help. Where should that help come from?

- **Legal**—The legal department is most likely the best source of information on known issues facing the company. The legal team gets a bad reputation in some marketing circles, but it is their job to protect the company. As such, they are constantly researching and identifying issues that may affect the brand's value.

- **Human resources**—The HR team will be aware of any employee issue that might make its way online. Ask them to be involved in your crisis SWAT team, but if they won't, at least pick their brain for potential issues.

- **Customer service**—Customer service folks are often your first line of defense with customers. They are aware of issues your customers might be having with the product or service. There is a very good chance they will have a list of known customer issues that you can use to begin the online research process.

- **Business unit heads**—The men and women leading the individual business units are very close to the business. They will know issues with the product or service that you can build upon.

- **Senior executives**—The executive team might direct you right back to any one of the four different groups already mentioned, but conducting an interview with the CEO would not be out of the question. He or she will respect the fact that you are trying to protect the brand.

What do you do after you have talked with each of these constituent groups and listed issues you are already familiar with? You begin the research process, of course! The first step is knowing the issues. The second step is researching whether people are already talking about those issues online.

Knowing the Share of Conversation Online

After you have identified your issues, you can begin conducting research to see if people are talking about or searching for them. It is imperative that you know where the brand stacks up in terms of share of conversation online. As a reminder, share of conversation is the amount of conversation taking place that mentions the brand versus the amount of conversation that is happening about the entire product category.

How do you know whether people are talking about or searching for these issues? You can follow these five easy steps:

1. **Develop keyword strings**—Based on the issues, develop a list of keywords that match those issues. This will take a little bit of time to properly hone, but it is the most important step to gathering the most relevant content.

2. **Build a dashboard only for issues**—If you are monitoring for multiple things (customer service, marketing, public relations, and so on), be sure that one of your listening dashboards is dedicated to known issues. This dashboard can sit in your social listening or social publishing platform, depending on how your organization manages issues.

3. **Check frequently**—Do not assume that building the dashboard is the last step. It is important to check frequently to see if anything pops up on the known issues. Also, do not assume that just because you only see one mention of the issue that a crisis is not under way. These are known issues for a reason, and any small post can turn into a big deal online. Also, most dashboards have alert systems that you can create. Consider creating an alert as your dashboard allows.

4. **Continually regroup for new issues**—Do not assume that the issues you previously identified and built dashboards for will be the only issue your company ever faces. It is important to bring your crisis response team together constantly to ensure you are tracking the right issues. If it turns out a new issue is on the horizon, be sure to go through the same series of steps we've identified here to begin tracking them.

5. **Formulate a response plan**—If one of these issues crops up online, do you have a plan to respond? If a response is warranted, who within the organization will deliver it? Who approves the messaging? Several years ago, David Armano of Edelman Digital developed an excellent community management map that still works well today. It can double as a response protocol (see Figure 11.2). It might look daunting, but the biggest step in developing this map is listing the known issues, which you should have done already.

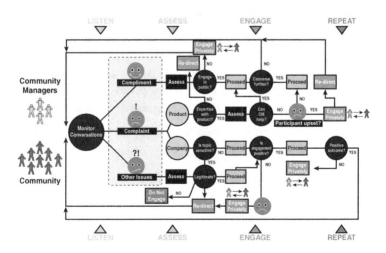

Figure 11.2 *Sample crisis response protocol.*

One of your other dashboards should be actively tracking overall brand mentions, and that is where you can ascertain the current share of the conversation. Knowing it before a crisis is important so you can benchmark how big the crisis was when you assess your response after the crisis subsides.

Profiling Pro and Con Influencers

A component of listening to the known issues and identifying any that are currently being talked about is nailing down the people who are driving the share of conversation online. These people could be talking about your brand or the issues positively or negatively. They could be talking in forums, on blogs, or on Twitter. Regardless of who they are, where they are talking, and the sentiments they express about the issues you care about, you need to identify who those top people are. If you spend the time to identify who these people are, then when a crisis does hit, you know who to share content with to spread your message.

In Chapter 8, "Understanding Digital Influence," we talk at length about identifying influencers, the tools available to help you do so, and how you can conduct this analysis yourself on an ongoing basis to stay current. Be sure to reference it as you go through the process of identifying pro and con influencers on a given topic.

Briefing and Getting to Know the Influencers

Before a crisis hits, take the time to really know who your influencers are and where they typically produce content. This is Essential Public Relations 101. Building a relationship and offering something of value to these people helps you if a crisis does hit. If you wait until a crisis hits and you have never talked to these people, they are not likely to help you. Take all the opportunities that are presented to you in peacetime to build those strong influencer relationships.

We cover how to get to know the influencers in Chapter 8, where we walk through the four different levels of outreach: VIP, exclusive access, pitch list, and listening only. The listening-only influencers are those who are difficult to "pitch" or might be more negative toward the brand.

Placing the Right Content

In Chapter 2, "Understanding Digital Analytics Concepts," and Chapter 3, "Choosing Your Analytics Tools," we talk at length about using listening data to inform content development in real time. It is a similar idea here: After the known issues and influencers have been identified, you should be looking for any opportunity to share relevant content with the community. This content does not need to be 100% issues related, however. If it is, it obviously cannot be something that would tip the community off to a potential product or service issue.

A good example of placing the right content is related to the customer service applications mentioned earlier. If you have talked to your customer service team and identified that long hold times are an issue and then realized after analyzing social conversations that this is the subject of some discussion online, what should you do? Well, a practical approach is to interject pieces of content on shared channels (such as Facebook or Twitter) that talk about how you are addressing longer-than-normal hold times. Although it isn't a full-blown issue yet, it could be if it got into the hands of the right influencer. However, if you have taken the time to put out specific pieces of content about the issue, you can neutralize some of that impact.

Knowing the Positive and Negative Words

It isn't enough to just know the issues and the influencers. You need to be intimately familiar with the words people are using in conversation. Chances are good that there are anywhere between 10 and 15 "money words" that people use in connection with one of these issues. Do you know them? If not, spend time doing research, looking at social conversations, and identifying those words.

How do you identify the money words? A number of tools are available to answer this question:

- **Wordle**—If you have ever developed a word cloud showing the most popular terms, it was probably developed by Wordle. Wordle is a free web-based application that enables users to copy and paste a large number of words into the system to see which words are used most frequently. Figure 11.3 shows an example of a Wordle.

- **Google Keyword Planner**—Google Keyword Planner can give you search volume, traffic forecasts, and keyword suggestions for a variety of keywords and phrases.

- **KWFinder**—KWFinder is a long-tail keyword tool with a helpful interface that allows its users to see search volume, average cost per click, average pay per click, and regional trends for a keyword or phrase.

- **SEMRush**—SEMRush is a more sophisticated solution that gathers in-depth information on volume trends, cost per click, and number of results for a specific keyword, and sample ad copy that brands or individuals are buying. It will also help its users identify new keywords and phrases that are related, but are ones people are also searching for. Lastly, it provides helpful competitive intelligence on what your competitors are ranking for and the estimated value of those rankings.

- **Keyword Explorer from Moz**—Keyword Explorer works in a very simple way. A user simply enters a keyword or phrase, and then what returns is SEO volume on that word, related keywords, and competition surrounding that word. Identifying adjacent words using this tool can be invaluable so you have the full picture of what the online community is searching for. Knowing the volume can also help you gauge just how active the community is on a particular topic.

- **Content Insights from BuzzSumo**—This tool provides insights into the types of content, keywords, and domains that are resonating with a specific audience. BuzzSumo is an invaluable tool for competitive research as well.

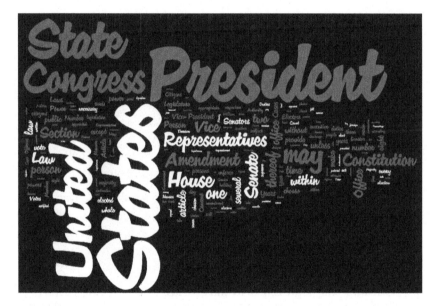

Figure 11.3 *A sample word cloud identifying the top keywords/phrases.*

These tools are excellent examples of tools that can work for visualization and research purposes. Each has its own benefits so we won't make a specific recommendation, except to say use the tool you feel gives you the most complete information. Remember, it is being used for crisis preparedness, and it is your brand at stake.

Tagging the Right Words

After you have identified the keywords people are using online, cross-referencing those words against the words you are using on all your properties is important. Do they match the words you are tagging on your website? If not, why? The goals should be to customize your content to what the community is looking for and also to make it as visible as possible.

Are these words the same words you are using in social media posts? If not, why? Again, you need to ensure that you are giving the right content and that it is very visible. What about on your blog? The same idea fits. Conduct an inventory of the words you are using in tags versus the words you have identified that match these issues.

If you go through the seven steps detailed in this section, you will have a firm grasp on the identity of known issues and will create a best-in-class crisis communications plan. Not only that, but these steps help make facing the day of a crisis a little easier. What happens when the crisis hits, though? How do you ensure that you are taking the right steps from an analytics perspective? Read on.

Crisis Day Monitoring and Ongoing Reporting

So a crisis has hit, and you have done your upfront research. Obviously, on the day a crisis hits, everyone is frenzied. There is certainly no time to do any in-depth research, which is why the steps we outlined in the preceding section are so important. What are the next steps?

1. **Deal with the issue hitting**—For the sake of this discussion, we assume that you have done the upfront research. When the issue hits online, you should activate the crisis protocols you have put into place.

2. **Develop a content plan**—When you know who is calling and who is talking online, it is easier to know what types of content you should be posting. Again, if you have done the upfront research, this should not involve much heavy lifting. A component of the content plan is also determining how frequently you will be posting.

3. **Determine your reporting plan and cadence**—There are things you should be reporting on in real time, and there are others you should save for after the crisis.

Let's dig into each of these steps in a little more detail.

Dealing with the Issue Hitting

On the day an issue hits, you do not have time to identify influencers, determine the share of conversation, or figure out what words people are using in conjunction with this issue. If a known issue comes to light and you have done your research, all that should be required is to activate your crisis protocols. These are the specific protocols that should be in place:

- **Form a monitoring team**—If you are a marketer or corporate communicator, you will not have time to monitor online conversations on the day of the crisis. Before a crisis hits, you should identify who needs to be on the monitoring team. It could be more junior members of your team, but this is also an excellent place to utilize an outside partner. When an issue hits, this team will need to be activated to offer real-time support.

- **Activate the war room and crisis response team**—You should have a previously designated physical location where you and the crisis response team will gather. It should have phones and computer access, and it should be away from the rest of the team. You need to focus on what's happening with the crisis, and you can't risk any distraction. The crisis team members vary from organization to organization, but most times this team involves marketing leaders, corporate communications, HR, legal, and senior executives.

- **Develop a schedule**—Depending on how big the crisis is, you will likely want to create a schedule that shows who is on duty and who is off duty. You should assume that everyone is on duty until some sort of formal schedule is created.

When the issue hits, you should be ready with all these things. Trust us: The online world will not wait for you to have all your ducks in a row.

Developing Your Content Plan

You know the issues people talk about online. You know the issues facing your business. You know the words people are using online. You know what people are searching for. Based on all this research, you should develop pieces of content that you can utilize if a crisis hits. It might be necessary to develop content on-the-fly, especially if an issue is unknown. However, developing that content is challenging.

Your posting cadence is also critical. It depends somewhat on the news flow, but as the crisis evolves, you should determine how often you should be posting online. It could be once, with a simple statement after the crisis breaks, or it could be frequently, as news develops. Either way, you should be prepared to post content within six hours of the crisis breaking.

As you develop your crisis content plan, you should also keep the following in mind:

- **Consider the social platform**—You can probably repurpose content on Twitter and Facebook, depending on what the crisis is about. However, developing something more unique for each channel might make sense, if the crisis warrants.

- **Ensure that the initial response is on the channel where the news broke**—If the news broke in an online mainstream news outlet, then that is where you should respond. (In the initial research, you will have identified influencers, including those from mainstream news, and your list should make the initial response easier.) If the crisis was spawned on Twitter, then you should develop a piece of content that fits the Twitter audience.

- **Keep the top keywords in mind**—You have already identified the top keywords in your research. The posts you develop, regardless of channel, should utilize those keywords.

- **Use senior executives**—This would be a good time to take advantage of your senior leaders who are already using social media. If they aren't using social media, use their voice in your posts. After the Domino's Pizza crisis in 2009, the company's CEO, Patrick Doyle, became the immediate face of the content they were posting. Positioning your senior leaders in this way gives your constituents confidence that you are taking the crisis seriously. This can also be an opportunity to convince your executives that they should be more active online.

- **Be flexible**—We said just a few paragraphs ago that developing some static content would be a good tactical move, and it is. But you should be flexible with your content, based on how the news cycle develops.

Developing Your Reporting Plan and Reporting Cadence

Depending on how big the crisis is, you might be inundated with thousands of posts over a very short period of time. Digesting and offering insights on that much data in a crisis situation is very challenging. If you have activated your monitoring team (internally or externally), you will also need to determine how frequently you are reporting, what you are reporting on, and what your postmortem reporting plan will be.

A component of the reporting plan is utilizing a tool that provides information in near real time. Check Chapter 3 and Chapter 4, "Digital Analysis: Brand" to find out more about tools that could fit the bill. If your business is in a category that is constantly under threat of crisis (for example, the airline industry), you should ensure that your monitoring tool can handle volume as it comes through in a timely fashion.

The following sections talk a little more about reporting frequency, contents, and how you should be reporting after a crisis ends.

Reporting Frequency and Contents During a Crisis

In the early days of a crisis, you should be planning on reporting fairly regularly. If the crisis is generating a lot of online attention, you might want to consider developing a report every hour. If the crisis is generating some attention but the news is not changing much, doing a couple of reports might make sense. What should be in your reports, and in what format should you present them?

- **Email**—If you are in the middle of a crisis, it will probably not be practical to create a fancy PowerPoint presentation. An email should be perfectly sufficient to deliver the news.

- **Executive summary**—Every report should contain a few sentences on what is happening online. Think about developing something that's very high level—even a bullet point format that sums up the period's activities.

- **Volume of conversation**—This is an obvious one, but it is helpful to see how much conversation is taking place online about the crisis.

- **Locations of conversations**—Do the conversations take place in blogs or forums? Most crisis situations see mentions coming from news and Twitter, but every situation is slightly different.

- **Sentiment**—Do not try to have someone on the team read the conversations and then assign a sentiment score to them, but it is helpful to offer a qualitative snapshot of the sentiment of the online conversation.

- **Top sites**—Which sites are generating the most buzz? Buzz in this case is most often a proxy for the number of shares on Twitter and Facebook that an article is receiving.

Do not obsess about making the report beautiful. What you really want to convey is a pulse check on what's happening, and content flow can change based on what is happening in conversations at that moment.

Reporting Frequency and Contents After a Crisis

After a crisis is over, you should plan on doing a deeper dive into how the crisis unfolded online. This is your opportunity to highlight what happened, how it happened, and how you reacted to make sure further brand value was not lost as a result of the crisis. Your monitoring team should be involved in putting together this report, whether that is your agency or an internal team. The following should go into the post-crisis report:

- **Executive summary**—One slide that talks about what happened during the crisis is an imperative. This might be the only slide your executives read, so be sure it tells the story you want to tell about the crisis.

- **Volume of conversation**—Again, seeing how much conversation took place during the crisis is helpful.

- **Locations of conversations**—Identifying whether Twitter or blogs drove the crisis coverage will help provide a barometer for where you can expect crisis coverage to originate the next time.

- **News cycle analysis**—Analyzing how the news cycle unfolded is important. How many mentions did it take before the peak was reached? How long did the news cycle last? Who drove that initial spike? These are all things you should be trying to answer in the report.

- **Sentiment**—Depending on the crisis, looking at overall online sentiment during that period would be helpful. You can then further break down sentiment by media type to see where the most positive, negative, and neutral conversations came from.

- **Influencer coverage**—If you have done your upfront analysis, you will know who typically drives share of conversation for the brand. Did they cover the crisis? If so, how did they cover it? This does not need to be a quantitative analysis. Rather, showing how the influencers covered it is most important.

- **New influencers**—Are there people who generated a lot of news attention who could be considered influencers in the future? If so, consider adding them to the list of sites/sources you are actively monitoring.

- **Key subtopics**—If the crisis is long enough, there is a good chance that subtopics will develop. What are they, and should you add them to your known issues list in the future?

The post-crisis report should be viewed partially as reporting on what took place during the crisis, but also as an update to the benchmark research you conducted in the first phase of the crisis planning process. To ensure that you have gathered all the relevant data, you should wait at least a month after a crisis to conduct this report. You might be able to glean valuable intelligence as mentions continue trickling in after the heat of the crisis begins to subside.

Correcting the History After a Crisis Is Over

After a crisis is over, you have the opportunity to assess how the team performed. How effective was your team? How effective was your pre-crisis research in saving you valuable time during the crisis? How good was your reporting during and after the crisis? Are there things you wish you would have reported on either during or after the crisis? The good news is that none of these things are set in stone. In fact, the best crisis plans set up the company for success during the crisis but are fluid enough to change based on a specific crisis experience.

For measuring the impact of your initial crisis planning, after the crisis subsides is the best time to evaluate some of your original research. Identifying important third parties who came to your aid and tweaking your content syndication plan are also helpful.

Evaluating Your Preliminary Research

You shouldn't be surprised that we advocate ongoing measurement of your communications efforts—crisis situation or not. There is no better time to evaluate how effective your initial crisis planning research was than after a crisis is over. Here's what you should be looking at when you evaluate your preliminary research:

- **The right influencers**—Did you reach out to the right people during the crisis to help spread your message? Were they effective in spreading that message beyond their initial post? Did any new people emerge as influential whom you could use in a future crisis? These are some of the questions you should answer to ensure that you can continue pumping out content that helps you correct the perceptions people might have developed about your brand during the crisis.

- **The right words**—The keywords you identified by using some of the tools we listed earlier should have been used in the posts you issued during the crisis. Were they used appropriately? After doing the post-crisis report and looking at the keywords people were using, do they still match up?

- **The right content**—Your preliminary research should have shown what types of content resonated most about a particular issue. Is that content still the same, or is there some nuance you can make to ensure that you keep reaching people with the right content?

- **The right story**—Does your message about a particular issue need to change in the wake of the crisis? Maybe you will never talk about that issue again unless another crisis develops, but analyzing whether the message is still resonating is critical.

Identifying Key Third Parties and a Content Syndication Plan

When a crisis situation ends, you have a great opportunity to see which third parties came to your aid. These are not necessarily individual bloggers, mainstream news reporters, or Twitter users. It might be that key third-party organizations utilized their own social properties to defend your point of view. If a crisis event crops up again, these groups will likely come to your aid again. Identifying any potential "friendlies" that could help you in a future negative situation is important.

Also, this is the time to test whether your content syndication plan was effective in spreading the message. The following are some key questions to ask yourself about the content syndication plan:

- **Did the influencers move content?**—When you reached out with a specific message, did they accurately portray your point of view? If not, it might be best to think about another source as the "tipping point."

- **What channels drove the most syndication?**—We know that Twitter tends to be a strong driving force for additional mentions, but was it really during the crisis? Or was Twitter just a megaphone for other people's content?

- **Did you have the right blend of original and static content?**—We mentioned earlier that having some canned content at the ready would be helpful, but you also need to be flexible enough to develop content based on how the news cycle develops. Did your mixture of new and old content work for you?

- **Did you achieve the volume you expected?**—You benchmarked the volume of conversation before the crisis, so you can see how much volume—generated by both you and other parties—occurred during the crisis.

Crises can be painful. However, if you take our advice, your crisis situation will be a little less painful. We promise. Utilizing social data before, during, and after a crisis can be invaluable in finding the right content mix, issues, and channels, and, most importantly, protecting your brand from future attacks. What are you waiting for? Start tapping into social data today to prevent or mitigate the effects of a crisis tomorrow!

12

Launching a New Product

Launching a new product or service is a significant under-taking for any company, even for the big brands like P&G and Coca-Cola. In most cases, the market, regardless of category, is saturated, and consumers are creatures of habit. According to strategic brand positioning expert and consultant Jack Trout, consumers repeatedly buy the same 150 items, which constitute as much as 85% of their household needs. In addition, only 3% of new consumer packaged goods meet or exceed their first-year sales goals. Thanks largely to the shifting dynamic from B2C to C2B, the opportunity of the role of digital analytics has expanded to support these significant investments. When applied intelligently, digital analytics can inform the full product life cycle. In this chapter, you learn how to support informing the lifecycle from perception and messaging to consumer utility to ultimate viability.

Some of the reasons product launches fail are internal issues within a company, such as the inability to support fast growth after a product gains some traction in the market. Or a product might be truly original and revolutionary, but the company finds there isn't a market for it. (The Nook, several years ago, being a classic example of this.) Most common is a scenario in which consumers feel that a product has failed to live up to its claims and/or benefits, and so the product receives harsh criticism and consumer bashing. A recent example came in 2016 when Samsung's Galaxy Note 7, one of its flagship phones, was known to catch on fire or explode. It was rumored that a car burned down because its owner left the Galaxy Note 7 in the car. The phones have since been banned on all flights (foreign or domestic), and Samsung was forced to recall the entire line. Ever since, Samsung's phone business has taken a hit against Google and Apple, and might never recover fully from the incident; time will tell.

Having a clear understanding of where new opportunity exists in a market depends on knowing consumer needs, wants, and preferences. This is absolutely crucial to new product success, and failure to do due diligence, where possible, to gather insights is akin to failing to prepare and increases the likelihood of mistakes and missing the mark during product launch.

Failing to conduct due diligence is not a one-time problem, either. Products that start out strong can quickly have trouble remaining successful during a growth phase. Before we talk about how to apply some of the digital analytics capabilities discussed earlier in the book, it's worth spending some time looking at the product lifecycle. Understanding the different phases of the product lifecycle and what you need to do in each one, from a marketing and/or advertising perspective, will provide a structured approach to guide your decision making on how and when to best apply digital analytics capabilities in the support of any product initiative. Let's take a look at the product lifecycle.

General Overview of the Product Lifecycle

The concept of a product lifecycle is essential to any professional in marketing, and it's taught as part of the curriculum at many colleges and universities. However, it needs to be augmented by appropriate digital analytics capabilities at specific phases to truly help you make informed marketing decisions. Essentially, any product goes through a lifecycle that has the phases shown in Figure 12.1. Within each of these phases, companies alter their marketing mix (product, pricing, distribution, and promotion) to account for the unique challenges faced within each phase:

- **Development**—Development is an internal phase that some omit completely when discussing this concept. During this phase, the product is being developed and made ready for release to consumers. At this point, the product is not in the market.

- **Introduction**—During this phase, the product is launched to the market, with the goals of generating awareness and achieving market penetration. Basically, the company is establishing a foothold for the product in the category.

- **Growth**—After the product has been accepted by the market, the company seeks to build brand favorability and increase market share.

- **Maturity**—At this stage, aggressive growth is no longer possible, as the category has matured and competitors offer similar products. The company seeks to defend its market share and maximize its profit margin.

- **Decline**—Inevitably, sales decline because a product is less desirable among consumers. The company must decide to either discontinue the product or relaunch it with new features and benefits.

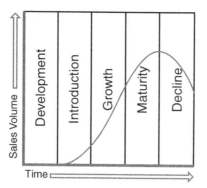

Figure 12.1 *The product lifecycle.*

The opportunities to reduce risk and refine product marketing initiatives are realized through preparation and continuous optimization. Fortunately, you now have the ability to accomplish these things because the consumers you're trying to reach are hyperconnected and have a propensity to share their product opinions and brand experiences across the digital landscape. By harnessing digital analytics capabilities, specifically social listening and search analysis, you can begin to improve your understanding of what the consumers you're trying to reach truly think, want, need, and expect from your brand and your competitors. (After all, open data cuts both ways.)

In this chapter, our approach has a goal of shifting (upward) product diffusion curves across the entire lifecycle by capturing deep consumer insights that enable you to make the necessary optimizations or course corrections. The diffusion curve is represented by the top line spanning all the phases in Figure 12.2. Digital analytics can help you realize the goal of optimizing a new product launch by capturing consumer feedback and behavior and distilling it down into specific answers that ultimately tie back to product success or failure.

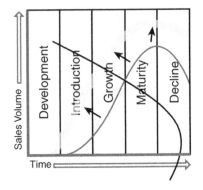

Figure 12.2 *New product launch—diffusion curve.*

The next sections outline each of the middle three product lifecycle phases, with unique considerations for each, along with the specific digital analytics you should consider as you answer questions associated with the goals and challenges for each phase.

The Product Lifecycle Introduction Phase

Recall that during the introduction phase, the product is introduced into the wild (see Figure 12.3). During development, assumptions have been made about the target audience, how the audience will perceive the new product, how the product is positioned to address specific end customers, and the value the product will provide to users. These assumptions will have been thoroughly examined, discussed, and vetted internally prior to launch. That said, they are simply hypotheses based on the best data available during the development phase.

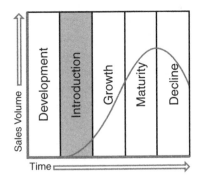

Figure 12.3 *The introduction phase of the product lifecycle.*

The rubber meets the road when a product is launched, so there likely isn't a more important time to be collecting and analyzing consumer data and feedback about the product, as well as the specific product attributes that you've positioned in your marketing mix and messaging. This analysis will enable you to identify bad assumptions and make adjustments as quickly as possible, as well as identify new opportunities that weren't discovered during the product development phase.

The introduction phase has fairly simple business objectives:

- Generate awareness

- Establish a foothold in the market

You need some initial considerations (the "what") as a starting point to guide the activities you'll perform (the "how") to generate the outcomes and benefits of this analysis (the "why"). The following are some examples of considerations:

- What are the emerging trends in the category regarding new product usage and repurposing? What trends are developing?

- What factors of influence are fueling consumer advocacy for Product X's new usage?

- What are the consumer likes/dislikes about current promotions and offers? Which promotion/offer channels have the most impact on consumers?

- Where do consumers find the most utility for Product X?

- Which meal occasions are the most relevant for Product X? Why?

Figure 12.4 lists activities that revolve around collecting, tracking, and monitoring key performance indicators and consumer feedback throughout the introduction phase, by customer segment (if applicable).

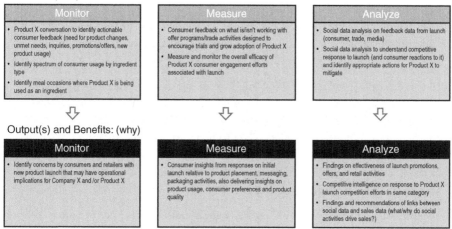

Figure 12.4 *Examples of activities during the introduction phase of the product lifecycle.*

Let's apply social listening analysis to solve this problem and capture data that can help you understand if you're generating awareness and penetrating the market to effectively lead to sales. The first step is planning. Remember that you get out of social listening what you put into it. A concrete and specific plan will yield detailed insights that you can actually act on. Let's walk through a hypothetical scenario in which you will generate a learning agenda (covered in previous chapters) for a mainstream consumer household product you might buy from a company such as P&G, Kraft, or General Mills. The following sections examine some of the broad questions you might want to answer after a product launch.

What Is the Consumer Reaction to Product X?

Are consumers responding favorably to their initial exposure to the product? Are there specific product attributes they like/dislike? Are there specific product attributes they prefer over others or prefer against competitors? Specific queries can be created within your social listening tool to reveal consumer conversations that answer these questions. This specificity, when combined with sentiment analysis, can produce insightful findings.

It's not enough to count mentions of the new product, use automated sentiment analysis, spit out the answer, and call it a day. That might produce eye-candy charts, but it won't generate anything the business can use to validate that a new product launch is heading down the right path in terms of acceptance or to point out a fatal flaw. Context is key here, and the more specific you can get with questions to guide your analysis, the better. It's more effective, yet more time-consuming, to break down the "consumer reaction" according to the specific product attributes and any key messaging being used in the marketing and advertising of the product. This is easily done today through a process of either hand-coding the set of data, or using crowdsourcing technologies like Amazon's Mechanical Turk or Crowdflower. With some simple setup, you can use either technology to achieve extremely granular (and clean) insights from your social listening data set.

In this example, Product X—a cooking ingredient, let's say—has four specific key attributes. Consumers are reacting favorably to the first three (for example, taste, price/value, quality) but unfavorably to the fourth, a new use for the product (for example, as a cooking ingredient). The product's growth strategy might rely on positive consumer reaction to the new use. It's imperative to monitor this closely and not let the overall picture (three out of four positives) alter consumer perspective on that specific product attribute.

In summary, remember to think critically about both product performance and market acceptance as a whole but also about product attributes that are strategically important to both the short- and long-term business plans. After you've identified those attributes modeling your social listening around those items becomes simple.

What Are the Consumer Concerns About Product X?

This is an important question to answer, but it is one that is difficult to predict ahead of time. What specifically should you be using to find and collect the relevant consumer conversations? Our experience has shown that it's an organic activity that is best done after you've already performed social listening and analysis about general consumer reaction (as described in the previous section). The reason for this is simple: You don't know what you don't know.

You can identify certain categories ahead of time, but there are always some categories (sometimes a few, sometimes many) that weren't on the radar earlier and need to be factored into your plans, based on how consumers are reacting. As described earlier in the book when we discussed digital analytics tools, segmenting your social listening data is critical. Your data for Product X can be first categorized into a bucket for "consumer concerns." Within that data set, you can further refine the data into subsets of concerns, using either hand-coding or some of the technologies we listed earlier for more granular analysis. For example, the concerns could be extensions of the four attributes we listed earlier. Detailed analysis of the fourth attribute (a new use as a cooking ingredient) could possibly reveal that awareness is high for the new use for the product, but the actual experience is poor. Consumers could be citing issues with inconvenient packaging or saying that the product itself isn't living up to the new use claims. Perhaps Product X isn't moist enough and needs to be reformulated.

These are examples of the specific types of consumer feedback that can be gathered and applied to product attributes, in sufficient detail, to take action. You don't necessarily need to change the product. It could just as easily be that the target audience in this case needs education about the new product use and the content/messaging in the marketing and advertising needs to be adjusted to clarify and eliminate any confusion in the minds of the consumers.

What Are the Consumer's Unmet or Unstated Needs?

Meeting consumer needs is obviously critical, but identifying those needs can be tricky. This is another activity best performed after your broader consumer reaction data collection has been done. Trying to predict unmet needs and search for consumer conversations via social listening tools is difficult because of the previously mentioned "don't know what you don't know" condition. The broad search will collect all types of reactions/conversations about the product. After the segmentation has been done, there will be a set of data that just doesn't fit into another category. Call it miscellaneous or other—the label doesn't matter. This is often one of the most revealing areas for identifying unmet needs. Consumers will provide opinions and ideas that don't fit neatly into another category. Taking the time to perform a qualitative analysis on this data set is worth doing and might very well uncover that elusive diamond in the rough.

The Product Lifecycle Growth Phase

In the growth phase of the product lifecycle (see Figure 12.5), the market has accepted the new product, and it's a race to grow and build market share. Here, the goal is not to generate awareness, because that has been done, but to differentiate the product in the category, building brand preference and capturing customers from competitors. This is more difficult, and the challenges associated with this phase are very different from those in the introduction phase.

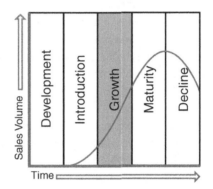

Figure 12.5 *The growth phase of the product lifecycle.*

This phase focuses on the triggers that are responsible for generating product advocacy, brand favorability, and adoption among the target audience. Knowing how and why these triggers occur can reveal how to fuel them through marketing and advertising efforts, which in turn drives growth. Robust analysis helps you clarify the appropriate marketing mix to deploy during the growth phase in order to achieve your growth objectives.

As in the introduction phase, you need some initial considerations: (the "what") as a starting point to guide the activities you perform (the "how") to generate the outcomes and benefits of the analysis (the "why").

The following are some examples of considerations in the growth phase:

- What online communities and dynamics are shaping the conversation about Product X and driving incremental adoption of cooking by consumers with Product X?

- What efforts can be made to fuel/grow customer advocacy within these communities?

- Which events and/or triggers are responsible for generating spikes in conversation about Product X? What can the company do to increase the volume of these triggers?

- How do these spikes in conversation correlate to sales of Product X?

- What is the appropriate media mix to drive growth and adoption?

Figure 12.6 lists activities that revolve around monitoring and measuring both consumer and retailer promotional efficacies to identify optimal marketing and engagement levers across specific marketing channels. Applying social listening can help play a significant role in solving any issues while also enabling your organization to understand how to drive product promotions. Effectively following the trends in social conversations can enable you to introduce marketing strategies and tactics to drive spikes in advocacy that eventually could lead to further sales.

Activities: (how)

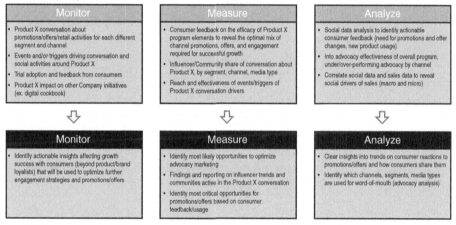

Figure 12.6 *Examples of activities during the growth phase of the product lifecycle.*

Again, the first step is planning. Let's continue with our example of Product X and generate a specific learning agenda that supports the growth phase. The following sections examine the broad questions you might want to answer in a growth scenario.

What Are the Communities, Sites, and Social Platforms in Which Product X Is Being Discussed, Shared, and Evaluated?

Engagement is one thing, and activity on any social platform is another. What's important to take away from both engagement and activity is understanding what advocacy looks like for your product/brand within that engagement and activity and to identify the strongest sources of that advocacy. It's important to remember the goal and to identify insights, trends, or patterns that can be fueled to emerge in other areas of the market. This will drive direct sales growth and also generate more advocacy, which in turn drives future growth.

When we use the term *advocacy*, we are using a specific definition. Many of the social listening and analytics tools covered in this book provide the ability to identify advocates or influencers using their own formulas/secret sauces. That's okay, as each one has pros. In this case, however, we're focused less on identifying a specific individual advocate and more about the source of that advocacy (what caused it) and where it occurred (the digital property).

For example, there are several potential sources of advocacy, such as ratings and reviews on Yelp and Google, as well as sharing and endorsements of coupons and special offers across social platforms like Facebook, Twitter, or Pinterest. Was it the positive review about the quality of Product X (a specific attribute, not the product as a whole) that drove new interest and consideration? Or was it the discounted offer for first-time buyers that was shared heavily on Facebook? Assessing qualitative feedback from consumers via social listening data and comparing it with quantitative data from social sharing of offers and coupons will help you find the answer.

These are a few of many potential sources that play an important role in the brand marketing mix when you're attempting to achieve growth through acquiring customers. You need to understand which sources to ignore and which ones to double down on, in terms of investment to fuel more growth. For that you need to create and develop specific channel tactics, but doing so will help you optimize the entire marketing mix, from a strategic perspective.

One important channel that will not be available through traditional social media monitoring tools is Amazon reviews. Your company should investigate whether you can access a tool to scrape these reviews, or you'll need to conduct a more qualitative assessment. Either way, data from reviews is extremely valuable to gather consumer insights.

Who Are the Influencers in the Product X Conversation?

This question is related to the previous question, but it's unique. We don't cover this in great detail here; read Chapter 8, "Understanding Digital Influence" for more information. It's a point worth mentioning here, though, because an outreach program might be a component for driving growth, particularly in an established category. There may be a set of key influencers on topics relevant to your product who can play a role in driving growth through word of mouth to their followers, thus reaching friends of friends, who are consumers not currently exposed to your brand and/or product.

What Is the Consumer Reaction to Retail or Promotions for Product X?

Brands discount heavily to lure new buyers in many categories, and this one is no different. However, each promotion is trying to resonate across a specific product attribute or set of product attributes to entice new customers. Is it all about the quality of the product, the best possible ingredients? Or is it a balance of price and value? The buyer wants to feel like the value and benefits are there for a reasonable price. Targeting promotions highlighting different product attributes across different segments of the target audience is a complex process.

It's not about the numbers or conversions associated with each promotion. Those are obviously key inputs for assessing marketing performance. However, the role of social listening in this phase, and the theme throughout this chapter, is to give brands a tool or mechanism to capture consumer opinions and attitudes about specific promotions in order to optimize their promotional marketing mix. That might mean changing where certain promotions are being executed or the specific language and pricing associated with a promotion.

In the example of Product X, the conversation associated with promotions cover many subtopics, but the common ones revolve around the following categories:

- **Product evaluation**—Consumers express intent or consideration for a trial to give the product a chance.

- **Sales**—Consumers share specific offers or coupons with their friends, along with their opinion of the value of an offer relative to the product.

- **Recipes**—Consumers share or describe their planned or favorite recipes for the product, along with the promotion.

- **Nutrition**—Consumers share nutritional information about the product, including their opinion on the health benefits of the product (or lack thereof).

- **Consumption**—Consumers share their favorite ways to consume or use the product (snack, in certain dishes, and so on).

- **Other/miscellaneous**—Consumers share something related to the promotion that doesn't fall into the other five categories. As indicated earlier, this category can be a rich source of insights for unmet needs or unanticipated uses. Do not discard this data without analysis just because it looks minimally useful in an unattractive category. Dig in and explore.

The Product Lifecycle Maturity Phase

In the maturity phase of the product lifecycle (see Figure 12.7), the product strategy is simple: "Defend your turf." This means staving off threats from mature competitors that offer similar products and squeezing every cent out of each transaction to maximize profit margins. Competitors might introduce new features to differentiate their product from yours. Keeping an eye on consumer reactions to competitors, whether established or new, and how they view differentiation is a high priority in this phase. Another important area of focus is understanding what changes have occurred since the product introduction and growth phases. It's important to understand what has changed from the baseline data and benchmarking regarding consumer awareness of the brand and product, consideration and intent to purchase the product, brand loyalty, and even sentiment of specific product attributes. Have those changed over time, and, in the maturity phase, are they declining? If so, why?

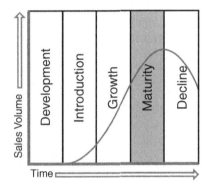

Figure 12.7 *The maturity phase of the product lifecycle.*

Another possible way to extend the maturity phase of a product for longer volume and sales is to utilize cross-selling opportunities with other products in the company's portfolio. What products could be packaged together for combination sales? How do consumers view the various packaging options, and are they helping extend the mature product's sales?

As with the other phases, we establish initial considerations (the "what") as a starting point to guide the activities you'll perform (the "how") to generate the outcomes and benefits of this analysis (the "why").

The following are some sample considerations in the maturity phase:

- What activities are most commonly performed and/or discussed among consumers that can be highlighted to extend the length of the maturity phase for Product X?

- What consumer trends and preferences have emerged for Product X? Of these, what has changed from the original data, baselines, and assumptions?

- What topics should the company monitor continuously throughout the maturity phase for Product X?

- What key brand advocates and influencers have emerged in the maturity phase, and how should they be engaged moving forward?

- What other related products do consumers show interest in that could be opportunities for combination meals and occasions (cross-selling)?

- What are consumers saying about direct competitors and their products? Are they citing any perceived differentiation or new features?

Figure 12.8 lists activities that revolve around identifying aspects of consumer attitudes that identify relationships between components of Product X program and business performance, with a focus on maximizing sales volume and closely monitoring competitors. Again, the first step is planning. Let's continue with our Product X example and generate a specific learning agenda that supports the maturity phase.

The following sections examine some of the broad consumer questions that were asked in the initial product introduction phase to understand changes in the market and consumer attitudes about the product.

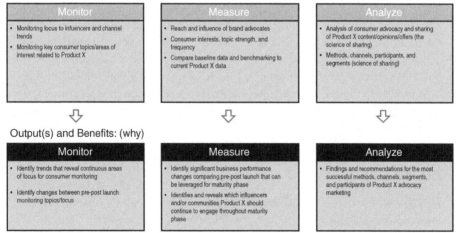

Figure 12.8 *Examples of activities during the maturity phase of the product lifecycle.*

What Consumer Trends and Preferences Have Emerged Around Product X Use?

When we walked through the introduction phase earlier in this chapter, we looked at important aspects of how consumers are reacting to the product and product attributes that we made a point to collect and analyze. You use this baseline information to build a marketing mix and a go-to-market strategy for the relevant channels. As mentioned previously, consumer attitudes, opinions, and behaviors change over time. The information distilled from the introduction phase has a shelf life. It expires, and you must gather and compare new information against the original to understand changes and trends that directly affect the length and duration of the Product X maturity phase.

This means dusting off those queries in your social listening tool and using them as a starting point for this phase. You might need to make tweaks and edits to refine the focus, but the exceptions will be minor.

What Related Products Do Consumers Show Interest In?

For a company with a diverse, yet related, product portfolio, determining what related products consumers are interested in can help extend the life of a mature product. The focus is on trying to collect data on any related uses and topics consumers associate with conversations about Product X and to identify any potential complementary products that can be combined into a more attractive package.

For example, Product X could be paired with other cooking ingredients to make a variety of recipes. Are consumers talking about specific recipes or ingredient pairings that coincide with any products in the current portfolio? Such conversations provide opportunities to examine in this phase. Any social listening tool will suffice, as the ability to capture relevant consumer conversations, and thus data, is dependent on the specificity and relevance of your search queries, not the technology or the tool.

Conclusion

This chapter has described an approach you can adopt to harvest relevant consumer feedback about your product, regardless of where it falls in the lifecycle. This information, while not the end-all, be-all, can have tremendous value. It can also be used to make near real-time optimizations to marketing and advertising campaigns or identify how competitive products are getting a leg up on you in the minds of consumers, based on differentiated positioning and relevance to consumer demands.

Will everything you find be valuable to your brand or product marketing? Absolutely not. We hope you understand that the approach described here is yet another key way to capture critically important consumer feedback about a product throughout the course of its lifecycle. You should not rely on it as the single source of truth but should combine it with other product feedback and consumer data to paint a comprehensive picture of product performance against consumer attitudes and needs. In the next chapter, you'll discover more about how to formulate your research plan.

13

Building Your Research Plan

Throughout this book, we have dissected many of the various tools you can use to gather and analyze digital data for the betterment of your marketing or communications programs. In Chapter 3, we dissected the tool landscape, gave you a framework to use in order to ensure you pick the right tools for your organization, and outlined how we thought the market would continue to evolve. Having access to the right tools enables you to build better campaigns, optimize more effectively, and truly understand performance. However, understanding a crowded and ever-growing tool landscape is only one part of the puzzle. Companies of all sizes are also looking to use cases. If a company is to select a social analytics tool like Crimson Hexagon, for example, how can it expect to use it? Similarly, how are other companies utilizing tools like Crimson Hexagon? In Chapters 9 through 12, we drilled into use cases, such as using data to inform a product launch, customer service, marketing programs, and anticipating a crisis.

It is important to outline the foundational elements as explained in the first several chapters of this book. Four years since the initial release of *Digital Marketing Analytics*, our experience shows that companies are still not clear on how to select tools, analyze data, and then apply it. They are weighed down by the amount of available data and the lack of internal headcount that is required to push a digital analytics agenda forward. The first few chapters of this book have shown you an adaptable roadmap for not only tool selection but also how you can ultimately use the data you're collecting.

Those chapters are also the foundational elements for the next several chapters in the book. In the following sections, we dive deeper into developing reports for manageable consumption, measuring campaign performance, and understanding how this all ladders up to understanding the effectiveness, efficiency, and effect of your digital marketing and advertising initiatives.

A critical part of any digital analytics program is a research plan. You don't need to have a panic attack. This is not a return to your high school science class, but it is a critical step to informing your eventual reporting. Without such a plan, your digital analytics program runs the possibility of being unclear, unusable, or misaligned with the marketing objectives. Where do you begin? The research plan starts and ends with sources and methods.

Developing Your Source List

One of the reasons we have focused on several different kinds of digital analytics tools in this book is that we firmly believe in the interplay between the various channels. Developing a new piece of content for your website can affect search, social, and paid media programs. Similarly, social media activities can have a profound effect on search visibility and can provide valuable input to the development of paid media programs.

Think about it for a moment: If you do a Google search for your name, what typically appears? The social platforms that you are currently using, right? On occasion, you also see a particular piece of blog content near the top of the results—social content you post or that is shared affects search results and vice versa.

We don't want to belabor the point, but it is important to understand that we are talking about digital media for a reason. All the types of digital media, social media included, rely on a cumulative effect of working together to deliver maximum value for the brand. When you are developing your research plan, you should take into consideration all forms of digital media.

The first step in developing the plan is to identify your sources. (Well, really, the first step is to identify your goals, but we assume that you're following best practices in strategic planning and have already done that.) As we've mentioned several times throughout the book, in addition to having a lot of data available to you, you could potentially select from among many tools and third-party services for the job. We assume that if you have reached the point of developing a research plan, you already have selected a set of tools that can help get you there. If you haven't, go back and read Chapter 3 before finishing this chapter. Next, we dig into each of the pieces of the source list.

Identifying Data Sources

This is likely to be very obvious, but a critical part of a research plan is identifying your data sources. Again, the data can come from a number of digital analytics tools or third-party data providers. It's increasingly common for companies to augment their own data with third-party data for purchase. According to a December 2017 study on data spending by eMarketer, U.S. companies will spend more than $10 billion on audience data from external providers.[1]

Smart marketers are filling in their audience and audience segments' blind spots by creatively combining their own data sources with data from third parties to develop insights and identify actionable steps they can take. We do not necessarily have a preference, for either tools or data providers, as each has strengths and weaknesses, and all play different roles. In addition, you should take into account the objectives of your program. For example, if it is a traditional public relations activity, some of these tools might not apply.

Although each tool has different strengths and weaknesses, there is a standard toolkit that you should assemble when building your research plan, including the following things:

- **Social listening tools**—You expected this one, right? Regardless of the tool you are planning to use, your research plan should include gathering data from this source. It offers insights into who your audience is, what content they engage with and share, whom they interact with on a daily basis, and where you can reach them by identifying which channels and platforms they are spending time on.

- **Search tools**—Throughout the book we talk about using search tools to understand the "intent" of your target audience. Search and social media are inextricably linked. One of the most popular search analytics tools is Google Trends, a.k.a. Google Insights for Search, and it should be in your research plan toolbox not only because of its usefulness but also because it's free! Google AdWord Keyword Planner is another option, especially if you are trying to assess keyword possibilities, affinities, and overall volume.

- **Web Analytics**—The role of an owned property, like a company website, in a marketing campaign has changed significantly since we wrote the first version of this book. However, in many instances it is still the central point of engagement companies uses with their customers. Whether your organization uses Google Analytics or Adobe Analytics, it is a critical data source to understand what user traffic has come to your site, how they've engaged, how long they've spent on the site, and if they have taken any of the desired actions (for example purchasing, downloading a whitepaper, sharing content). It's the most useful way to determine how your audience behaves on owned media properties you may have.

- **Paid Media Data Sources**—When we use the term *paid media* we mean everything from television, to display advertising, to online video, to native advertising, and pretty much every media format in between. Paid media performance data comes from a variety of sources, including the publishers where advertising was placed, data service providers (DSPs), and data management platforms (DMPs). Which of these paid media sources you use as part of your media plan is entirely dependent on the goals of the research you are conducting. To help guide you, however, consider using the sources that allow you to understand your audience better, where you should place your media, and then if you have the available data, what types of creative assets you should use.

- **Social platform insights**—Facebook Insights and YouTube Insights, for example, are great sources of data if you are conducting an analysis of social media activation and how each of those networks has performed for the brand. Typically, we have used the data provided by these insights platforms as a good complement to data and insights derived from reading social conversations analyzed using social listening tools. This is particularly helpful if you are trying to understand whether top-performing content themes on Facebook match top social media conversation themes on other platforms. These platforms also give you a good sense for how engaged the audience is, what types of content they like to consume, the virality of your content, and how efficient the brand is at spending its media dollars.

- **Traditional media monitoring tools**—Traditional media monitoring is not the focus of this book, obviously, as we are focusing on digital marketing, but it can be an important tool in your toolset. Social listening tools capture a significant number of online news sites, but tools such as Factiva and Cision have even greater news media capture capabilities.

- **Third-party research tools**—As much as we would like to have our own digital analytics tools give us everything we need, oftentimes it is important to call on third-party data to help fill in whatever story you are trying to tell. As we indicated earlier in this chapter, companies are spending on third-party audience data like never before. An example of a third-party data source would be Forrester's Technographics reports or eMarketer Trendpacks, which give you access to media consumption habits, audience demographic characteristics, and how your audience goes about making a purchase decision. These sources can also be supplements where digital data doesn't have every answer.

These are not the only data sources, obviously, but they are the most popularly used types of sources. Remember that not every tool is required for every job. Think about the overall goal of the program and your research before narrowing down the tool selection. A common mistake many companies make is to be sucked into the universe of tools and data sources without a clear and specific plan, and then to begin to collect, store, and analyze data and sources they don't need. Avoid "collecting it because you can" and only prioritize what your objectives depend on.

Picking the Channels for Analysis

After you have selected your data sources, the second most important step is picking the channels and/or platforms you are going to analyze. Picking the channels and platforms is not as simple as saying you are going to track everything (nor should you). If you glean nothing else from this book, we hope you take away that providing proper scope around what you are collecting leads to better insights.

What do we mean by picking the channels or platforms for analysis? When you are developing your research plan, we want you to figure out whether you are going to track only blogs, for example. If you are planning to use this data to inform a traditional public relations program, then maybe you only want to utilize news. If you're planning to do an audience analysis in support of planning for a digital marketing initiative, you'll utilize many of the channels and platforms listed next. Here are some channels that are typically analyzed when conducting this type of research:

- **News**—News outlets are the usual suspects that you should be familiar with by now. The *New York Times, Wall Street Journal*, and *USA Today* are examples.

- **Blogs**—Discerning a blog from a news outlet is becoming increasingly difficult these days, but blogs are the most common channel identified for developing research plans.

- **Comments**—Blog and news comments can also be a source of conversation data to analyze, as well as fodder for the research plan.

- **Groups or forums**—These are often closed networks of people who are talking about single, or related, subjects online. A good example of a group or forum is Babycenter.com, which is dedicated to all things "mom."

- **Owned properties**—Again, by owned properties we mean your corporate website or blog. It is often one of the most important sources for understanding how your audience behaves.

- **Paid media sources**—We mentioned earlier that paid media could be display advertising, television, online video, or native advertising. If your campaign or company is running any sort of paid media, and we're imagining that they are, especially in this day and age, it'll be an important channel to analyze.

- **Facebook**—Facebook is the most dominant social platform in the world with 2 billion monthly users and is most commonly included in research plans. It's important to understand, however, that listening tools do not capture all available Facebook content, only publicly posted content on their platforms. The walled garden label for Facebook still applies in 2018. One potential data source for information on what's happening on Facebook is DataSift's STREAM for social data product. If you are going to use Facebook in your research plan, be sure to determine how you will get the data (either through a provider like DataSift or by going directly to the platform).

- **Twitter**—Twitter currently boasts more than 328 million monthly users and is one of the most common channels analyzed, as brands of all sizes attempt to determine how it can be best leveraged. It is also typically a large source of mentions for brands. One thing to note, though, is that not every tool pulls in the entirety of Twitter mentions. Over the last several years, Twitter has restricted access to its data to only a handful of providers. Be sure that the tool you are using to capture Twitter data has as comprehensive a data set as possible. This is why a product like STREAM from DataSift can be so helpful, as it gives you a one-stop resource for all major social platforms. The data from all the priority social platforms listed here can be obtained via the DataSift STREAM for social data product.

- **Instagram**—Instagram currently has more than 800 million monthly users due to the rise in popularity of visual communications and sharing. Visual analytics tools or features within social analytics tools like Sysomos or Brandwatch can be used to identify insights from social data containing image engagement.

- **Snapchat**—Snapchat currently reports more than 255 million monthly users and is heavily dominated by the highly coveted cohorts of millennials and Gen Z consumers. Snapchat data that is available for analysis and reporting isn't as robust as some of the other platforms here, but can still provide a window into audience engagement, content consumption behaviors, and affinities.

- **YouTube**—YouTube currently reports 1.5 billion monthly users and is nearly the largest search engine in the world, second only to Google. YouTube insights give video content engagement data and social listening tools can help with the commentary and discussion around video content.

- **Pinterest**—Despite having the lowest monthly audience at 175 million active users, Pinterest can be a valuable source of data for insights around image-based content and sharing.

- **Reddit**—Long ignored by marketers, Reddit has risen in potential importance due to its thriving and highly engaged community of 234 million monthly active users. Analysis of Reddit discussion can yield important indicators about consumer intent, perception, or expectations.

Depending on your business and research goals, these channels will probably vary. We cannot emphasize the importance of not collecting data because you can. Do not feel obligated to track them all. Only track those that help you meet your goals!

Identifying Search and Source Languages

Identifying what search parameters and source languages you will use has as much variability in the research plan as any we have talked about so far. One of the reasons there is so much variability is that a lack of clarity exists around what tools to utilize in what markets. Throughout the book we talk about a variety of different tools, and those tools capture wide-ranging amounts of digital data, depending on the source and market in question.

The other reason for the variability is available resources. *Resources* in this case can refer to money and human resources. Not many people are floating around who have experience conducting global digital analysis programs, especially in the more remote parts of the world. These tools and people can be expensive.

Many tools, though, have strong capabilities in markets outside of North America, if you are trying to gather English-only mentions. In almost every case, companies start with global English and expand from there. Organizations with heavy operations overseas need to think about global analytics. Where is a good place to start?

It probably does not make sense for your organization to analyze in every language around the globe. Nor would it make sense for your organization to monitor every country's activity. The most sensible place to begin is by narrowing down to the markets in which you currently do business. From there, you can select the right tool(s) to gather that data. If that isn't an option, another possibility is to narrow down by a specific set of languages.

According to data from Nielsen Online, GfK, and the International Telecommunications Union, 10 languages reach approximately 77% of the world's online population. English is the most prominent language online, reaching more than 25% of the world's online population. Chinese is second with almost 20%. If you are looking to conduct global analytics, these are the other languages you should be capturing:

- Spanish

- Japanese

- Portuguese

- Arabic

- German

- Russian

- French

- Bahasa (Indonesia)

Capturing all these languages is not imperative, certainly, but this list is a good starting place if you are launching a global analytics project. After you have identified the data sources, the languages for analysis, and the channels for analysis, you have completed about half of your research plan. The next step is to clearly define the methods for the analysis.

Nailing Down the Research Methods

A critical part of a research plan is the research methods you will utilize after the data has been identified and gathered. In the first part of this chapter, we talk about what the right data sources are and which languages and channels you should capture. That is only part of the equation. It is a critical part of the process, obviously, but without a consistent set of methods, the analysis or project can fall apart.

Several components are involved in finalizing your research methods:

- **Hypothesis**—Do not worry about whether your science teacher is looking over your shoulder and grading your hypothesis, but it is important to have some general statements about what you expect to see in the analysis.

- **Time frame for analysis**—Gathering all the available information on the Internet is not practical, nor is it practical to gather information for all time. You need to select a specific time frame to properly scope your analysis.

- **Project team**—Not everyone in the organization is going to be involved with your research project, so clearly defining roles is important.

- **Depth of analysis**—It might sound like we are beating a dead horse, but the amount of data available to you is incredible! According to an IDC report, the world is expected to generate 180 trillion gigabytes annually by the year 2025; this is up from 10 trillion gigabytes in 2015 (Forbes, 2016).[2] Because of the volume of information, your analysis can be very granular. Before you start analyzing the data, determine how deep you want to go with the project.

- **Coding framework**—You should have a standard approach to coding mentions or pieces of data as you are conducting the analysis. By coding, we simply mean a method for categorizing or notating the topic mentioned in the post, the sentiment of the post, or the location of the post (blogs, Twitter, forums, and so on).

- **Sentiment approach**—How people are talking about your brand online (positive, negative, or neutral) is important. Is it the most important metric? No, it is not that important in every case. If you have a consumer brand, though, it might be very important to understand. As with the coding framework, you should have a standard approach to measuring sentiment; otherwise, the results could be inaccurate.

- **Spam/bot filtering**—Because of the way the tools we have talked about in previous chapters work (that is, using keywords to gather information on the Internet), you are likely to capture mentions that you do not care about or that are spam. Before conducting the analysis, your team should have a clear understanding of how to treat those mentions.

Over the course of the next several sections, we dive into each of these components in more detail.

Developing a Hypothesis

The hypothesis development process is the single best way to ensure that your research is focused. Without a clearly defined hypothesis, you could end up producing a research report that does not tell a clear story. It does not need to be a hypothesis in the way that you learned all throughout your high school and collegiate education, but it needs to be a statement you can use to guide the data collection and analysis processes.

Simply put, a hypothesis is a proposed explanation for some kind of phenomenon. There are several kinds of hypotheses, but the most common form is the scientific hypothesis. A scientific hypothesis can be tested using the scientific method.

This book does not include a discussion of the scientific method (consult your old textbooks if you would like to take that trip down memory lane), but it is important to note that the hypotheses that you develop for your digital analytics programs should be testable. That is, it should be a statement (or statements) that you can prove or disprove using data.

What is the most important element of a hypothesis? Simply put, unless you have outlined the behavior you are trying to analyze, your hypothesis is incomplete. The following are a few examples of hypotheses you might come up with:

- Conversations mentioning the brand are taking place in news and blogs, and they are not representative of our target audience.

- When consumers come to our website from paid media sources they are less likely to engage than other channels.

- The most effective way of reaching our target audience is through online video advertising.

- The most engaged audiences for our brand are on Facebook.

- Our brand is not relevant compared to our competitors in social media.

- Corporate responsibility mentions will be the most referenced messaging pillar from the list of five core messages.

- People talking about our brand online will be offering new product ideas or requesting a heightened level of customer service.

- Industry conversation themes will be in alignment with the brand's messaging pillars.

✉ Note

These are just a few examples of potential hypotheses. Note that these hypotheses do not apply to a specific brand, and you should consider your own situation before developing a hypothesis statement. Do not fall into the lazy marketer trap of copying and pasting what we have listed here. Think critically about what matters most to your brand and business objectives.

Those statements seem straightforward, right? It should be relatively easy to develop hypotheses for your brand. However, if you are struggling to develop your own brand's hypotheses, what can you do? Try the following:

- **Preliminary research**—You probably have a set of media-monitoring terms laying around that you can pop into Google for some initial searching. By this time, you have also selected a social media listening tool. Input some of the social media monitoring words into that tool and see what you come up with after a cursory review. The key is that it does not need to be an exhaustive search.

- **Gathering existing market research**—See if you can obtain the volumes of offline testing your market research team has already done. It can be a valuable source for developing a hypothesis statement.

- **Interviewing marketing or communications colleagues**—Some of your compatriots in the communications or marketing functions might have some knowledge based on work they have already completed.

- **Looking at existing paid media or website data**—If your brand has a large media or website presence, this might be a daunting exercise before developing hypothesis statements. If that is the case, frame the data you plan to gather and analyze in the context of the objectives you are trying to achieve. The historical behaviors on these channels, though, should provide you with a good basis to develop hypothesis statements.

- **Asking your online community**—If this is a standalone research project or you're just attempting to verify some assumptions after you have launched an online presence, asking your community to provide input can be helpful. There is a very good chance that your community will offer up an opinion if asked and that can serve as a good behavior (or question) to test.

Creating a hypothesis is the most important step in developing the methods portion of your plan. Without it, all the work you have done to narrow and identify sources of data will be for naught. You will just end up testing everything, which will make your final report a lot less helpful for those who read it. **Do not skip this step, even if it takes you an additional week to land on the right hypotheses after an internal review.**

Time Frame for Analysis

Gathering every single mention about a brand, its competitors, and the industry for the entire time the Web has existed would be impossible. Not only would you be unable to digest that amount of information, it would also lead to a serious issue with spam collection. (We discuss the issues with spam later, in the section, "Filtering Spam and Bots.")

The other reason capturing all the available data is impractical is incomplete data. It is not discussed much within digital analytics, marketing, and public relations circles, but oftentimes a shortcoming of this kind of research can be incomplete information. By that we mean that a blogger might mention the brand in January but delete the post in March. When you conduct the analysis in April, you cannot capture that piece of content. Another example is an individual who is active on Twitter when he mentions your brand but then goes several months without activity or has his account suspended.

Aside from the issues related to data degradation and spam, another important reason to identify a time frame for the analysis is the length of time it takes to properly analyze behavioral trends. Looking at a short window might provide some interesting information, but establishing any long-term trends in consumer behaviors would be very difficult.

On the flip side, looking at a time frame that is too long is also possible. For example, if you were to gather two years' worth of data, a trend that you identify at the beginning of that cycle might no longer be a trend 20 months or so later. It could very well be a trend, but you would need to do additional testing with more recent data to verify that.

Where is the happy medium? Best practices suggest that data should be captured over a 12-month period. Utilizing a 12-month window lessens the possibility that holidays (if applicable), quarterly earnings events (if applicable), and crises (if applicable) will unnecessarily bias the data. It also enables you to accurately assess behavioral trends online. The 12-month time window also eliminates a lot of concern about data degradation. If collecting data for 12 months results in too much data to analyze, a compromise solution is to gather 6 months of data.

✉ *Note*

> Although narrowing down the window might cut down on the amount of data to gather and analyze, it might also create a seasonality bias in the data. If your company has clearly defined "busy seasons," and your analysis does not include those times, you might get inaccurate results and develop poor insights.

Identifying the Project Team

The project team is one of the most crucial elements of the research plan. It is not enough to develop your hypotheses and identify the data sources. Without a team behind the project, there is a good chance the project will not be completed and the organization will not benefit from its insights. These are the most crucial roles to identify within the project team:

- **Project leader/champion**—This person does not necessarily need to be the one who does the work, but she needs to be the person who assembles the research plan. She also should be the one who helps to evangelize the need to complete the project and gather the insights.

- **Research leader**—The research leader could be the same person as the project leader, but oftentimes the roles are separated. The research leader is the one who ensures that the parameters identified in the research plan are followed.

- **Analyst**—In all likelihood, the analyst is the person who completes the research in conjunction with the research leader. He could come from any part of the organization, but the best analysts understand the tools and the business needs. They are the people who can properly blend those two elements into actionable insights for the business.

- **Research Quality Assurance (QA)**—Someone on the team should be designated to double-check the coding. This could be the analyst working on the project or the research leader. Read more about coding in the following sections of this chapter.

- **Content strategist/engagement leader**—This person works hand-in-hand with the analyst, research lead, and project lead to develop insights from the data. Without this person, all that is completed is the collection of a massive amount of data.

These people can come from any part of the organization. Ideally, you want to form a hybrid team between marketing and market research, but if the team members are coming from one area or the other, that is okay. As long as the people have knowledge of the tools and the business, the project will be successful.

Determining the Depth of Analysis

Depending on the volume of data in question, the time frame you are using, and whether you are expanding the scope behind your own brand (to competitors and the broader industry), reading and coding every mention might not be possible. We will talk more about the coding process in a moment, but the depth of your analysis is an important consideration. You can pick from four different methods of analysis for your project:

- **Automated**—Many of the tools we have talked about in this book offer automated dashboards that count mentions across a variety of potential metrics. This is not a very desirable state, though, as the data has not been vetted for spam or checked for relevancy.

- **Manual**—Whether or not you decide to go with a manual process of reading and analyzing every post depends on the size of the project and the resources available to you. If you decide to analyze only content that mentions your brand, and there are not many mentions, then doing the analysis manually can work. If yours is a company the size of Disney, however (which means you have tens of thousands of mentions per day), then a manual process won't work.

- **Hybrid**—Most companies take a hybrid approach, in which they rely on an automated dashboard and supplement it with manual analysis.

- **Random sampling**—This method utilizes all the data you can gather from the tool(s) you are using and then randomly samples a selection of those mentions. How large the sample is depends on the confidence interval you are comfortable using. The confidence interval indicates how reliable your data will be. If you are familiar with political polling, you have no doubt seen mention of plus or minus 5% next to the results. It is similar with digital data. After the random sample is pulled, a manual process ensues.

Which method you choose depends on your particular project, but we recommend that you use a random sampling method. Such a method boils down a large number of mentions into a manageable size and offers the best approach to manually reading posts and offering insights.

Building the Coding Framework

Before you freak out at the term *coding*, let us explain what we mean by it. Coding the random sample—assuming that you choose the random sample method—involves applying a qualitative label to a much larger post. Think of it much like a categorization exercise. For example, if a mention of a brand took place in the *New York Times*, then a possible code for that mention could be "news." It really is not more complicated than this. However, it is important that the team working on a project agrees on the set of variables that will be coded for at the start of the project. The following are some examples of codes you can use for your project:

- **Media type**—This basic tag assesses whether the mention came from a news, blog, forum, Twitter, comment, video, or image site.

- **Sentiment**—Sentiment coding is simply understanding whether a piece of content is positive, negative, or neutral. Read more about sentiment in the next section of this chapter.

- **Messaging pillar**—Most companies have a set of messages they are trying to convey to the marketplace. One of your tags should be which bucket that mention falls into.

- **Company spokesperson**—This is an obvious yes or no tag to include in the analysis.

- **Type of post**—Is the post a customer complaint, or is it a product mention? Could the mention be categorized as an HR issue? Capturing the type of post helps you segment and share the data with other parts of the organization, if appropriate.

- **Target journalist or media outlet**—Again, this is an obvious tag, but you should be able to sort based on the tag and see whether a majority of mentions came from target publications.

Depending on your particular project, there could be dozens of different codes you can use. The most critical thing is to establish them ahead of time.

Taking a Sentiment Approach

Online sentiment is still one of the most controversial subjects in the digital analytics community today. The debate is centered around two different core topics:

- **Automation versus manual**—The social listening tools we have mentioned throughout the book all have an automated sentiment-scoring tool. Unfortunately, those automated sentiment-scoring tools are far from accurate—primarily because they have a hard time discerning sarcasm from authenticity. However, manual sentiment analysis introduces issues of human bias and scale that have yet to be overcome.

- **Value to the brand**—It is important to note that online sentiment is not necessarily a proxy for overall brand reputation. It is possible that during a period of crisis, the two could be related, but it is not always the case. Some brands place too much emphasis on online sentiment, whereas others do not look at it at all. The answer lies somewhere in the middle of those two extremes to yield sentiment analysis that is actionable and useful to brands rather than just interesting.

The most common scale for online sentiment analysis is positive, negative, and neutral. However, this scale does not allow for very much interpretation. In addition, not every post is overly negative or positive. In longer-format posts (such as blogs or news), there will likely be elements of positive, negative, and neutral mentions woven throughout. Our preference is to utilize a five-point scale for scoring sentiment:

- **Positive**—The positive posts will likely be the most obvious. They are the posts that advocate for the brand in some way or that complement an action the brand has taken. These posts are also often endorsements of the brand to friends and family members.

- **Somewhat positive**—A step below the positive mentions, somewhat positive can be tempered endorsements of the brand. These mentions might mention the brand positively but may do so only briefly in the course of a post.

- **Neutral**—The neutral posts are probably the hardest to classify because determining the intent from a casual read of the posts is often difficult. Furthermore, some posts say positive and negative things in a period of a couple of paragraphs. Typically though, these posts don't advocate for the brand in anyway, and they likely just mention the brand's name.

- **Slightly negative**—These posts often use negative terms in association with the brand, but one of the key differentiators between slightly negative and negative is that slightly negative posts do not focus on your brand exclusively. The person might say that he or she "dislikes" the brand but in the context of a post that is totally irrelevant to you.

- **Negative**—Negative posts focus exclusively on the brand and are hyper-critical of its actions, behaviors, or messaging.

There is no perfect solution to the sentiment question. Tools currently on the market, such as Clarabridge, are trying to lend more validity to automated sentiment scoring. Until that process becomes more accurate, brands need to rely on manual scoring by humans. As long as the scale and types of posts that fall into each part of the scale are decided upon ahead of time, it is still the best solution.

Filtering Spam and Bots

The final portion of your research plan should be an outline of how to deal with spam and bots. A tremendous amount of spam exists on the Internet, and it varies in volume, depending on the brand you are analyzing. In some instances, we have encountered a spam-to-real content ratio of 90%:10%. In niche markets, such as business-to-business technology, there is often less spam because there is not the ability to capture traffic from genuine sources.

Spam and bot filtering is only one part of the process. The other part is factoring in news or press release syndication. Some tools filter out press release syndication, but others capture it. Those instances are, technically speaking, a mention of the brand, but they are mostly noise. They do not necessarily contribute anything to brand reputation or value. Our recommendation is to exclude such instances from your analysis.

So there you have it. These are the elements of a research plan. The plan is a critical component to direct your research and ensure that actionable insights follow the analysis. These steps do not necessarily need to be done in sequential order, but mapping out the sources and methods completely is important.

References

1. Chadha, Rahul. "Audience Data: Where Marketers Are Investing Their Spending," eMarketer, December 11, 2017. https://www.emarketer.com/content/this-is-where-marketers-are-spending-on-us-audience-data

2. Kanellos, Michael. "152,000 Smart Devices Every Minute In 2025: IDC Outlines the Future of Smart Things," Forbes.com, March 3, 2016. https://www.forbes.com/sites/gilpress/2017/01/20/6-predictions-for-the-203-billion-big-data-analytics-market/#4612b7de2083

14

Building Reports that Will Actually Be Useful

In the last several chapters, we have talked at length about the different use cases for digital data. You should now have a better understanding of how that data can be valuable for groups other than public relations and marketing. Remember the maxim that we have reiterated throughout this book: "Knowledge is power." If you are the person feeding information to product planning, strategic planning, or customer service, then you are at the seat of power within your organization.

Knowing the different applications of digital data is helpful, but unless you have a firm understanding of how to build a research plan (see Chapter 13, "Building Your Research Plan") and deliver insights, you will be sitting on a pile of data with little meaning. Insights are critical in fueling the communications strategies and tactics for your organization. A component of developing insights is knowing how to deliver a report.

It's important that you get reports right. Why? Because if you do not, all the research you have done on tools and all the time you have spent building your research plan will go to waste. This chapter provides an overview of what your reports should contain. We dig into the following specific topics:

- **Report construction**—If you have developed your research plan, building a report should be a piece of cake. We'll offer some tips and tricks on how to construct a report.

- **Report delivery**—If we do nothing else in this chapter, it is our hope that we arm you well enough that you do not fall victim to data dump syndrome. The reports themselves must present insights that inform strategies and tactics; they cannot be slide after slide of only data.

- **Report use cases**—Not everyone in your organization needs to see every piece of data that you have collected. For example, you will likely need to create a report for just your executive team. That report should include the key takeaways, a few of the most important data points, and a description of how the data is going to be used.

- **Central repository of information**—The reports that you construct will have limited long-term value unless you develop a program or repository for the insights that you have gleaned.

Reports are where the rubber meets the road. Taking the time to build an appropriate internal toolset will pay off for your organization. This is where understanding the digital data applications will benefit you the most. This is also where building your research plan in advance will save you a tremendous amount of time. It is our view that the information in this chapter will be applicable best practices for any use case your business might need to solve. Without further delay, let's get into how to build reports.

✉ *Note*

In the coming sections we talk about how reports are constructed for public relations and marketing. However, the concepts are broad enough to be applicable to other parts of the organization, if such a use case exists for your company or client.

Constructing Reports

This chapter is about building better reports, and it makes sense to start with an explanation of how to construct reports. When you read this section of the chapter, it'll be obvious if you did not read Chapter 13, in which we talk at length about building a research plan. If you launched right into data collection and analysis, your report is likely going to fall victim to "data dump syndrome." What does that mean? It means putting together dozens of slides that tell a quantitative story. The quantitative story is only one part of the equation. If you are telling only the quantitative story it's likely that your reports are missing insights or, at best, it is the potential victim of interpretation. By that, we mean interpretation of what the data means to the organization. You do not want to fall victim to interpretation in your reports. You want to be the one offering the data and the insights.

How do you combat this problem? Much of the answer to this question lies in Chapter 13, you can do a few other things to prevent being infected by this syndrome:

- **Build your reports from back to front**—This is not necessarily intuitive for most people; the next section includes more explanation of this concept. The idea is that you start with what you want the reader of your presentation to take away and move forward.

- **Ensure that you have a reasonable hypothesis**—If you have a set of hypotheses, your presentation will be focused. If you cast the net wide, collect a lot of data, and then try to put all that data into a presentation, you will be swimming upstream without a paddle.

- **Focus on the Five Ws**—It is easy to lose track of the story you are trying to tell as you are sifting through a mountain of data. Every slide or insight you deliver should be based on the five Ws (who, what, when, where, and why). You'll learn about this in the section, "Focusing on the Five Ws," later in this chapter.

- **Formatting reports**—Some of this will be covered in this chapter in the section, "Building a Report from Back to Front," but we cover some tips and tricks to properly format your reports that throughout the chapter.

- **Watching your report time frame**—In several chapters we have talked about ensuring that you have a large enough data set to properly identify trends and develop insights. The actual development of the report is no exception, but there are some subtle nuances.

In the next several pages, we dive into each of these topics individually.

Building a Report from Back to Front

Again, building a report from back to front isn't intuitive. You might be saying, "Are you telling us to start with the last slide first?" Yes, that is exactly what we are telling you to do. Why? Because doing so can help you deliver cohesive, concise, and focused reports. This approach ensures that your report clearly conveys the most important takeaways. Otherwise, your takeaways might get buried.

How do you go about building your report in this way? There are four key steps to pulling it off successfully:

1. **Conduct initial research**—At this stage, there is no need to build a comprehensive digital data profile, but it's great if you do have one. Whether you use a social media listening tool, data from a DMP (data management platform) or Google Analytics you should do some initial searching to get a sense of the current online landscape. This research does not need to be comprehensive but is meant to be directional.

2. **Develop your hypotheses**—If your hypotheses lack focus, the report will, too. An example of a hypothesis statement that you can use to properly build a report might be, "We expect to see the majority of conversations online mentioning a particular product." If, when conducting the research, you realize that the hypothesis statement is true, you can spend several slides digging into the details of that conversation. If it proves not to be true, you can spend several slides discussing what was being mentioned online. (Chapter 13 really digs into how to format a research hypothesis.)

🔍 *Tip*

How many hypotheses should you have? There is no clear-cut answer to this question, unfortunately. However, three to five different hypothesis statements is typical. This number of hypotheses will give you a solid foundation of data and will result in a sufficiently concise report that people in your organization can digest.

3. **Build your strategic and tactical recommendations**—You can refine these recommendations as you start to collect data to either prove or refine your hypothesis statements, but before you put the final report together, jot down a few things you might be able to do tactically as a result of developing the report.

4. **Create the report outline**—Ultimately, the outline of the report will be in the front of the presentation. After you do your initial research, write your hypothesis statements and formulate initial strategic and tactical recommendations, it is time to start creating the outline. The outline will lead to a more concise and clear final report.

If you use the method of building reports from back to front, your final reports will be clearer and likely containing insights that you can take action on.

✉ *Note*

We are aware that this approach might seem like a self-fulfilling prophecy. By developing hypotheses ahead of time, you could introduce bias into the data collection and analysis process, and you could possibly miss out on valuable intelligence. The hypothesis statements are meant to be a guide only. When you dig into the data, if you realize that some new groundbreaking insight deserves to be reported on, you should report on it. Nothing is stopping you from expanding beyond your initial hypotheses.

Ensuring That You Have a Reasonable Hypothesis

As mentioned in Chapter 13 and the preceding section, you need to have a reasonable hypothesis before you can develop a concise and cohesive report. The hypothesis statement should be based on your initial research and knowledge of the business. Similarly, you should take into account what the goals of your marketing program will be. The more input into the hypotheses that you can offer, the better the hypotheses and the report will be.

The following are some examples of hypothesis statements that you can use for the purposes of your report:

- "A majority of conversations taking place online reference customer service issues."

- "When people come to our website they are not advancing beyond the initial landing page."

- "The people who engage with our content online do not look like our target audience today."

- "There are a large number of searches about our brand, but not a lot of engagement. This might mean that our audience is more passive than we would like."

- "We suspect that the majority of our online audience is engaging in video content versus imagery."

A hypothesis statement should represent some element of the five Ws, which are covered in the next section. For the moment, though, it is important to note that you should not skip the hypothesis step. Doing so is a sure-fire way to develop "data dump syndrome."

Focusing on the Five *W*s

Aside from building your hypothesis statements and your initial recommendations, there is no more important component to a clearly laid-out report than focusing on the five *W*s:

- **Who**—The "who" is the people who are talking about or engaging with the brand, its competitors, or its industry online. The "who" could be the demographics of the people who are talking, whether they are influential or not, or even whether they are employees of the company.

- **What**—The "what" is the key topic people talk about and search for online. It can be based on the hypothesis statements you have outlined in the previous step, or it could be based on your deep-dive research. This can also be used for creating both paid and earned content that affects search engine optimization (SEO).

- **Where**—The "where" is the location of the conversations or engagement taking place online. You will most often see "where" defined as news, blogs, Twitter, Facebook, YouTube, forums, and other social networks.

- **When**—The "when" is the date/time element of your research. Are people talking on the weeknights, or are they talking on the weekends in the early morning? Are they coming to your website during the day? Do they conduct most of their searches Monday through Friday? The good news is that most digital analytics tools offer the capability to identify this data point. Identifying when people are talking can be helpful as you line up your content schedule.

- **Why**—The "why" involves understanding the rationale for the behavior of people mentioning or engaging with the brand, competitors, or industry online. It can partly be answered through an understanding of digital data points but requires additional research inputs—namely surveys and focus groups. Digital data should serve as an input to those surveys and focus groups to try to answer that "why," however.

Every slide or bullet that you put together for your report should attempt to answer the five *W* questions. You won't be able to answer all five *W*s in every bullet or slide, but your goal should be a minimum of three. When the report or bullets do not include enough of those elements, you often are left with very ambiguous statements that are difficult to act on.

🔍 *Tip*

An example of an ambiguous comment would be noting in the report that 40% of the conversations are taking place on Twitter. Although it's helpful to know where people are talking, this statistic leaves out who is doing the talking, when they are talking, and what topics they are talking about.

Formatting Reports

Presenting digital analytics reports in Microsoft PowerPoint or Keynote is common practice. In our view, creating such a presentation is the best way to compile the mountain of data you have collected and then convey a story to your key internal or external stakeholders.

The following elements should be in every one of your reports:

- **Project overview**—Every presentation you create should have one slide that outlines the goals of the project. In our experience, it's amazing how often reports do not clearly articulate the goals for the research. We can tell you that without clearly setting this expectation, it is likely that your presentation is going to fall flat.

- **Hypotheses**—If you are testing hypotheses—and we sure hope you are!—they should appear on a separate slide. It is also worth noting on this slide whether the hypotheses were proven to be true or slightly off, just to provide context.

- **Methodology**—The methodology should include how much data you collected, where you collected it, who collected it, when it was collected, and what was collected.

- **Executive summary**—The executive summary should include the top three to five findings from the research. The key element here is that every bullet you put on the executive summary slide should be actionable. There should be some way for the organization to develop a marketing strategy to combat or amplify what you have found.

- **Top-level data**—The handful of slides that follow the executive summary should focus on the most important data and analysis captured in your report. They should seamlessly flow from the executive summary and are likely to be based on your original hypotheses.

- **Top-level recommendations**—The recommendations should flow from the executive summary slide previously presented. They should appear on a series of slides—likely three to five tactics or ideas that can be executed. They can include social media tactics or any other communications medium, based on your findings. Something to consider for top-level recommendations is including them in the beginning of your report after the executive summary. It isn't necessary to do so, but if you are in an organization that has challenges focusing, consider moving this up in your presentation might make sense.

- **Everything else**—We do not mean to minimize the amount of work you have done to put together the report, but the rest of the report is just backup. It shows that you have done the work required to develop the insights and recommendations but really is valuable only to the numbers junkies (we mean that in the nicest way possible) on your team.

How long should a report be? The answer, as you might suspect, is that it depends on the depth of the research and the number of questions you are exploring. A typical report following the format described in this section would be anywhere from 15 to 20 slides. You should reasonably assume that getting your audience to pay attention after about 20 or so slides will be challenging. Keep it brief and stay focused on the story you are trying to tell. Large amounts of data can often lead to large amounts of slides, which can often lead to presentations that are not digestible. Keep the presentation simple and germane to the story you are trying to convey.

Understanding Your Report Time Frame

How much data you collect and present is entirely based on the scope of the project. However, you should always err on the side of including more data in your upfront analysis. Why? There are two primary reasons:

- **More data eliminates anomalies**—Major news events tend to skew the data either positively or negatively. However, when you include an ample amount of data, those news events have less of an effect.

- **More data is a more accurate predictor of how behaviors have changed**—If you have been actively communicating with your audience(s) and want to see how the behavior has changed, the best course of action is to look at the 12 months leading up to the communications and then as much time after as possible. The behaviors you are trying to change and influence do not change overnight. Putting out an advertisement today does not mean people will be aware of your product tomorrow. Similarly, just because you begin posting a link to new content today does not mean people will engage with it over the long term.

Other data sources should follow a similar rule. If you collect 12 months' worth of social media conversations, you should also collect 12 months' worth of search data. Or, if your research project calls for website data, then you should collect 12 months' worth of that as well. Consistency is key. It will be very easy to poke holes in the methodology if you do not follow the same script with all the data you are gathering.

Now that you know the key tips and tricks for developing a report, it is time get down to creating it. You can then deliver it, as described in the next section.

Delivering a Report

You have done a lot of work on collecting a pretty large amount of data, ideally over the past 12 months. You have developed hypotheses. You have built slides that outline what the data is telling you. You have created some preliminary recommendations based on that data. The bottom line is that you have done a tremendous amount of work to get to this point. But you are not done yet. There still is the very important step of delivering your report.

One consideration is to whom you should deliver your report; we talk about that in the next section. Another important consideration is *how* to deliver the report. Compiling the report and sending it out via email is not enough. You could do that, but you would be leaving the report open to wild interpretation that might not be helpful. You have likely spent hundreds of hours compiling the report, and you want it to be well received. Providing a voiceover with additional context can help.

If sending out the report via email, even with a voiceover, is not the right approach, how should you deliver it? The best approach is to deliver it in person. How should that meeting be structured? There are four steps to a successful review of a report:

1. **50% review**—Your report may be further along than 50%, but this is the opportunity for your stakeholder group to provide feedback on the report itself. It is also their opportunity to ask questions or make additional data requests, based on their specific needs. This review session will ultimately lead to a more focused report for all of your stakeholders.

2. **Final review**—After you have incorporated the input of your stakeholder group, you should set up a second meeting where you can go through the report in more detail. Ideally, you should set up a one- or two-hour meeting in which you go through the slides described earlier in this chapter. In this session, you can talk through the findings with your stakeholder group and begin discussing how to act on the recommendations.

3. **Strategy and tactical workshop**—Now that you have a mountain of data and some initial recommendations, it is time to put that information to good use. The group you invite to this workshop is likely smaller than the first two review session groups, including mostly the people who will be executing against the data and recommendations.

4. **Debriefing and next steps**—You need to debrief with the larger stakeholder team, discussing what worked and what didn't with the research project. This is also an opportunity to discuss what project the team will undertake next. Will the next project be a continuation of the research already done? Will it be an exploration of a theme or themes you have identified in this report? Those are just a couple of the things that could be discussed in the debriefing meeting.

You must do a lot of work to put together a research report, and you don't want to miss out on the chance to deliver your findings in person. Presenting strong insights in person about your customers to senior executives will help them to remember you. In the executives' minds, you will forever be the person who understands the customer. Remember: Knowledge is power.

Understanding Report Use Cases

Until now, we have been speaking in generalities about what should go into a report. We have talked about ensuring that your slides include some reference to the five Ws (who, what, when, where, and why). We have talked about how to deliver a report, how to structure a report, and how much data to include in a report. What we have not talked about yet, however, is to whom you should deliver the report.

If you sat down and listed all the people who would be consuming the report you are developing, you might find yourself with a list of about 10 use cases. I am sure you could guess without us telling you that developing 10 different versions of the same report is silly. If you tried to develop 10 different versions of the same report, you would be working on it for quite a long time. In most situations, there are just three primary use cases that you should always consider:

- **Executive**—The executive within your company is not going to read a 50-page research report. Yes, we are sure that there are exceptions who will read the whole thing, but the majority of people will not. They probably won't even read the 15 or 20 slides that we described earlier. You have to create a slimmed-down version for your executive team.

- **Management**—The management level includes the people who are likely to take action based on your data and findings—typically the public relations and marketing people within your company. They will be the ones expected to develop strategies and tactics based on your findings.

- **Analyst**—Analysts want data. They will find value in the recommendations, but these folks will be "geeking out" on all the additional data slides in the back of your presentation.

Let us dig into each of these use cases in a little more detail.

The Executive-Level Use Case

The executives in your company are busy. They deal with operational challenges, human resources problems, product issues, and many other things that come up during a normal workday. Most of them find value in new research, even if it is in a marketing channel they do not fully understand. This is especially true if you offer significant consumer, product, or customer service insights. If your research and data focus on those three areas, you will likely get their attention.

However, you will not have their attention for a long period of time. You might have a grand total of 15 minutes with an executive to share your findings (if you are lucky). That does not give you much of an opportunity to go into great depth. You probably cannot even utilize the slide format outlined earlier for your report. Here's what you can share that will get the executives' attention:

- **Project scope**—Keeping this part brief is important because executives do not care about the intricacies of the tool or date range you selected. They also do not care about the total volume of data you collected. The project scope should be very high level on the project's goals and its approach. You should use no more than three or four bullets on this slide.

- **Key data points**—As with the project scope, the executives are not going to care about all the data you have. They will likely appreciate that you have gathered it, but they will not have time to get into it in great detail. You should give the executives two or three things that they should take away from the meeting.

- **Key recommendations**—We have presented these types of reports to a number of executives over the years, and the response is almost always the same: "This is great, but what are we going to do with it?" The recommendations do not need to be finalized, necessarily, but they should be ideas that could be executed based on the data. You will either get a "go" or a "no," and having preliminary ideas is a great way to get immediate sign-off on any sort of tactical implementation you have considered.

- **Next steps**—You don't need to say much about next steps, but giving executives an understanding of what will happen when you all leave that room is important. It could be more research, or it could be more meetings to develop the tactics as a result of the research. Whatever it is, make sure the next steps are concretely outlined for your executives.

With executives, you might have an opportunity to present 4 or 5 of the 50 or more slides you've prepared. You might find this scary, or you might feel like your work is being minimized, but set those feelings aside. Presenting those 4 or 5 slides could give you greater visibility to the executive team. That is a pretty big deal at most companies. (And remember: Knowledge is power.)

The Management-Level Use Case

Those in the management level are the people who are going to be using the data most often within your organization. If your project has executive-level sponsorship, the management-level people will also be responsible for developing strategies and tactics as a result of the research. Most often, they are the marketing and public relations people within your organization.

Some people in the management level will want to see the entire report. We know plenty of people in the marketing and public relations professions who love to see numbers. Unfortunately, we know just as many who are so numbers averse that their peers who are effectively using data to hone strategies and tactics are lapping them. What does the management-level use case look like? It looks a lot like the executive-level use case, with a few notable additions:

- **Project scope**—Like the people at the executive level, those in the management layer care about how the project was completed. Unlike the executives, though, this audience is likely to care more about the tools, the date ranges, and the volume of data collected.

- **Key data points**—Again, like the executives, the managers want to know the key data points. During your 50% review, this team might identify those for you, but if not, err on the side of including too many. You can always cull the list down after the broader team has an opportunity to review it.

- **Additional "noteworthy" data**—You might have excluded elements from the executive report to prevent the report from being too long. If so, this is the group to share that information with.

- **Recommendations**—Based on the data you have collected, the managers are going to want to know all the potential applications for it. This is where you can go above and beyond what you share with the executives and discuss more ideas. The managers are likely closer to their particular piece of the business on a day-to-day basis, and therefore they might be able to use the data to identify some recommendations that you would not. That is perfectly okay. In fact, we encourage it with the reports we prepare for companies.

- **Next steps**—The managers care about next steps, and the next steps can be the same as what you share with the people at the executive level.

Tip

Based on how numbers hungry or averse your organization is, the preceding list may change. However, in our experience, following this outline is best practice. It will set you up for success every time.

The Analyst-Level Use Case

The analysts—the "data geeks" as we like to affectionately call them (and ourselves sometimes)—are the men and women who sift through mountains of data and deliver insights to make communications programs (and the business overall) more effective. They are your organization's eyes and ears—and oftentimes the brain. Without consumer insights people, many communications programs would miss the mark, leaving many people in the management level looking for new employment.

We are obviously biased as we ourselves come from the analyst-level world (at least we started there). We can't overstate the importance of the role analysts play in the digital analytics process. They are most often involved in selecting the tool, creating the project scope, writing hypotheses, crunching the data, developing the insights, and determining how best to mesh what they have found with existing research. These are significant tasks. All the while, they must measure the progress of existing communications programs.

What do the analyst-level people care about in this context? Well, there is a good chance that these folks put together the report. If they did not, however, they are sure to care about everything the managers care about, plus all the available raw data. That raw data might lead to additional research projects or the refinement of existing projects.

🔍 *Tip*

Although the analysts are not involved in executing the tactics that result from the research, you should not consider them less valuable. The analysts can be your friends, especially if you are trying to test certain ideas. Befriend them and make sure you provide as much value to them as they do to you.

You have a lot of data, and you have reported on its various findings to the different internal stakeholders. It is time to move on to the next project. But before you move to the next project, there is still a critical question that needs to be answered: How is this information stored to ensure that you are constantly able to tap into it and learn about what your customers are saying? The last section of this chapter covers how to build a central repository of information.

Building a Central Repository of Information

The field of digital analytics has come a long way in the past five years. Significant innovations in the area of data capture and analysis have taken place as social media has exploded and presented much new information for public relations and marketing. There has even been progress with combining multiple data sources to offer the best insights. We know it sounds silly, but until very recently, the people who held the search data were not always excited to compare notes with the person who held the social data.

What we as an industry have not gotten good at yet, however, is building a central repository for information. You see, in most cases, the reports are developed as we have outlined in this chapter, put into PowerPoint, shared, and then stored on a hard drive somewhere. That is useful only for the person who has the report on his or her desktop. Nobody else in the organization will see consistent, long-term value from it. This model also opens up the organization to knowledge-management issues if the person who owns the presentation leaves the company.

You can see the problem, can't you? Well, the good news is that a couple solutions are available for building a central repository:

- **Command center**—No, we are not talking about the bridge of the *Starship Enterprise*. Many companies, including Dell, Gatorade, and Cisco, have created social media command centers to serve as central repositories of data collection and insight development.

- **Web-based application**—Several companies specialize in the development of dashboards that live remotely on individual desktops.

Command Centers

The command center concept became popular after Dell developed a physical location (see Figure 14.1) where people on Dell's Social Media and Community team could monitor conversations around the globe. These command centers capture all kinds of data, much of it centering on the five Ws concept covered earlier in the chapter.

A command center is usually a single location with multiple monitors and multiple individuals reading conversations on a nearly 24/7 basis. It can also be a source of information for public relations, marketing, customer service, social media, crisis managers, community management professionals, and consultants within the organization. The people who work in the command center utilize listening tools and categorization/routing techniques to put the data in the hands of the people who need it most.

The command center is the primary source of data, but it is not the only place for gathering information on key stakeholders online. The people who work in the command center could be market research professionals, but quite often they are a random collection of people from within the organization who have some social media responsibility.

Figure 14.1 *Dell's Social Media Command Center, located at the company headquarters in Round Rock, Texas, serves all of the company's global needs.*

A command center can provide an organizationwide rallying point for social media, but some drawbacks exist:

- **Physical and technological infrastructure costs**—The tools and the physical space needed to power a command center in this way are not cheap.

- **Scalability questions**—If all the data is being collected in the command center, how do people who are not near the room take advantage of it in real time? They need someone who is actively monitoring within the command center space to send them the details. This is not an efficient use of anyone's time.

- **Available talent to work in the command center**—There is a dearth of available digital analytics talent, and command centers require strong communications and technical skills to operate effectively.

Command centers are very cool spaces, but they require a significant investment. Technology—in terms of data gathering and display, human talent, and physical location—costs need to be considered. However, using a command center is one effective way to centralize data gathering and insights development within your company.

Web-Based Applications

An alternative to creating a physical command center location is to build a web-based application that can live on multiple desktops within the organization. You might have even seen these web-based applications being referred to as *data lakes*. These data lakes or web-based applications provide a central repository for the organization to gather data in near real time. There is often an interface by which users from all walks of the company can query based on the question(s) they are trying to answer.

The most valuable part of this type of centralized data application is that it is completely customizable. If you want to see only social media conversations about your brand, you can do that. If you want to see only social network data, you can do that also. If you only want to see web data, you can do that, too. What is key is that you develop a set of goals, use cases, and requirements before building an application like this.

The market will continue to go down one of these two paths—command center or web-based application—as the centralization of data becomes more important. Not every company is there yet. Plenty will continue to execute reports as we outlined at the beginning of this chapter, and that is okay. However, as your organization becomes more familiar and more interested in this kind of data, the need to build a repository of information will grow. Do not wait to be asked. Get ahead of it and start thinking about how you can build either a command center or a web-based application to house the information.

15

The Future of Digital Data

Throughout the course of this book, we have armed you with everything you need to use digital data to make your marketing programs better and your business smarter. We have explained the basic digital analytics concepts, provided guidance on setting up your marketing technology stack, offered some use cases for digital data, and provided details on how to formulate a research plan and measurement scorecard. Each chapter should help your organization harness the tremendous power of digital data to understand how your audience behaves, how content performs, how to make sense of the channel ecosystem that you can use to engage your audience, and then understand the impact your programs have had on the business.

After going through the first 14 chapters, you might be thinking that implementing everything we have outlined is going to be difficult for your business—but don't worry. Think about the concepts that we have talked about throughout this book as a journey. If your organization is just starting to effectively use digital data, this book should give you a serious jumpstart on that evolution. If your organization has been using digital data for years, hopefully what has come before this chapter has provided you with some tips on how to optimize the program you have been running. In an ideal world, you will eventually take advantage of everything we have discussed in this book.

It is important to keep in mind that many of the companies that marketing industry professionals view as best-practice organizations have taken years to get to that point. Organizations such as Intel, P&G, Cisco, PepsiCo, American Express, and Coca-Cola have been investing in this capability for years.

You might be surprised to know that even with the explosion of digital data, a large number of organizations still aren't using it to its full potential. For example, more than half of the organizations rely on educated guesses or gut feelings to make decisions based on digital data according to a recent survey from Experian. Similarly, according to the bi-annual survey from Deloitte, Duke University,[1] and the AMA1, 68% of senior marketing executives do not use data to make everyday business decisions. That's all while there are 2.7 Zettabytes of data existing in the digital universe today. What is a Zettabyte? A single Zettabyte contains one sextillion bytes, or one billion terabytes. That means it would take one billion terabyte hard drives to store a single Zettabyte of data. Said in a simpler way, we have a lot of data available to us as marketers. If you read the first part of this book and thought you were behind, you should think again.

If you are not currently using digital data to its fullest potential, then now would be a good time for you to start. If you are looking for a formula to get started, here are some good places to begin your digital analytics program:

- **Develop company goals**—If you would like to develop a digital analytics capability, what are you trying to achieve by doing so? Is it to simply understand your customers better? Is it to understand how your digital marketing programs performed? You could have many goals, but before you go down the road of picking tools, knowing what you would like the end result to be is imperative.

- **Identify internal resources**—In almost every one of the chapters so far, we have talked about the importance of human and financial resources. You also need to think about your digital analytics program holistically. The resources need to be in place before you start picking tools, determining use cases, and putting the data to use.

- **Build reporting requirements**—If you have the go-ahead to create a digital analytics program, you should also start thinking about reporting requirements. Your bosses will want to know what they are getting for their investment in this program.

- **Develop a program schedule**—In all likelihood you will not be able to launch your program with every tool available from day one. You will need to create a Gantt chart or a program schedule that outlines how this new function will be built. This chart can include everything from when new tools will be researched to how head count for this new group will be acquired.

- **Achieve participation from other parts of the organization**—We have been involved in many digital analytics launches with clients of all sizes. One thing that consistently happens is that companies attempt to start small, but they don't stay small very long. When people in other parts of your organization realize the power of digital data, they will want to participate. Before launching your program, give thought to how other parts of the organization can participate. It could be something as simple as a financial contribution or something more rigorous, such as a set of digital media readiness standards.

At this point in the chapter, you might be wondering what getting started in digital analytics has to do with the future of the industry. The truth of the matter is that many companies that have implemented digital analytics programs are going through the motions. At one point in time, an organization may have realized that using digital data to understand was important, so the organization purchased some tools and got started. Organizations often did this without thinking through the five things in the preceding list or any of the other best practices we have outlined throughout this book. It is our hope that in the future, companies will think about the items in the previous list and everything else we've talked about throughout the book before launching a program and hoping.

Watching How the Digital Analytics Disciplines Evolve

Over the course of the next several pages, we'll take a look back to the first edition of this book at how we thought the future would unfold. We think it's helpful to take stock of where we were four years ago, and whether or not we have made much progress against these projections. Then, we'll conclude this chapter by looking forward to see what the next several years hold for our industry. As we've reiterated throughout this book, the digital marketing and analytics industries are evolving at a rapid pace, which makes predictions difficult. What follows are simply our observations having been in the industry for more than 15 years.

Looking Back at How Social Media Listening Has Evolved

Very few specialties under the digital media umbrella have gone through as much transformation over the last 10 years as social media listening. When some of the original companies like Visible Technologies, Radian6, and Sysomos hit the scene, they provided a window into what was happening online but had largely incomplete data with several user interface challenges. Fast forward to 2018 and those providers have either gone out of business, been acquired by larger organizations seeking to create a full suite of marketing capabilities, or been replaced as market leaders. Social listening tools now have sophisticated user interfaces that allow customers to do everything from pulling social media conversations to analyzing those conversations using sophisticated machine learning and artificial intelligence techniques.

As we look back to some of our predictions in the first edition of this book, we indicated that it was our expectation that we would see further consolidation in this industry. At that time, literally hundreds of options were available on the market to monitor social media conversations. While there are still many tools available on the market, the larger enterprises have really focused on six primary social media data providers. Those providers include Sysomos, Crimson Hexagon, Synthesio, NetBase, Sprinklr, and BrandWatch. Radian6/Salesforce, while still a provider of this data, has fallen off in our estimation as a potential alternative for large enterprises.

We also speculated that even with consolidation, the social media listening market would continue to evolve. We felt this way because, for the most part, social media listening data could still be paired with other digital data sources far more often by large companies. We were partially right with this prediction. For the most part, social media listening vendors have not evolved very much. They have incorporated other data sources, but they haven't necessarily done so to the point where organizations are turning to them for all of their digital data requirements. Where we were correct in indicating that the social media industry would continue to evolve is in the area of usage of social media listening data. More organizations than ever are using sophisticated techniques (that is, linguistics, machine learning, artificial intelligence) to understand how consumers are talking about their brands. Similarly, more often than not, social media listening data is being paired with search (or other digital) data to have a more complete view of online behaviors. We would expect this trend to continue, if not continue evolving over the coming years.

We also predicted that the social listening vendors who gave dashboards to clients would see those dashboards' value diminish, Again, we think we were largely correct with this prediction. Many clients are still accessing the social media conversation data within the platform itself, but we are seeing more companies exporting the data to either integrate it with other sources or perform more advanced analytics techniques to understand behaviors. This is why most of the social listening vendors have integration with major social media management systems (SMMS) tools such as Hootsuite and Spredfast. To the credit of the social listening vendors, they have made their dashboards easier to use, too, which we think has kept most of their clients from exporting the data. However, as digital analytics programs have gotten more sophisticated, we see many companies focusing on an internal customer data management platform that all data feeds into. So, we expect the trend of gathering the raw data only from these platforms to intensify.

Finally, in the first edition of this book we talked a lot about the development of social media listening command centers. Dell and Gatorade, being two of the early pioneers of these centers, have continued to maintain them, but they have evolved immensely. No longer are these command centers for social media listening only. Now, brands such as Intel have launched command centers that listen to social conversations, identify trends that might not have fully taken off yet, identify content opportunities as a result of those trends, and optimize their media spend according to real-time performance.

Do we think value exists in continuing to invest in these centers? Our answer is yes, assuming you are doing one of the things we listed earlier with Intel's use case. As Mason Nelder, former director of social media and digital strategy at Verizon said at South by Southwest Interactive several years ago, these centers are a symbol to the organization that listening to your customer is important and that digital and social media are important to the organization's communications and marketing goals.

In that context, you can see how the command center space might be valuable.

Do you need a command center? The answer, as usual, is that it depends. If you are looking for something around which your organization can rally, then creating a command center might make sense. If you are looking to build a strong listening capability to more fully understand your customer's behaviors, then building the space might be a secondary concern. This isn't to say that you cannot have both goals and build the space; rather, it is typically one or the other in companies. Most companies have not evolved the command center concept beyond a singular use case.

The social media listening market has changed substantially since 2007, and we have no indication that the next five years will be any less tumultuous. Our hope is that over the next several years more organizations use social listening data as a means to understand consumer behavior in ways that deliver actionable insights to all areas of a company, beyond marketing, and also blend it with other digital data sources.

Diving into Search Analytics

The difference between search analytics and social analytics is that the former is very well established. For search analytics, established tools such as Google AdWords help a marketer understand what words are being used most often and in what volume. An established set of metrics are accepted by the industry, such as click through rate (CTR), total clicks, cost per click (CPC), and cost per acquisition (CPA).

The way those metrics have been calculated hasn't changed in years. It could be argued that it might be time to change the search analytics model or at least examine whether the established metrics are still appropriate, but that would require a significant amount of "reprogramming" within companies. Companies have used the same method of calculating the effectiveness of their search programs for years, and we don't see that changing anytime soon.

With that in mind, what do we see changing? Think about your own online behavior for a moment. There is a very good chance that you will read about a brand or product on a social media platform and turn to a search engine to learn more about the product. Similarly, knowing what words people are searching for most often in conjunction with your brand or product name can be instructive as you develop your social media content.

In this book's first edition we intimated that most marketers instinctively understand the link between search and social but rarely look at the data side by side. While that was true four years ago, we think this trend has started to change for the better. We see more marketing organizations blending search and social data and seeing search as more than just a tactical counting exercise. Search data is a critical input to fully understanding the customer journey for your brand. Our expectation is that search data will grow in importance for organizations as they start to further explore its linkage to other sources.

Looking into the Audience Analysis Crystal Ball

We predicted that the area of audience analysis would likely see significant innovation over the next several years, and boy, were we right on the money. Tools from social listening vendors have begun to provide rich data on demographics, geographies, and audience characteristics, relying heavily on data from channels such as Facebook and Twitter. There have also been significant enhancements made by industry professionals, such as Seth Duncan, Chief Analytics Officer at W2O Group (the company that Chuck Hemann is currently employed by). Seth and his team discovered an ingenious method of identifying social behavioral signals and then applying advanced statistical techniques to develop audience affinities that can be used for creative development, media targeting, and/or digital strategy development.

Looking back to 2013, we talked a lot about how brands can use hand-coding techniques to more fully understand audience characteristics. While that is still a method used by organizations and agencies alike, more sophisticated techniques powered by companies such as Crowdflower and Amazon's Mechanical Turk have made the process of understanding audience characteristics faster and cheaper. We would expect that as machine learning and artificial intelligence become more mainstream within marketing organizations, the process of understanding audience behaviors will become even easier.

The key for audience analysis to continue to evolve will be in how the tools themselves continue to evolve. Much innovation is happening in the artificial intelligence and machine-learning worlds, and so it is our expectation that the tools will get even better in this area. Knowing that understanding the audience is at the core of every marketer's job description, we suspect that we're only scratching the surface with these capabilities. If we write a third edition of this book, it is a fair assumption that the audience analysis market will have changed even more dramatically.

Forecasting the Content Analysis of the Future

In many parts of the book we talk about the importance of understanding content performance. While this is not a book about content marketing, we think it's important to understand how to analyze content because it is the lifeblood of any marketing program, digital or otherwise. If your content is not appropriately tailored for the audience you are trying to reach, the program will fail. It really is that simple.

In the first edition of this book, we talked at length about tools such as Chartbeat and Woopra to understand content performance. Those tools have continued to evolve and incorporate other digital touchpoints within their platforms. That's the good news. The bad news is that it's still a very labor-intensive effort for most organizations to understand content performance. What do we mean by labor-intensive? Think for a moment about where you get your data on the performance of your content. If you are part of a large organization, the most likely source for data on performance would come from an agency. Setting that aside, the place that they get the data from is most often from the channel in which that content was distributed. That's a fine approach to take for understanding content performance, but it's limiting. This approach only allows you to understand the impact a piece of content had on that channel. It does not allow you to understand how that piece of content impacted the customer journey overall.

Similarly, it doesn't help you to understand how one piece of content might have performed against another piece of content on another channel.

Over the past several years, a number of advancements in the tools and technology markets have aimed to understand this holistic performance more effectively.

Google, Adobe, and others like them have developed sophisticated attribution modeling offerings that allow marketers to understand either the collective impact channels have had on a key business performance indicator, or how content itself contributes to the bottom line. Our hope is that these tools continue to evolve, and that more companies adopt them to truly understand how content is performing.

What else are we expecting as content analysis evolves? It isn't necessarily an innovation as there are some in the industry who have taken this approach, but we expect content indexes to become more prominent. It sounds like a very complex topic, but in practice, executing it is very easy if you have knowledge of Microsoft Excel.

The idea behind a content index is that you are presented with a series of metrics to evaluate your content (for example, likes, comments, shares, and clicks on Facebook) that are on different scales and carry different levels of importance for your business. A content index would take every piece of content you have created on that channel, gather the relevant metrics, and apply a weighted score to each metric. This approach allows you to more accurately assess content performance based on your organization's priorities instead of just counting a particular activity (likes, comments, shares, and so on).

Content analytics will continue to evolve as more marketing organizations pivot from a channel-first to an audience-first approach. As that continues to happen it will become increasingly important for those same organizations to look at the performance of content holistically. How did a piece of content on social media impact the customer journey on our website? That's just a sample question that we, as digital analytics professionals, will need to answer more often over the coming years.

Understanding the Influencer Analysis Landscape

Next to social media listening vendors, the area where we have seen the most change since the first edition of this book is in the area of influencer analysis tools. As an example, we predicted that Klout, given its ubiquity in the market at the time, would not be going anywhere. We also predicted that it wouldn't be unseated by any other tools in the market place. Lastly, we predicted that Klout would be a part of the landscape for the foreseeable future. Boy, we could not have been more wrong about that prediction. Following the acquisition of Klout by Lithium Technologies in 2014, almost all innovation with the core platform has stopped. There are still changes being made to it, but the advancements it had made in understanding online influence have all but stopped.

It isn't just Klout, however, that has seen significant change. Tools such as PeerIndex, Appinions, Little Bird, and Kred have all been marginalized by the marketing industry. It isn't that online influence, and engaging influencers for the purposes of achieving marketing goals, isn't important. It's that these tools did not deliver on the solutions that most organizations really needed.

As we said, online influence (and the engagement of online influencers) is still central to many marketing programs. So why, then, have so many tools gone by the wayside? We think the answer to this question is threefold. First, although these tools helped to identify influencers, they did not help organizations with the more fundamental challenge of engaging with them online. By this we mean, what is the best way to reach that person? How do we manage the relationship long term? Tools such as Sprinklr that specialize in content distribution and social channel management can aid in this effort, but they do not help to solve the identification problem. Second, there is still considerable dispute within many organizations about who "owns" influencer marketing. Does communications own influencer marketing? Does marketing own influencer marketing? Is there some other part of the organization that manages the programs? We do not see an end in sight to this organizational problem, which means the influencer analysis market will continue to be disrupted. Lastly, influencer analysis is challenging to scale without a heavy investment. To build a full-scale influencer analysis program, you need people, tools, and processes. None of those things are cheap or come together quickly. If some of those things change over the coming years (to be clear, we do not think they will), perhaps the influencer tool market will stabilize. However, we think most marketing organizations have bigger fish to fry so these issues will continue to be unresolved.

This leads us into the last section of this chapter, in which we discuss the future of digital analytics more broadly. Before we leave this section, it is worth repeating that tools and approaches continue to evolve at an insane pace. Regardless of whether we are talking about search, social, influence, or content analysis, we're expecting that pace to continue for years to come.

Understanding Where Digital Analytics Goes from Here

The tools and individual disciplines that we have discussed are only one part of the equation. The other part—and it is a big part—is the enterprise itself evolving. Recall at the beginning of this chapter that we cited several statistics indicating that the amount of digital data was growing, but that the number of companies taking advantage of it is not. This is troubling for many reasons, but primarily because marketers should be looking for as much intelligence on their customers as they can glean. Not only that, but listening to social media conversations and gathering digital data are just smart reputation management.

Part of the reason why adoption has been slow to materialize has been an issue of talent. We talked about the talent gap issue in the first edition of this book, and it is still an issue today. There are not many people with the appropriate skills to effectively implement a best practice digital analytics capability within a company. There are more of us than there were four years ago, but for the moment many companies are still struggling to find the right talent to not only create the function but also manage and evolve it over the course of a long period of time.

The following sections discuss the challenges and the solutions to building robust digital analytics capabilities. We firmly believe that digital analytics will become a growing part of the enterprise's marketing function, but some steps must be taken first.

Bridging the Analytics Talent Gap

Over the past few years, marketers have had a ringside seat to the biggest shift in their profession since, well, the creation of broadcast television. Consider for a moment that Facebook has now crossed 2 billion users, Pinterest reached 70 million unique visitors faster than any standalone site ever, and Twitter has more than 320 million active users. Marketers are now faced with a burgeoning community of creators, not consumers. Sure, the largest online population is still composed of those who consume content, but the number of people who contribute and share is growing substantially. This has several implications for marketers, not the least of which is factoring in new channels.

The other implication—and this is something that is more difficult to control—is the number of people looking to break into the business for companies or agencies. Unfortunately, the digital media space is moving at a pace that far outstrips the availability of quality talent. We don't mean to be unfair about this, but the number of people who have executed digital media campaigns for the Fortune 500 is still very small. It isn't a matter of setting up a Facebook page or managing a Twitter account. The best professionals are part marketer, part behavioral psychologist, part businessperson, and part number cruncher. Ah, the numbers. You knew we were getting there eventually, right?

If the talent gap in digital media is huge, the analytics talent gap is equally big. Whenever someone tweets, likes, comments, or clicks, she has created a data point that requires analysis. However, analyzing those top-level metrics is only one part of the equation. Can you take those metrics and turn them into a business insight? Many people know how to collect data and put it into a presentation. Fewer people know how to collect the data and put it into a presentation that highlights insights that improve the business or a communications program.

The addition of digital marketing analytics professionals to corporate teams is not going to be a trend that slows down. We have seen a significant uptick in the number of openings at agencies and companies for positions of director or vice president in digital analytics since the first version of this book. These organizations hope that by hiring such a person, a digital analytics capability will follow. Will it work? Only time will tell, but hiring a leader of digital analytics is a prudent first step in making it happen. Unfortunately, as two people who have been looking to fill these roles at several agencies and served on the inside of a large corporation, we can tell you that they do not grow on trees. Most of the people who have been successful in the analytics world come from diverse backgrounds.

If you are currently looking for such a person, what can you do to land the correct talent? Aside from scouring colleges and universities for more junior talent (not a bad idea, by the way), you can take a few other steps:

- **Understand what goes into a proper analytics job description—** Knowledge of social media listening tools is important, but it is not nearly the only thing you should be looking at to evaluate candidates. A senior analytics person should be able to help your organization source talent, have familiarity with a broad range of analytics and marketing concepts, and have the ability to present to upper management when necessary. Keep in mind that this is someone who will be responsible not only for understanding your customer but also building the capability. Strong business acumen is just as critical as the math and tool skills.

- **Have an open mind—**More people than ever have experience with digital analytics, but it still isn't a large group of people. Sometimes you have to step outside your hiring comfort zone to hire the right person. You might want to consider someone from the social sciences who has strong research skills. It is our experience that strong research skills translate to these roles better than weak research but strong digital media skills.

- **Remember that some skills do not show up on a resume or LinkedIn profile—**You need to find someone who is naturally inquisitive, but when was the last time you saw "naturally inquisitive" on a resume? I know we haven't very often. That's probably something that you'll have to snuff out in an interview. This speaks a little bit to the point we just made, but the skills of an analyst don't easily translate to the traditional resume or LinkedIn profile.

- **Look for those people evangelizing on behalf of the space—**Not many digital analytics bloggers are active writers. If you do encounter someone who is writing often, it would behoove you to check him out. He might be someone who does a lot of writing and not a lot of doing, but it is worth investigating to see whether he can back up his knowledge in a real-world environment.

Let's assume for a moment that you have the right person inside the organization already or are at least close to bringing someone in. Where should this person sit within your organization? This is a very important decision because that person's career trajectory will be greatly affected by where she sits within the organization. Many digital analytics professionals sit with the marketing team, and that does make some sense. However, we believe that digital analytics professionals should sit within the broader market research function because digital data is valuable, but it's infinitely more so when paired with other data sources. The market research team has access to a lot of proprietary business performance data that can be valuable as you are assessing overall digital marketing programs. It is the source of offline market research, which is very helpful in understanding consumer behavior. Finally, an important factor is the existing headcount within that team. As we just mentioned, teaching digital media skills is often easier than teaching strong research skills. Having a group that consists of strong researchers will make the development of a digital analytics capability easier.

The integration of market research and digital analytics teams leads us to our next point, which is the internal gathering and application of this data.

Housing Your Customer Data

If you think about all the tools we have talked about here and throughout the book, you see one common denominator: You do not own any of the data. What does this mean exactly? It means that every time you embark on a new digital research assignment, you must go to one of the tools, develop something akin to a profile, export the data, and then analyze the data. That is certainly fine if you are familiar with the tools and research processes. What happens, though, if you aren't as familiar but need information on how your customers behave online?

Herein lies what we think is the biggest revolution coming to digital analytics. Over the coming months, and most likely years, companies will be building internal repositories for this data. We have mentioned this throughout, but these tools have very easy-to-use APIs, which allow users to easily extract data. There are also data sources that your organization likely has (sales data being the biggest one) that aren't publicly available to many stakeholders or even your agencies. Wouldn't it be nice if you could build a tool that is easily accessible for all and includes all the available data inputs? It certainly is possible, and we think it should be done more often. If you are going to build such a repository, these are some things you should take into consideration:

- **Build a cross-functional team**—This sort of effort isn't going to be completed by one person from the social media or marketing team. The likelihood that someone on the marketing team has the technical skills required isn't very high. To build this capability, you need a cross-functional team that includes marketing, market research, IT, social or digital media, and analytics.

- **Detail all the data inputs**—Housing this much data could quickly go from manageable to completely unwieldy. Before moving toward the actual build and implementation, ensure that you have catalogued all the data you would like to capture and which tool it is going to be captured by.

- **Gather technical specifications**—Your IT team will come in handy in developing the technical specs to build this tool. However, do not let the IT folks create the tool in isolation. If you do, there is a very good chance that it will be written in a language that will not be easy for everyone else to decipher.

- **Ensure that you have the ability to query the database**—Whichever data inputs you select, there is probably going to be too much data available for the brand marketer. That is okay, as long as the user has the ability to select the data inputs or variables that matter to her.

- **Make it easy to extract the data**—Having the data all housed in a dashboard is one thing, but making it easy to extract is another. Make sure you build in an export function to get the data out of the tool for further manipulation.

This sort of approach is not for companies that are just getting started with digital analytics. It is for those that are utilizing the tools we have discussed here, analyzing and implementing findings, and looking for a greater level of sophistication with their digital analytics approach. If you are just getting going, follow the steps we have outlined throughout this book. Before you know it, you'll be building an internal analytics repository for your organization.

Continuing Consolidation of Data Sources Just as New Sources of Data Emerge

Over the course of the last several years, we have seen technology behemoths Google, Adobe, SalesForce, and Oracle add more data sources to their ever-growing marketing capabilities. We suspect that trend will continue, especially as businesses of all sizes work to lessen the complexity of data collection, cleansing, and usage across their organizations. One hypothesis for why businesses are still making decisions based on so little data, as we outlined earlier, is the number of sources they have to go to in order to pull together a nearly complete picture of an ecosystem (accessing 100% of the data should never be a goal). If the companies listed previously are successful in continuing to centralize and consolidate the data sources available to marketers, it should lead to easier decision making and greater adoption of digital data.

All of that being said, if you follow the marketing, digital, and analytics industries closely you know that the number of public data sets is exploding, as is data coming from Internet of Things (IoT) devices. Companies of varying shapes and sizes are trying to understand at a more granular level how end consumers are engaging with their products, and then integrating that data with legacy data sources (for example, digital data). We know that inter-connected devices are a trend that's only going to continue. We also know that those devices are spitting out more data than organizations can reasonably manage today. One thing we will be watching is how organizations begin to gather this data and integrate it with other sources. We suspect consolidation within the traditional digital data sources will continue, but sources outside of that ecosystem will explode. The management of that data will be the new issue facing marketing and IT organizations, alike.

Dealing with Growing Concerns About Consumer Privacy

Beginning in 2018, global governments are taking a number of steps to provide privacy to consumers who might have had their data used for malicious purposes in the past. For example, the General Data Protection Regulation (GDPR) is a regulation by which the European Parliament, Council of the European Union, and the European Commission are intending to use to strengthen and unify data protection for all individuals within the European Union. This new regulation extends to all foreign companies processing data of EU residents. While this regulation is still relatively new, and its impact on your business should be discussed with internal counsel, we think it is safe to assume that it will only slow the amount of data businesses will be able to collect on the people they are trying to reach with marketing and communication programs. It seems improbable that this regulation will be able to stop the data train completely, however.

The GDRP is indicative of a broader trend toward protecting the privacy of consumers and eliminating (to the degree possible) the unlawful collection and usage of data to further business objectives. What's noteworthy, however, is how few organizations are actually ready for this change. The World Advertising Federation published a study recently asking companies how prepared they were for GDPR.[2] Unfortunately, only 65% of respondents said they expected to be fully compliant, with 70% saying that marketers were not fully aware of the implications. This is troubling on many levels, and we encourage you to speak to your in-house counsel on how you are collecting and using data immediately.

To be clear, a number of people favor the doom-and-gloom scenario that GDPR is bringing to the market. Many feel that this, and other regulations like it, will mean the end of personalized communications. We are not in that camp. We think that there will continue to be some push toward personalized communications because at the same time consumers are concerned about privacy, they are also demanding the best experience possible from brands. However, the passing of data from consumers to brands will require a transparent and informed value exchange. These regulations do represent the end of the secret data collection for companies. A trend, in our estimation, that's positive for all parties involved.

Making Social Data Become More Available to Brands

If you have spent any time with IT organizations in your career, you will know that one thorn in their side is the collection of data from social media channels. The challenges IT organizations face are endless in regard to social data but include varying metric definitions, which leads to dimensionalization challenges, privacy restrictions, dark posting done by advertisers, and API limitations. Due in no small part to the 2016 United States presidential election, Facebook and Twitter have recently announced that they will be revealing any ad to anyone, regardless of the targeting the advertiser is using starting in 2018. Will we ever get to a place where 100% of the data on social media platforms is available to businesses? No, we find that hard to believe for a variety of reasons, the most important one being privacy. However, the move toward greater transparency by exposing dark ads to all users is a step in the right direction toward demonstrating whether or not social media contributes to business or marketing results.

One issue that continues to plague social media is its contribution to the business. For years, the industry has been "stuck" managing impressions and engagement with little ability to understand how Facebook, Twitter, LinkedIn, YouTube, and so on contribute to more bottom-line metrics. The exposure of data from dark advertising is a step toward a more complete picture of channel performance. Additionally, the social media platforms have continued to evolve their measurement offerings so that brands can truly understand the impact that they desire. We suspect that this trend will continue, and more brands will start to incorporate social media planning into their overall campaign planning mix. All in all, this is a positive trend for social media within large companies. The more that it can be measured like more traditional channels, the more the investment will grow in those channels by large companies.

Continuing Struggle by Companies to Get Clean and Accurate Data

If you have been a digital marketing professional for almost any length of time you know that the subject of bots isn't that new. Website analytics platforms such as Google and Adobe have created sophisticated filtering software to ensure companies are capturing accurate data for years. Now, it is coming to light that a large number of social media users are fake or are bots. According to estimates published toward the end of 2017, approximately 270 million fake accounts are on Facebook and 48 million are on Twitter. Those are staggering numbers, but bots and fake accounts are likely to grow in sophistication and number as the opportunity to influence people and advertising dollars grows.

While digital data is plentiful, it is also extremely messy. Digital data is still largely unstructured and requires a significant amount of cleaning, organizing, and transforming before it can be used to make business decisions. This isn't something that will likely change as digital data grows, though we hope we are wrong with this prediction. How can organizations deal with this problem, though? The best path forward is planning for it and understanding that it will always be a part of the data collection process. Building in the required business processes for cleaning is something we recommend to every organization. We don't suspect that we'll be changing that recommendation any time soon.

Continuing Measurement Challenges for Chief Marketing Officers (CMOs)

If you recall some of the data from earlier in this chapter, you know that organizations are struggling to use data to make business decisions. To add an even finer point on it, in a 2017 study by Forbes and Neustar,[3] only 42% of CMOs said they could fully attribute sales results to marketing investments. The reasons for this are many, but include a lack of available data, lack of clean data, not having data in a centralized and accessible location or, in the worst-case scenario, not attempting to track the bottom-line performance at all. Our peers in the digital analytics profession do not do ourselves any favors when we make up metrics like return on engagement or return on influence, just to name a couple.

Now, as we've pointed out in several cases throughout this book, we are not a fan of tracking only return on investment. We think other metrics are just as critical to people planning marketing campaigns inside of companies. However, not trying to solve this return on investment conundrum will reach a tipping point. Our hope is that we make progress on this issue in the coming months and years because a better ability to measure leads to greater accountability and transparency. We think you will agree that being accountable to the business and being transparent about performance is something worth striving for, right?

Scratching the Surface of Machine Learning and Artificial Intelligence

The number of applications of artificial intelligence and machine learning technology continues to grow. Everything from Siri that is a part of your iPhone and other Apple devices, to self-driving cars, to Google AI, which can learn how to beat video games in a matter of hours, artificial intelligence technology has become significantly more mainstream over the last several years. Thanks to social media and a significant amount of data left behind through casual browsing of the Internet, artificial intelligence holds great potential in digital marketing and is already being used to improve digital advertising buying and optimization. Using AI to provide better customer experience, predict the outcome of marketing programs, and target end consumers will surely bring great return on investment to businesses.

The idea of artificial intelligence is not new, but the pace of new breakthroughs is. Several factors are at play, including the advancements in machine learning algorithms, the increase in computing capacity to train larger models more quickly, and the massive amount of data that can be used to train machine-learning models. These breakthroughs have led to some spectacular technologies such as Google's DeepMind, Amazon's Alexa, and Google's Assistant devices. While not perfect, the benefits many consumers and businesses are seeing from these technologies are many.

We could go on for pages and pages about artificial intelligence and its applications and benefits for marketing. Things such as chatbots are becoming central parts of customer experience programs implemented by many companies. The new use cases and breakthroughs are coming at a much faster pace than most marketers can keep track of, while still maintaining their day-to-day responsibilities. In the interest of giving you some concrete ways we see artificial intelligence and machine learning helping marketing, here are a series of use cases you should be familiar with over the coming months and years:

- **Predictive modeling**—One of the more straightforward marketing applications for artificial intelligence is in its ability to aid in predictions. Because of the high volume and quantifiable nature of marketing data, models can often be trained much more quickly on marketing data than on other information such as HR or inventory data. Being able to predict the success of a marketing initiative, as you might imagine, would be an enormous benefit to companies. We can expect more companies to crop up in the future that offer just this sort of capability to companies.

- **Image recognition**—In the relatively near future, it is likely to be possible for consumers to search for images. This might be as simple as snapping a photo of a pair of shoes you want to buy, or using a web app to select a certain image that you found within a Google search. As more of the web moves from being text-based to image- and video-based, we should expect some significant enhancements in the use of AI to understand visual content.

- **Customer segmentation**—If you are familiar with customer segmentation, and if you are reading this book we assume that you are, you know that it is typically an arduous process that takes weeks (if not months) to complete. Artificial intelligence is starting to be applied to aid in this process as well. Companies such as AgilOne are allowing marketers to optimize email and website communications by continually learning from user behavior. Applications such as this should allow for companies to scale personalization efforts far more effectively in the future.

- **Content generation**—You are likely already aware that a large percentage of sports-and finance-related content is written by machines, not by humans. As artificial intelligence technology becomes more sophisticated, we should expect more of that in the future.

- **Recommendation engines**—Today's sophisticated recommendation engines, like the ones many of us access through Amazon or Netflix, go way behind a simple human-determined set of guidelines. A recommendation engine powered by artificial intelligence can pull from a significant amount of nuanced data to draw conclusions from behaviors or actions.

- **Search improvements**—As we've mentioned throughout the book, search is a critical part of the journey. It's a behavior that almost every Internet user uses on a daily basis. Because of that, there are a number of improvements to search that have been generated by artificial intelligence. For example, technologies such as Elasticsearch are now relatively mainstream, allowing many brands to have search that goes beyond simply matching keywords. Similarly, data-as-a-service vendors such as Indix make it easier than ever to draw conclusions from search trends. Consumers should expect more and more websites to follow in the footsteps of Google (and other providers) in implementing autosuggest, suggested corrections, advanced search options, and other similar improvements to search behaviors.

We're just starting to scratch the surface on the applications of artificial intelligence for marketing. Over the coming months and years, we expect the technology to only get more sophisticated. The most likely place to see significant advancement and adoption first by marketers is in the area of speech and image recognition. These two areas are likely to become mainstream before we know it.

The field of digital analytics has grown significantly since we published the first edition of this book, and it will continue to grow for the foreseeable future. Companies are beginning to realize the true power of digital data and its impact on marketing programs. That impact is not going to lessen, and the companies that are leveraging this data and technologies effectively will be the ones that win. Wouldn't you like to be on the winning side?

References

1. "CMO Survey: Analytics More Influential, But Talent Lacking," Deloitte Digital and Duke University, August 29, 2017. https://www.fuqua.duke.edu/duke-fuqua-insights/cmo-survey-aug-2017

2. "70% of global marketers are not fully aware of the implications of GDPR," World Advertising Federation, September 13, 2017. https://www.wfanet.org/news-centre/70-of-global-marketers-are-not-fully-aware-of-the-implications-of-gdpr/

3. "Marketing Accountability," Forbes and Neustar, October 2017. https://cmo-practice.forbes.com/wp-content/uploads/2017/10/Forbes-Marketing-Accountability-Executive-Summary-10.2.17.pdf

Index